DATA ENGINEERING FOR CYBERSECURITY

DATA ENGINEERING FOR CYBERSECURITY

Build Secure Data Pipelines with Free and Open Source Tools

by James Bonifield

no starch
press®

San Francisco

Printed in the United States of America

First printing

29 28 27 26 25   1 2 3 4 5

ISBN-13: 978-1-7185-0402-8 (print)
ISBN-13: 978-1-7185-0403-5 (ebook)

Published by No Starch Press®, Inc.
245 8th Street, San Francisco, CA 94103
phone: +1.415.863.9900
www.nostarch.com; info@nostarch.com

Publisher: William Pollock
Managing Editor: Jill Franklin
Production Manager: Sabrina Plomitallo-González
Production Editor: Sydney Cromwell
Developmental Editor: Frances Saux
Cover Illustrator: Josh Kemble
Interior Design: Octopod Studios
Technical Reviewers: Andrew Eastman and David Sanchez
Copyeditor: Lisa McCoy
Proofreader: Daniel Wolff

Library of Congress Control Number: 2025007905

For customer service inquiries, please contact info@nostarch.com. For information on distribution, bulk sales, corporate sales, or translations: sales@nostarch.com. For permission to translate this work: rights@nostarch.com. To report counterfeit copies or piracy: counterfeit@nostarch.com. The authorized representative in the EU for product safety and compliance is EU Compliance Partner, Pärnu mnt. 139b-14, 11317 Tallinn, Estonia, hello@eucompliancepartner.com, +3375690241.

For Abby, Ruby, and Lily

About the Author

James Bonifield is a cybersecurity professional with over a decade of experience analyzing malicious activity, implementing data pipelines, and training others in the security industry. He has built enterprise-scale log solutions, automated many aspects of security operations, and led analyst teams investigating major cyber threat actors. He holds numerous certifications, including the OSCP, GXPN, and CISSP. He enjoys spending free time with his wife and kids, traveling, and tinkering with all things security and Python related.

About the Technical Reviewers

Andrew Eastman is a seasoned cybersecurity professional with over a decade of experience in threat detection, incident response, and network defense. He currently serves as a cybersecurity professional for Microsoft's internal corporate blue team, where he focuses on safeguarding enterprise assets against advanced cyber threats. He holds a master's degree in cybersecurity and information assurance from Western Governors University and has earned a suite of industry-recognized certifications, including CASP+, CySA+, CEH, and CCNA.

David Sanchez is a consulting architect at Elastic, where he specializes in detection engineering, artificial intelligence and machine learning integration, and comprehensive cybersecurity solutions. He is adept at collaborating with clients to design and implement tailored, scalable security strategies that address unique challenges and drive business success.

BRIEF CONTENTS

CONTENTS IN DETAIL

7
WORKING WITH SYSLOG DATA   127

PART III: DATA TRANSFORMATION   147
AND STANDARDIZATION

8
DATA MANIPULATION PIPELINES   149

9
TRANSFORMATION FILTERS   173

PART IV: DATA CENTRALIZATION, AUTOMATION, AND ENRICHMENT   201

10
CENTRALIZING SECURITY DATA   203

ACKNOWLEDGMENTS

First, I want to thank my amazing wife, Abby, for always supporting my projects. Thank you for listening to me talk about this book all day, every day. I also want to thank my girls, Ruby and Lily, for being great kids. Thanks to my parents, Jeff and Leigh, and my brother, Jerry, for encouragement along the way.

Thank you to Bill Pollock and Jill Franklin for extending an offer to write for No Starch Press. Thanks to my developmental editor, Frances Saux; to my production editor, Sydney Cromwell; to my copyeditor, Lisa McCoy; and to the rest of the amazing team at No Starch Press.

Thank you to Andrew Eastman and David Sanchez, the technical reviewers for this book. I've had the pleasure of knowing these gentlemen for many years, and I appreciate their insights.

INTRODUCTION

Data engineering is the practice of creating infrastructure that can receive data from multiple sources, format or consolidate that data, then store it in databases for analysis. Many organizations require data engineers to track information like customer engagement metrics, financial transactions, and stock market movements. But when it comes to cybersecurity, data engineers are critical to connecting sensors to the analysts who can detect incidents.

Although generally invisible to all but those who manage them, the tools that ship data from one place to another are foundational to cybersecurity programs. Before an analyst can identify a problem, the relevant alerts and event logs must leave the organization's workstations and servers and land in a central database.

In this book, you'll learn how to extract, transform, standardize, and streamline events using free and open source tools. You'll learn how to centralize log management, perform data enrichment, and distribute events to various technologies and databases for analysis.

Who This Book Is For

This book is for anyone tasked with creating a cybersecurity monitoring system or centralizing a business's logs. It may be particularly useful for those operating with constrained budgets, but it is relevant to those operating with enterprise-level funding as well.

Network defenders can use this book to transform events taken from a multitude of systems and tools into a standard format before storing them. Administrators and engineers can also use this book to manage the many device health logs flowing through the network.

Offensive testers can also use it to read and transform the variety of outputs from hacking tools to store them for client reports, automate the comparison of results, and dispatch additional tool actions. Those seeking to automate defensive or offensive actions may find centralizing and standardizing logs useful as well.

What's in This Book

We'll cover a data engineer's toolkit for tasks including encrypting network communications, extracting data from hosts, and transforming and cleaning that data. We'll also cover tools that ship data to other places, automation software, and caching tools. Here's a breakdown of the book's parts and what you'll learn in each chapter:

Part I: Foundations of Secure Data Engineering
This first section lays the foundation for the rest of the book. You'll configure your own TLS infrastructure, prepare SSH keys, and use Git to centralize and manage your project files.

Chapter 1: Data Engineering Basics   Learn about the goals of a data engineer: building pipelines that centralize, standardize, and enrich data. Explore common architectures for an organization's logging infrastructure. Then, survey the JSON, ECS, and YAML formats and install tools we'll use throughout the book.

Chapter 2: Network Encryption   Encrypting network data is important for protecting data, but some people find it daunting to configure, so they bypass it when learning a new tool. In this chapter, you'll become comfortable with using network encryption and set up a TLS infrastructure that you can use to encrypt tool traffic in subsequent chapters. You'll also become familiar with configuring SSH to connect to remote servers.

Chapter 3: Source and Configuration Management   Learn to use Git for source management so that, as you create configurations throughout this book, you can track any changes you've made and revert them if needed. You'll use Git locally to manage files and remotely to act as a backup and a hub for your work.

Part II: Log Extraction and Management

To begin creating data pipelines, you'll have to extract data from various hosts and the network. This section covers tools and approaches for doing so. You'll use tools for Linux and Windows as well as ones that receive network data from appliances or sensors.

Chapter 4: Endpoint and Network Data   Work with Filebeat to extract data from Linux hosts and connect to network services to receive logs. You'll interact with local files, receive data over the network, and proactively reach out to external sources for data.

Chapter 5: Windows Logs   Use Winlogbeat to read the Windows event log. Enable and use Windows security features such as Sysmon and enhanced PowerShell logging, and explore uncommon event logs containing useful security data.

Chapter 6: Integrating and Storing Data   Explore the Elasticsearch database and its frontend user interface, Kibana. Learn to work with Elastic Agent, which combines features from Filebeat, Winlogbeat, and other tools in a browser-based GUI. Read host-level data, then collect network metadata directly from the host. Also learn about ingest pipelines and assets needed to transform log data inside Elasticsearch.

Chapter 7: Working with Syslog Data   Use Rsyslog to read and write local files and to receive and transmit data over the network. Explore Rsyslog's plug-ins for OpenSSL and Kafka.

Part III: Data Transformation and Standardization

Standardization is an important part of data engineering. You'll learn how to convert and parse multiple data formats from various technologies into one standardized naming convention using JSON structures. This data transformation step is useful for security analysts, automated response tools, and machine learning.

Chapter 8: Data Manipulation Pipelines   Learn about Logstash's inputs and outputs, connect systems to Logstash, and link the tool with services such as APIs, Amazon S3, and Redis.

Chapter 9: Transformation Filters   Use Logstash's filters to transform and manipulate incoming events to correct timestamps, enrich and delete data, standardize key-value data pair field names, extract values, and write custom Ruby code.

Part IV: Data Centralization, Automation, and Enrichment

In this part, you'll use Kafka to centralize your data feeds, enabling you to distribute and analyze your logging events in real time. You'll learn to automate many of the processes described in previous chapters using Ansible. Finally, you'll use caching tools to add a cyber threat intelligence enrichment process to your data pipeline.

Chapter 10: Centralizing Security Data Configure Kafka to act as central plumbing for your data pipelines. Create topics to keep data organized and then use tools such as Filebeat and Logstash to send and pull data from Kafka.

Chapter 11: Automating Tool Configurations Explore Ansible, which allows you to script and automate system administration tasks across multiple hosts at once.

Chapter 12: Ansible Tasks and Playbooks Learn various ways of using Ansible to install and configure the tools discussed in this book. Automate your TLS certificate creation and data pipeline deployment, and run multiple automated actions in sequence.

Chapter 13: Caching Threat Intelligence Data Use the caching tools Redis and Memcached to store data using an in-memory cache, which speeds up data lookups and enrichment activities. Create a distributed cyber threat intelligence enrichment process directly in your data pipeline.

Prerequisites

This book assumes a basic familiarity with the Linux operating system and its command line. We'll walk through all configuration steps and commands to run, but you'll find it easiest to follow along if you're used to working in the terminal. Here are some other topics you might want to familiarize yourself with before moving on:

Virtual machines

Virtual machines are virtualized computers running inside of other computers. For example, you might run a Linux virtual machine on your Windows desktop or laptop. The computer that hosts the virtual machine is called a *hypervisor*. Virtual machines are helpful for practicing new tools and concepts, as you can take a snapshot of their current state and then return the machine to that state if anything goes wrong.

TCP and UDP

The tools covered throughout this book make network connections using the Transmission Control Protocol (TCP) and User Datagram Protocol (UDP). TCP is a protocol that requires systems to acknowledge receipt of the data they exchange, making it resilient to connectivity issues. TCP is useful for tasks like file transfers and email delivery, where it's important not to lose any data. UDP doesn't require an acknowledgment from a recipient, and it's useful for tasks like watching videos or listening to audio without constantly being interrupted. If some of the bytes drop while traveling from the server to your screen, the show goes on without a hiccup.

HTTP and TLS

You'll use the Hypertext Transfer Protocol (HTTP) to request and receive data from the web. HTTP is an unencrypted protocol, meaning an overly curious or malicious actor on the same network could position themselves to inspect the content of your communications with a web server. Today, most websites use HTTPS, which encrypts traffic with Transport Layer Security (TLS), the "S" in "HTTPS." We'll cover TLS further in Chapter 2 and use it to encrypt all network traffic when able, including for data fetched from the web and communications between tools.

SSH

Secure Shell (SSH) is a technology that creates an encrypted *tunnel*, or network connection, from one computer to another. It's often used to remotely control a computer as if you're using its local keyboard. You'll configure several virtual machines in this book and then make extensive use of SSH to interact with them. You'll also explore an automation tool, Ansible, that uses SSH to orchestrate actions on many hosts at once. Chapter 2 discusses SSH in more detail.

Scripting languages

In this book, you'll write a few scripts using the Python programming language and use the Ruby programming language to transform data. We'll walk through these scripts' contents in detail. That said, you could also automate many of the commands we'll cover using shell scripts that execute Linux commands. Some experience creating shell, Python, or Ruby scripts is recommended, but not necessary, to follow along.

Online Resources

You'll find all of the commands and configurations in this book on GitHub, along with useful tidbits, at *https://github.com/bonifield/data-engineering-for -cybersecurity*. Each chapter has a corresponding directory containing its code and files. This repository will also contain any updates or corrections, if necessary.

PART I

FOUNDATIONS OF SECURE DATA ENGINEERING

In this part of the book, you'll explore the data engineer's role in cybersecurity environments and set up a lab environment in which to apply the techniques covered in subsequent chapters. You'll also learn how to work with core technologies helpful to data engineers. Chapter 2 covers the basics of network encryption with TLS and SSH, which you can use to protect your organization's sensitive security data while in transit, and Chapter 3 discusses working with the Git version control tool to organize the configurations you'll create in future chapters.

1

DATA ENGINEERING BASICS

Before we begin working with data engineering tools, let's survey the tasks a data engineer must accomplish when building their infrastructure. We'll also cover common logging architectures and discuss the data serialization structures frequently used by tools to format log data, including JSON and YAML.

Common Data Engineering Tasks

In this section, we cover some of the activities a data engineer is tasked with, including the challenges they might face and the strategies they can use to meet the organization's goals.

Getting Data to the SIEM

A *security information event manager (SIEM)* is a central database for security-related data. Analysts use SIEM tools to read logs from across the organization, view security alerts in various dashboards, and correlate disparate data points to understand activity taking place in the environment. In many organizations, the SIEM is crucial to incident response, as it allows analysts to, say, view ransomware indicators so they can quarantine a host or block malicious email senders.

Getting data to the SIEM can pose a challenge, however. Data useful for security analysis, such as logon events, processes started, and files downloaded from the internet, all come from different locations, such as Windows, Linux, and Unix operating systems; various network appliances; and even custom applications, all of which have differences. Throughout this book, you'll use tools that overcome these obstacles to acquire data from multiple sources. You'll also standardize this disparate data before sending it to the SIEM for analysis.

We'll assume the use of SIEM databases as the destination for the security data in this book, but you may send the data elsewhere if you desire. Many examples will show command outputs on the terminal; these outputs reflect the format of events transferred to a database for storage.

Managing Throughput and Latency

When designing pipelines, data engineers strive to reduce *latency*, or the delay between the time when an event enters a data pipeline or system and the time at which it exits. Latency might occur in several contexts. For example, a user might send a request to a database and then have to wait for a response, or a log might enter a computation-heavy pipeline before landing in a SIEM.

Latency can pose issues for security data pipelines. Pipelines may become congested due to too many events passing through, or server failures may reduce the number of available data processing nodes. These slowdowns might prevent important alerts, such as data theft or ransomware indicators, from reaching analysts in real time.

One way to address latency is to find ways of streamlining any processing and avoiding overly complex code. Delays may also stem from high processing requirements, the encoding and decoding of character strings, drive write speeds, or network bottlenecks. We'll find ways of avoiding unnecessary processing by using conditional logic, such as if-else statements, throughout the book.

As a data engineer, you'll also find it useful to understand the concepts of load balancing and throughput. *Load balancing* is the act of distributing a large data stream to multiple recipients so as to avoid overloading one single receiving server. Although you won't implement dedicated load balancers in this book, load balancing is a feature built into several of the tools we'll discuss.

Throughput is the total amount of data passing through a pipeline or system in a given amount of time. You should strive to maximize throughput; if your goal is to move vast amounts of security data, you should find a way to do so as fast as possible. We'll discuss throughput at a high level as we cover ways of avoiding bottlenecks.

Enriching and Standardizing Events

In addition to sending logs from various systems to the SIEM, data engineers might enrich and standardize those logs. *Enrichment* is adding useful information to the data. For example, you could add hostnames to network IP addresses in sensor alerts, add reputation scores or "malicious" tags to a website someone visits, or tag commands commonly used by intruders in living-off-the-land techniques for review.

Data enrichment can help analysts prioritize and reduce their workload. If they regularly need to look up a specific attribute related to some incident, such as the hostname corresponding to an IP address, it might make sense to enrich certain data feeds directly in the pipeline to save the analysts from having to perform the lookup themselves.

Likewise, standardizing data is important because the events that enter your data pipeline might have a variety of formats. *Structured data* is data organized neatly into rows and columns, such as relational database tables. *Semistructured* data is data saved in formats like JavaScript Object Notation (JSON), Extensible Markup Language (XML), and comma-separated value (CSV). Whereas structured data is likely already stored in a database and ready for querying via Structured Query Language (SQL), semistructured data generally encompasses output from tools and sensors, data being prepared for further formatting into structured data to be sent to a relational database, or data prepared to be stored in "document-oriented" databases. If you want to use semistructured data outside of a database, you'll likely have to read or parse it using command line tools. Many chapters in this book convert data to JSON before it reaches the SIEM.

By contrast, *unstructured data* might include images, blocks of raw text, audio files, or binary files, which are less conducive to storing in a database. When found in a database, unstructured data is commonly accompanied by metadata fields that describe the data's content.

Importantly, standardized data reduces the amount of work analysts have to do to correlate data across multiple sources. For example, if two network appliances send logs in different formats, a poorly implemented data pipeline might expect the analysts themselves to account for these differences, adding unnecessary overhead to analysis. A well-formed data pipeline should process the data into a single format, making the differences between tools irrelevant to analysts.

In this book, we'll primarily work with *time-series* data, or data with a timestamp used to determine a sequence of events. We'll parse timestamps and meaningful data from unstructured and semistructured event logs. We'll also briefly cover non-time-series data, such as the contents of Nmap scan results. Additional examples of non-time series include flat text documents, web page scrapes, names and addresses, product prices, and certain types of threat indicators.

Example Architectures

A data pipeline is essentially a transformation process that uses tools, scripts, and perhaps even user input to manipulate and store data. How might data engineers create data pipelines that meet the goals outlined in the previous section? Let's cover a few network designs you could implement using the tools and configurations discussed throughout this book.

Always remember that the enemy of usability is needless complexity. Avoid overengineering your data pipelines, and keep your goals realistic.

A Basic Data Pipeline

At its most basic, a data pipeline consists of a data source, such as a network device or host within the organization, that generates and transmits data; a system to receive and transform that data; and, finally, a system to store the data. For example, Figure 1-1 shows an example pipeline that receives log events transmitted from networked devices, formats them as JSON, then stores them in a database.

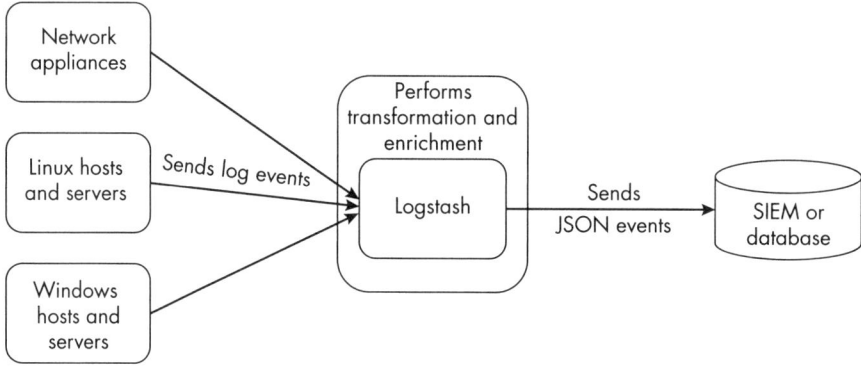

Figure 1-1: A pipeline that converts events into JSON before storing them in a SIEM

In this design, devices in the environment all transmit their log data to Logstash, a tool covered in Chapters 8 and 9 that receives and transforms events. Logstash converts all events into JSON and then loads the data into a SIEM or a database such as Elasticsearch. You'll use Elasticsearch in Chapter 6, but note that Elasticsearch isn't the only database capable of receiving JSON data, and JSON is just one of many formats that different databases may prefer.

You could use any number of tools to extract the logs from the hosts and transmit them to Logstash. In Chapters 4 through 7, we'll cover the tools Filebeat, Winlogbeat, Rsyslog, and Elastic Agent, respectively, for this purpose. These tools can retrieve logs from hosts like desktops, laptops, and servers or receive logs from network appliances and sensors.

The data pipeline shown here reflects the most common scenario: Users and computers send data somewhere for storage and analysis, and it's the data engineer's job to ensure that data reaches its destination. Data pipelines may also request data, however, as we'll discuss next.

Proactive Data Retrieval

Many applications and cloud services make data available via application programming interfaces (APIs), which allow you to reach out to the service to retrieve data. APIs may handle weather forecasts, commercial flight departures and arrivals, malware indicators, and millions of other data points. You could even use APIs to request data from the database to which you previously sent the data for analysis.

We'll explore using several tools, including Logstash, to receive streaming data from network appliances, servers, and hosts and proactively retrieve it from APIs, as shown in Figure 1-2.

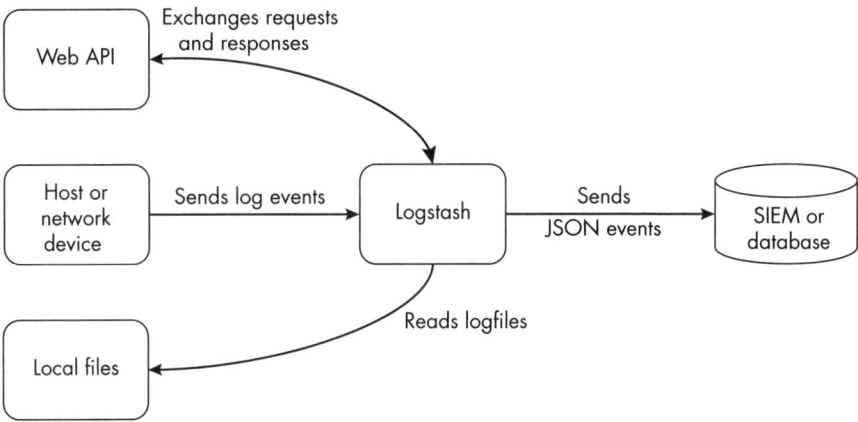

Figure 1-2: A data pipeline that both passively receives data and proactively fetches it

As in the previous example, Logstash retrieves all events and converts them to JSON before sending them to the SIEM or database. In this pipeline, however, Logstash both receives events from a server and proactively retrieves events from an API over HTTPS. For example, Logstash may send certain IP addresses, domains, or file hashes to an online service to determine a reputation score or tag phishing domains as malicious. As you likely don't have reputation scores for every website on the internet, you'd have to interact with an external service provider to receive this information. In this pipeline, Logstash also reads local files before sending them to the SIEM.

Temporary Data Centralization

You may need to centralize your data into one service so that multiple interested parties can receive a copy of it. For example, an organization's security data might be relevant not only to analysts but also to compliance teams, seasonal auditors, or insider threat teams. Kafka is a platform that links the parties that send the data to the consumers that may need a copy of it and allows analytics processing on the data streaming through it. The tool doesn't transmit data; instead, users and services connect to Kafka to provide (publish) or receive (subscribe) data. A pipeline that includes Kafka could look like Figure 1-3.

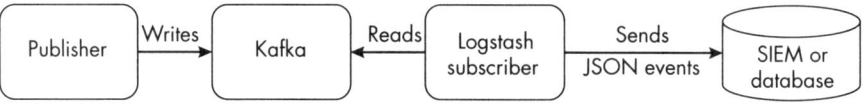

Figure 1-3: A pipeline that centralizes data using Kafka

In this pipeline, Filebeat *publishes*, or connects to and transmits, data to Kafka. Logstash *subscribes*, or connects to and then receives, data before transforming it and sending it to a database. We cover Kafka in Chapter 10.

Event Caching

A *cache* holds data in a database located in a system's memory to provide nearly instant access to the data. Adding a caching tool to your data pipeline can enable you to rapidly compare events traveling through your pipeline to values stored in the cache and modify the events before they make it to your SIEM. For example, Chapter 13 will use caching tools to search events for threat intelligence values, like malicious IP addresses or web domains, and enrich the events accordingly. We'll cover the architecture of such caching pipelines in more detail in that chapter.

Data Serialization Formats

One common task we'll discuss throughout this book is making data accessible to the tools in your data pipeline, which often involves converting different types of data and their fields into a standard format. Before you can do so, you should understand how to work with common serialization formats.

Serialization is the process of converting data from a format specific to a programming language into a format that can be sent across the network, exchanged with other tools or languages, or stored in a database. *Deserialization* is the reverse of serialization; it translates that common syntax back into some programming language's format. Serialization and deserialization aren't typically manual processes; most programming languages contain helper functions that, when explicitly invoked, serialize your data for you.

In the following chapters, we'll use the JSON serialization format to structure data. We'll also format log data fields using the Elastic Common Schema (ECS). Converting data to JSON and applying the ECS naming convention make it easier to add, delete, or edit values in your data pipeline. Lastly, this section covers the YAML format, which we'll use in later chapters to create configuration files.

JSON

JSON, short for "JavaScript Object Notation," formats data as a series of key-value pairs. All major programming languages (not just JavaScript) use it, as it's easy for both machines and humans to parse. Often, you won't need to create or alter JSON structures yourself; tools will do it for you.

JSON's syntax relies on quotations and brackets, as shown in the following example:

```
'{"first_name": "Lily", "has_pets": true, "num_pets": 4, "pet_types": ["dog", "fish"]}'
```

A JSON string is enclosed in single quotes (' ') and contains curly brackets ({}), which themselves contain one or more related key-value pairs. In this example, the brackets contain key-value pairs describing attributes of someone named Lily.

Keys must always be strings enclosed in double quotes (""), but values can have any of several data types. JSON uses the keywords true or false for Boolean values. It doesn't wrap numbers in quotations unless those numbers should be treated as text. Square brackets ([]) indicate an *array*, or a comma-separated list of values. This serialized string is ready for other tools to use and can be stored in a JSON-friendly database.

YAML

YAML is a recursive acronym of the phrase "YAML Ain't Markup Language." In this book, we'll use YAML to create and edit configuration files, not to transmit or receive data. You'll create many YAML configurations from scratch, so it's worth familiarizing yourself with the format.

YAML also uses key-value pairs, but it relies on whitespace and indentation rather than JSON's quotations and brackets to communicate relationships between data fields. The following snippet displays portions of *filebeat.yml*, a YAML file you'll configure in Chapter 4. The specific lines aren't important right now, but take note of the hierarchical, indented syntax:

```
output.logstash:
  enabled: true
  hosts: ["logstash01:5044", "logstash02:5044"]
  ssl.enabled: true
  ssl.verification_mode: full
  ssl.certificate: "wildcard.local.flex.cert.pem"
  ssl.key: "wildcard.local.flex.key.pem"
  ssl.key_passphrase: "abcd1234"
  ssl.certificate_authorities:
    - ca.cert.pem
    - ca-int.cert.pem
    - ca-chain.cert.pem
```

In YAML, indentation identifies how lines relate to one another. Within the output.logstash element, the format *nests* related settings, or indents them underneath. Lists can be enclosed in square brackets (similar to

Python lists or Ruby arrays), as with the `hosts` setting, or in a hyphenated sequence, as with `ssl.certificate_authorities`. Generally, quotation marks are optional; they're present for demonstration purposes on the `ssl` lines but omitted on the other lines.

Elastic Common Schema

The ECS is a standardized data naming specification, not a serialization format, that we'll use throughout this book. Logging tools that extract or process data often refer to any given field, such as a source IP address, using different names like `sip`, `src_ip`, or `sourceip`. Using ECS, these fields would standardize under the name `source.ip`. For an overview of commonly used ECS fields, see *https://www.elastic.co/guide/en/ecs/current/ecs-getting-started.html*.

Standardizing data in this way makes building your data pipelines easier, as you won't have to account for different field names from different tools for the same type of data, except for instances of renaming them to the standard, as you'll do throughout this book. Analysis becomes easier too, as analysts don't need to know that one tool produces important data using one name, while another tool provides the same type of data under another name; analysts only need to use one common name across all tools.

Next, let's cover setup requirements for the following chapters.

Virtual Machine Setup

This book primarily uses Ubuntu Linux, but many sections also show commands for Red Hat Enterprise Linux (RHEL) and similar builds. You can download Ubuntu from *https://ubuntu.com/download/desktop* and Red Hat from *https://developers.redhat.com/products/rhel/download* with a free user account.

To follow along with this book's examples, I recommend configuring three Linux virtual machines. One machine will serve as your main workstation, and the two others will enable you to practice sending data from one machine to another. That said, you could follow along with just two virtual machines, and even one will suffice in a pinch. If you run one virtual machine, however, you sacrifice the ability to create *clusters* of tools, or multiple instances of an application running simultaneously on different nodes.

In Chapter 5, we'll cover Winlogbeat, a Windows tool for reading event logs. You can download a free evaluation copy of Windows after registering for a Microsoft account if you wish to use a virtual machine to practice working with Winlogbeat. Alternatively, if you're running Windows on your computer, you could just install the software there. None of the steps in Chapter 5 are destructive or harmful, and while some portions do require you to change domain group policy, you can uninstall Winlogbeat from your host machine once you've finished and stop collecting event logs.

I tested every tool in this book using Ubuntu and Red Hat virtual machines with 4GB RAM, two CPUs, and 50GB solid state storage. You can increase resources as desired, however, and these numbers should be much higher in production environments. Use a network configuration such as Network Address Translation (NAT), commonly found in most virtual machine tools, that lets virtual machines on the same physical host communicate with each other and reach the internet to download files. Host-based NAT networks don't expose your virtual machines directly to the wider computer network.

There are many great installation tutorials for these virtual machines online, and I'll leave it up to you to determine what hypervisor tools to use to run the virtual machines. Once you've completed the installation and verified that it's working, take a baseline snapshot of each virtual machine. Whenever you configure a tool in subsequent chapters, I recommend shutting down the virtual machines and taking another snapshot to preserve your work. That way, you can revert the machine to a workable state if anything breaks later.

Windows File Transfer and Shell Access Tools

If you're using a Windows computer to host the Linux virtual machines, you should consider installing a couple of additional tools to make file transfers and shell access easier. The first is WinSCP, used for moving files between Windows and your virtual machines, available at *https://winscp.net/eng/download.php*. The second tool, PuTTY, is an SSH client that you can use to access your virtual machines' command line interface from a Windows host, without using each virtual machine's user interface. PuTTY is available at *https://www.chiark.greenend.org.uk/~sgtatham/putty/latest.html*. Note that Windows has an SSH client built in, but it lacks many features that make PuTTY worthwhile.

Other Useful Tools

The Linux tool jq reads JSON data and displays it on your terminal, adding indentation and colors for readability. While we won't use it in the book's examples, you might find it helpful for viewing some of the data we'll work with. Install it on your workstation virtual machine using **sudo apt install jq**. The basic syntax for reading a JSON file is jq '.' *file*.json, and the syntax to read a specific field, such as message, is jq '.["message"]' *file*.json.

Finally, you'll need a lightweight text editing tool to edit the many configuration files discussed throughout this book. I recommend Microsoft's Visual Studio Code or Notepad++ for Windows, which supports syntax highlighting, multiline operations, and find and replace with regular expressions. Visual Studio Code is available at *https://code.visualstudio.com*, and Notepad++ is available at *https://notepad-plus-plus.org/downloads/*.

Summary

Now that you understand the basic tasks of a cybersecurity data engineer and have set up your environment, you can begin learning how to collect, process, and store data for your home lab, business, or customers. The tools in this book will empower you to acquire and shape security data however you see fit to support your goals. Let's get started!

2

NETWORK ENCRYPTION

Data engineers should use encryption to protect the sensitive log data transmitted between tools. This chapter covers Transport Layer Security (TLS), a protocol that encrypts network connections to prevent the eavesdropping and manipulation of in-flight data.

Encryption might seem less critical when used between tools that are internal to an organization than when used for public communications, but internal encryption is important, as it protects an organization's most sensitive data. If an attacker or disgruntled employee gained access to communications equipment or a way to sniff data traversing a network interface, they could steal as much of it as they have storage space for. Internal encryption garbles what this person captures, so no sensitive data can be exploited or modified, and you should always apply it when setting up a data pipeline.

We'll begin by creating TLS certificate authorities, asymmetric keys, and signed certificates to enable the tools discussed throughout this book to establish encrypted connections with one another. We'll also configure

Secure Shell (SSH), a service that encrypts remote terminal access and file transfers between workstations and servers.

TLS Components

In a TLS connection between a client and a server, at least one party proves their identity to the other; then, both parties wrap their conversation in a secure channel before transmitting data. To achieve this, TLS requires several core components: a certificate authority (CA) that both parties need to trust, public and private keys for encrypting and decrypting data, certificate signing requests, and the final signed certificate.

The *CA* is a trusted entity that can issue signed certificates used by network services to encrypt data. Without a CA, nobody would be able to verify the identity of anyone else and no encrypted data should be exchanged. You can think of the CA as the Department of Motor Vehicles; the DMV issues you a driver's license (akin to a certificate), which you can then use to lawfully drive on public roads. If your license is inspected, it is validated using a central database.

A TLS connection relies on both parties having public and private key pairs. The *private* key is used to decrypt data previously encrypted by the *public* key in what is known as *asymmetric encryption*. The details of asymmetric encryption are outside the scope of this chapter, but in essence, everyone in the world can have a copy of your public key, and while they can use it to encrypt data, they can't decrypt that data; only your private key can do so.

Certificate signing requests contain details for inclusion in the final signed certificate, including but not limited to the public key and information about the key, which servers the certificate is valid for, and the organization and locality. A certificate signing request is akin to an application for a driver's license, as it contains everything the approver needs to make a decision and authorize the resulting signed certificate. The CA creates the signed certificate using the contents of the certificate signing request. The certificate signing request itself isn't signed; rather, OpenSSL generates a new signed certificate file. Web servers use this new signed certificate and its matching private key to form TLS connections between your browser and the server.

Interactions

Let's walk through an example that includes these TLS components. Say Bob wants to visit the website for Alice's Restaurant. He enters the website name, and his browser completes Domain Name System (DNS) resolution and the Transmission Control Protocol (TCP) handshake and then begins the TLS session setup. The browser first sends a *Client Hello* message, which tells Alice what TLS version and cipher suites his browser supports. Alice's Restaurant responds with a *Server Hello* message that includes its signed certificate, a random string, and its supported cipher suites.

Now that Bob's browser has Alice's signed certificate, it checks the certificate against the CA listed in that certificate. Since Bob's browser also trusts that CA, it generates a second random string called a *premaster secret*. It then encrypts the premaster secret using Alice's public key and sends it back to the server. The server uses its private key to decrypt the premaster secret from Bob. Since it was encrypted using Alice's public key, only Alice can decrypt it.

Using some very fancy math, both Bob's browser and Alice's Restaurant then generate identical session-specific symmetric keys based on the random string sent by Alice initially, as well Bob's premaster secret. Bob's browser and Alice's Restaurant both agree setup is finished by sending each other messages encrypted with the new symmetric session key. Now that setup is complete, the browser and the server will encrypt all data they send using these session keys, as symmetric encryption is generally faster than asymmetric encryption. Nobody else will be able to know what Bob is ordering at Alice's Restaurant.

Mutual TLS

Notice that in the TLS setup described in the previous section, only Alice's Restaurant sent a signed certificate. Alice didn't care who Bob was, only that Bob wanted to see the menu. But what if Alice's Restaurant needed to verify its customers? In that case, Bob would also send a signed certificate for Alice to verify, setting up a *mutual TLS (mTLS)* session.

Clients and servers use mTLS when both parties need to authenticate each other, in contrast to the more typical case in which just the client, such as a web browser, verifies the server. During an mTLS connection, both client and server exchange certificates with each other, and both are checked against a CA before encrypted data is exchanged.

In a security engineering context, using mTLS can protect against a variety of network attacks by limiting who can send data to your network services, including your logging infrastructure. For this reason, mTLS is a large part of the zero-trust movement, as it enables you to allow only those that can prove their identities before accessing internal or sensitive applications. Enforcing trust requirements before granting application access thereby limits what a network intruder can access, even if the intruder has working usernames and passwords.

Mutual TLS is meant for internal networks and zero-trust environments only. Don't use mTLS on a website or service meant for the public, as every potential customer would then need a trusted certificate to access your service.

Generating a Certificate Authority

In this section, you'll create your own root and intermediate CAs. You'll use the intermediate CA to sign certificate signing requests for all the tools in this book. In production environments, be sure to store CAs in highly secured systems used only to create intermediate CAs; the root CAs should be air-gapped and physically locked up. In your practice environment, you can forgo these security measures.

Before continuing, create the directory structure for the TLS files in your home directory on the Ubuntu virtual machine you're using as your main workstation:

```
$ cd ~
$ mkdir -p ~/tls/{configs,keys,csr,caroot,caintermediate,certs}
```

Stay in your home (~) directory for the following TLS commands, beginning with the creation of the root CA. Keep these CA files on your workstation, and don't delete them at the end of this chapter, as you'll use the CAs to create certificates for tools featured in each remaining chapter.

Root Configuration

OpenSSL is a free, open source tool for creating and managing TLS infrastructure, including CAs, keys, certificate signing requests, and certificates. It is packaged by default with most major versions of Unix and Linux systems and is estimated to be used by millions of websites. We'll use dedicated OpenSSL configuration files to set the options for the CAs instead of specifying these options on the command line. Using configuration files allows us to more easily revoke and create intermediate CAs in the future. Create *~/tls/configs/openssl-rootca.cnf* using the editor of your choice and add the following lines to it:

```
###############################################################
❶ [ ca ]
  # Section for the ca command; redirects to CA_default
  default_ca      = CA_default

❷ [ CA_default ]
  base_dir        = tls/caroot
  # Cert and key this config refers to
  certificate     = $base_dir/ca.cert.pem
  private_key     = $base_dir/ca.key.pem
  # Filepaths
  new_certs_dir   = $base_dir
  database        = $base_dir/index-root.txt
  serial          = $base_dir/serial-root.txt
  # Signed certificate specifics
  default_days    = 3650
  default_md      = sha512
  preserve        = no
  x509_extensions = ca_root
  # Required to copy Subject Alt Names (SANs) from CSR into cert
  copy_extensions = copy
  email_in_dn     = no
  unique_subject  = no
###############################################################
```

```
❸ [ req ]
  prompt              = no
  default_bits        = 4096
  default_md          = sha512
  distinguished_name  = ca_distinguished_name
  x509_extensions     = ca_root
  string_mask         = utf8only
  ############################################################
❹ [ ca_distinguished_name ]
  countryName             = US
  stateOrProvinceName     = MO
  localityName            = St. Louis
  organizationName        = Business, Inc.
  organizationalUnitName  = Information Technology
  commonName              = Root CA
  emailAddress            = none@localhost
  ############################################################
❺ [ signing_policy ]
  countryName             = optional
  stateOrProvinceName     = optional
  localityName            = optional
  organizationName        = optional
  organizationalUnitName  = optional
  commonName              = optional
  emailAddress            = optional
  ############################################################
  # v3 extensions
  ############################################################
❻ [ ca_root ]
  nsComment             = OpenSSL Certificate for Root CA
  subjectKeyIdentifier  = hash
  authorityKeyIdentifier = keyid:always,issuer
  basicConstraints      = critical, CA:TRUE
  keyUsage              = critical, cRLSign, digitalSignature, keyCertSign
  ############################################################
❼ [ ca_intermediate ]
  nsComment             = OpenSSL Certificate for Intermediate CA
  subjectKeyIdentifier  = hash
  authorityKeyIdentifier = keyid,issuer:always
  basicConstraints      = critical, CA:TRUE, pathlen:0
  keyUsage              = critical, cRLSign, digitalSignature, keyCertSign
  ############################################################
❽ [ client_cert ]
  nsComment             = OpenSSL Certificate for Clients
  subjectKeyIdentifier  = hash
  authorityKeyIdentifier = keyid,issuer:always
  basicConstraints      = CA:FALSE
  keyUsage              = digitalSignature, nonRepudiation
  extendedKeyUsage      = clientAuth
  ############################################################
❾ [ server_cert ]
  nsComment             = OpenSSL Certificate for Servers
  subjectKeyIdentifier  = hash
  authorityKeyIdentifier = keyid,issuer:always
```

```
basicConstraints      = CA:FALSE
keyUsage              = digitalSignature, keyEncipherment, nonRepudiation
extendedKeyUsage      = serverAuth
################################################################
❿ [ flex_cert ]
nsComment             = OpenSSL Certificate for Clients or Servers
subjectKeyIdentifier  = hash
authorityKeyIdentifier = keyid,issuer:always
basicConstraints      = CA:FALSE
keyUsage              = digitalSignature, keyEncipherment, nonRepudiation
extendedKeyUsage      = clientAuth, serverAuth
```

The ca section ❶ should contain only one key, default_ca, that points to a different section containing settings we've named CA_default. The CA_default section ❷ contains options for actions that CAs typically perform, including signing certificate signing requests using the command openssl ca, which you'll use shortly.

First, the CA_default section establishes the base_dir variable as the *tls* directory (which is relative to the configuration file's location); commands using this configuration will create new files relative to this path unless it's overridden on the command line. The paths specified for the root CA certificate and private key let OpenSSL know where to find these files when signing a certificate signing request.

This section also declares the location of new signed certificates and the location of the index and serial number trackers, which store a history of issued certificates. The CA creates new signed certificates valid for 10 years and creates SHA-512 message digests when signing certificate signing requests. We'll define the configuration's X.509 version 3 extensions, which describe the certificate's purpose, in the ca_root ❻ section.

Critically, we copy all subject alternative names (SANs) from the certificate signing request into the final signed certificate using copy_extensions = copy. A *SAN* is an X.509 extension that allows a certificate to list hosts or IP addresses for which the certificate is valid. We won't copy email addresses into the *Subject Distinguished Name (DN)*, which typically contains organization and locality information.

Next come configurations for OpenSSL's req ❸ subcommand, which we'll use to generate a new key pair, the root certificate, and the certificate signing request. OpenSSL won't prompt the user for the subject distinguished name, as those details are already in the configuration file. Keys created using this configuration will have 4,096 bits. We specify default_md using SHA-512 again for req to create the message digest, or key signature, for certificate signing requests. The distinguished_name and x509_extensions options point to their own sections because they each require several details to be specified.

The ca_distinguished_name section ❹ contains organizational and location information for the resulting signed certificate, which the signing_policy section ❺ requires, defining what fields must be present in a certificate signing request. The signing policy options in this configuration are all optional, but setting them to required means that anyone wanting a signed certificate must match some or all of the CA's location and organization values.

The next sections specify the roles this CA can assign. In the ca_root section ❻, the legacy-named Netscape comment (nsComment) briefly describes the certificate for anyone inspecting the comment. The subject _key_identifier is a hash of the Subject Public Key value, which helps to identify itself as corresponding to the paired private key. Defining keyid:always means the subject_key_identifier from the CA issuer must also always be present for verification; otherwise, a certificate error may occur during a TLS connection setup. Adding issuer means the issuing CA's distinguished name value will also be included in the signed certificate.

The option basicConstraints is critical and, per RFC 5280 section 4.2.1.9 paragraph 4, is required because this configuration is flagged as CA:TRUE, indicating a CA that we'll use to validate signatures. The keyUsage option is also critical, as it notably includes keyCertSign, which allows the certificate to perform signing duties.

The next section, ca_intermediate ❼, defines the intermediate CA. It has a slightly different basicConstraints option than the root CA's. The value pathlen:0 means it can have no subordinate CAs under it and can sign only user or server certificate requests. By contrast, the ca_root section doesn't include pathlen because it can create subordinate CAs.

Inside the client_cert section ❽, CA:FALSE explicitly states that certificates created with this extension aren't CAs. We also provide notably reduced options in keyUsage. The client_cert section's extendedKeyUsage option, clientAuth, means that any certificate created with this extension can initiate only TLS connections; it can't receive them. Similarly, the server_cert ❾ section's extendedKeyUsage option uses serverAuth only to receive TLS connections and cannot initiate them. Later in this chapter, you'll create and use a certificate with the flex_cert ❿ section, which applies both clientAuth and serverAuth extensions to a new *flex* certificate, so tools in this and later chapters can initiate *and* receive TLS connections.

Root Generation

With the root CA configuration in place, run the following command to generate a 4,096-bit certificate, valid for 10 years, with a SHA-512 message digest:

```
$ openssl req -x509 -config tls/configs/openssl-rootca.cnf -days 3650 -new
-extensions ca_root -keyout tls/caroot/ca.key.pem -out
tls/caroot/ca.cert.pem -passout pass:abcd1234
```

We don't need to generate a certificate signing request for a root certificate; instead, we immediately receive a signed certificate. Review the contents of the certificate using the following command:

```
$ openssl x509 -text -noout -in ~/tls/caroot/ca.cert.pem
--snip--
Issuer: C = US, ST = MO, L = St. Louis, O = "Business, Inc.",
```

```
OU = Information Technology, CN = Root CA, emailAddress = none@localhost
Subject: C = US, ST = MO, L = St. Louis, O = "Business, Inc.",
OU = Information Technology, CN = Root CA, emailAddress = none@localhost
--snip--
X509v3 Subject Key Identifier:
04:D7:9B:FE:08:A7:98:AC:0D:1B:A6:4B:4D:9B:A0:B4:68:D3:E5:20
X509v3 Authority Key Identifier:
04:D7:9B:FE:08:A7:98:AC:0D:1B:A6:4B:4D:9B:A0:B4:68:D3:E5:20
--snip--
```

Notice that the issuer and subject values are the same, as are the authority key identifier and subject key identifiers. For this reason, root CAs are considered self-signed.

Let's add index and serial trackers for the root CA to keep track of the certificates it has issued. The *index tracker* stores subject information about each certificate the CA has issued, and the *serial tracker* stores the next available serial number for use, generally incrementing from 00. Run the following commands:

```
$ touch ~/tls/caroot/index-root.txt
$ echo "00" > ~/tls/caroot/serial-root.txt
```

Next, we'll create a copy of the root CA configuration and modify it to make the intermediate CA configuration.

Intermediate Configuration

We'll use an intermediate CA, sometimes called a signing CA, to sign requests for tool-specific certificates. In production, intermediate CAs provide a buffer between the root CA and user certificates to limit the root CA's exposure to leaks or destruction. To configure the intermediate CA, copy the root configuration into a new file named *openssl-intermediateca.cnf*:

```
$ cp ~/tls/configs/openssl-rootca.cnf ~/tls/configs/openssl-intermediateca.cnf
```

Change all references to the root CA so they reference the intermediate CA in the CA_default, req, and ca_distinguished_name sections. Otherwise, this CA will function the same as the root CA:

```
--snip--
[ CA_default ]
base_dir        = tls/caintermediate
# Cert and key this config refers to
certificate     = $base_dir/ca-int.cert.pem
private_key     = $base_dir/ca-int.key.pem
# Filepaths
new_certs_dir   = $base_dir
database        = $base_dir/index-intermediate.txt
serial          = $base_dir/serial-intermediate.txt
# Certificate specifics
default_days    = 3650
```

```
default_md      = sha512
x509_extensions = ca_intermediate
# Required to copy Subject Alt Names (SANs) from CSR into cert
copy_extensions = copy
email_in_dn     = no
unique_subject  = no
################################################################
[ req ]
# Section for the req command
prompt              = no
default_bits        = 4096
default_md          = sha512
distinguished_name  = ca_distinguished_name
x509_extensions     = ca_intermediate
string_mask         = utf8only
################################################################
[ ca_distinguished_name ]
countryName             = US
stateOrProvinceName     = MO
localityName            = St. Louis
organizationName        = Business, Inc.
organizationalUnitName  = Information Technology
commonName              = Intermediate CA
emailAddress            = none@localhost
--snip--
```

The rest of the configuration is identical to the root configuration.

Intermediate Signing

To receive a signed intermediate certificate, we need a certificate signing request and a SHA-512 key pair. Run the following command to generate the intermediate CA's certificate signing request, named *ca-int.csr*, as well as the key pair:

```
$ openssl req -config ~/tls/configs/openssl-intermediateca.cnf -new -keyout
~/tls/caintermediate/ca-int.key.pem -out
~/tls/caintermediate/ca-int.csr -outform PEM -passout pass:abcd1234
```

Next, sign the intermediate certificate signing request using the root CA's configuration, *openssl-rootca.cnf*, to create the signed certificate, *ca-int .cert.pem*:

```
$ openssl ca -batch -notext -config ~/tls/configs/openssl-rootca.cnf
-passin pass:abcd1234 -policy signing_policy -days 3650 -extensions
ca_intermediate -out ~/tls/caintermediate/ca-int.cert.pem -infiles
~/tls/caintermediate/ca-int.csr
```

Note we've included the -notext argument in the previous command. This tells OpenSSL to output only the certificate content, whereas it would otherwise include the human-readable text viewable with the openssl x509 command.

Let's inspect the intermediate certificate's issuer and subject values:

```
$ openssl x509 -text -noout -in ~/tls/caintermediate/ca-int.cert.pem
--snip--
Issuer: C = US, ST = MO, L = St. Louis, O = "Business, Inc.", OU = Information Technology,
CN = Root CA,
emailAddress = none@localhost Subject: C = US, ST = MO, L = St. Louis, O = "Business, Inc.",
OU = Information
Technology, CN = Intermediate CA
--snip--
X509v3 Subject Key Identifier:   A3:A5:5D:C1:9C:C6:78:81:D9:ED:34:4C:3C:80:AC:05:73:8A:34:C6
X509v3 Authority Key Identifier: 04:D7:9B:FE:08:A7:98:AC:0D:1B:A6:4B:4D:9B:A0:B4:68:D3:E5:20
--snip--
```

The intermediate certificate includes its own subject and subject key identifier and the root CA's issuer and authority key identifier values.

Notice also that the intermediate CA's email isn't present in the subject, though it's present in the issuer field belonging to the root CA. This is because we set email_in_dn = no in the root CA's configuration, which applied to subordinate certificates only. The decision of whether to include emails in the subject distinguished name doesn't affect the tools in this book; organizations may use emails in distinguished names for certificate tracking purposes.

The intermediate CA's subject key identifier becomes the authority key identifier for all certificates it signs. The subject similarly becomes the issuer. This marks the beginning of a trust chain, in that a client certificate is issued by a trusted intermediate CA we trust, which was issued by the trusted root CA.

We also need index and serial trackers so we can keep track of what the intermediate CA has issued:

```
$ touch ~/tls/caintermediate/index-intermediate.txt
$ echo "00" > ~/tls/caintermediate/serial-intermediate.txt
```

OpenSSL has a verification command to ensure that certificate signatures match that of the issuing entity. The following command verifies that the root CA properly signed the intermediate CA's certificate:

```
$ openssl verify -CAfile ~/tls/caroot/ca.cert.pem ~/tls/caintermediate/ca-int.cert.pem
~/tls/caintermediate/ca-int.cert.pem: OK
```

This verification process, whether performed using this command or using connections across the internet, requires the entire *trust chain*, or root CA and any subordinate CAs, to be present. In this example, we're comparing only the intermediate CA against the root CA's signature. To verify certificates signed by the intermediate CA, we need a file that contains both root and intermediate CAs in one location.

Chain Files

A CA *chain file* is a single file containing both the root CA and all intermediate CAs' signed certificates and potentially any other certificate you wish to bundle for verification or distribution. This file should be distributed across your network to all users and services connecting to the tools in this book.

The CA chain file is just a text file containing all the necessary certificates needed to provide a full trust chain. That is, it consists of all entities in the signature process. Combine the signed certificates into one file named *ca-chain.cert.pem* in the *~/tls/certs* directory:

```
$ cat ~/tls/caroot/ca.cert.pem ~/tls/caintermediate/ca-int.cert.pem >>
~/tls/certs/ca-chain.cert.pem
```

It's a courtesy to include a CA chain file when sending a signed certificate back to its requestor within an organization.

Setting Up TLS for Logstash

We'll use Logstash extensively throughout this book to transform data streams, display test outputs on the screen, and send data into a database. Chapters 8 and 9 cover Logstash in depth. Let's create a TLS key and "flex" (combined client and server) certificate for Logstash so we can send data to it as we test tools throughout this book. We'll create flex certificates throughout the book for each new tool as needed, in addition to a special kind of "wildcard" certificate in Chapter 6 that contains multiple hostnames. In production environments, try to limit your certificates to either clientAuth or serverAuth extensions depending on service requirements.

Flex Configuration

We'll begin by creating the OpenSSL configuration, which is noticeably shorter than the CA configuration. This file declares only the server's identity; it doesn't need to sign anything else, nor does it contain signing policy settings. Add the following contents to *~/tls/configs/openssl-flex-logstash.local.cnf*:

```
###############################################################
[ req ]
prompt             = no
default_bits       = 4096
default_md         = sha512
❶ default_keyfile    = tls/keys/logstash.local.flex.key.pem
  distinguished_name = flex_distinguished_name
❷ req_extensions     = flex_cert
###############################################################
[ flex_distinguished_name ]
countryName              = US
stateOrProvinceName      = MO
localityName             = St. Louis
organizationName         = Business, Inc.
organizationalUnitName   = Information Technology
❸ commonName               = Logstash Flex
  emailAddress             = none@localhost
```

```
##############################################################
[ flex_cert ]
❹ nsComment       = OpenSSL Certificate for Client and Servers
❺ subjectAltName = @alternate_names
##############################################################
❻ [ alternate_names ]
DNS.1 = logstash
❼ DNS.2 = logstash.local
```

Include .local in the key name to identify the domain name that the key is for ❶. Place options for the req command ❷ in their own section, flex_cert; recall the openssl req command generates key pairs and certificate signing requests. The common name ❸ should contain the server's fully qualified domain name for backward browser compatibility, as modern browsers rely on the SAN to identify what a certificate is for. Note that many commercial certificate providers require you place an FQDN here. As this is a lab environment, you may also just use descriptions here, as you did with your CA certificates. The comment ❹ includes similar information so the reader understands the certificate's purpose. The SAN ❺ uses an at sign (@) to indicate an array of values located in the alternate_names section ❻. It's best to include any variation of the service name that could be used to authenticate, such as the base name logstash and the fully qualified domain name logstash.local ❼.

In production, don't include IP addresses in the list of alternate names unless you're certain they won't change during the certificate's lifetime. If you must include IP addresses, use the same numbered-dot notation for each IP address, similar to notation used for the hostnames in this configuration, such as IP.1 = 192.168.1.99, IP.2 = 10.10.1.99, and so forth.

Server Keys and Certificates

Let's generate the key pair and certificate signing request for Logstash. We protect the private key using the password abcd1234 and don't include the argument -keyout because the private key's filename is already specified in the configuration (though you may comment it out and use the command line; OpenSSL is very flexible):

```
$ openssl req -config ~/tls/configs/openssl-flex-logstash.local.cnf
-new -out ~/tls/csr/logstash.local.flex.csr -outform
PEM -passout pass:abcd1234
```

This command should have created your key pair and the Logstash certificate signing request. Use the intermediate CA configuration to sign the certificate signing request:

```
$ openssl ca -batch -notext -config ~/tls/configs/openssl-intermediateca.cnf -passin
pass:abcd1234 -policy signing_policy -extensions flex_cert -out
~/tls/certs/logstash.local.flex.cert.pem -infiles ~/tls/csr/logstash.local.flex.csr
```

View the new certificate to make sure everything is in the right place:

```
$ openssl x509 -text -noout -in ~/tls/certs/logstash.local.flex.cert.pem
--snip--
Issuer: C = US, ST = MO, L = St. Louis, O = "Business, Inc.", OU = Information Technology,
CN = Intermediate CA
Subject: C = US, ST = MO, L = St. Louis, O = "Business, Inc.", OU = Information Technology,
CN = Logstash Flex
--snip--
X509v3 Subject Key Identifier: C6:92:DF:FD:66:0F:B2:F3:57:04:F4:9E:1E:29:94:EF:17:15:23:DE
X509v3 Authority Key Identifier: A3:A5:5D:C1:9C:C6:78:81:D9:ED:34:4C:3C:80:AC:05:73:8A:34:C6
--snip--
```

Now we see that the intermediate CA is the issuer and authority key identifier and that Logstash appears in the subject and subject key identifier.

Finally, verify the certificate's signature; please note that the following bolded command should be one continuous line:

```
$ openssl verify -CAfile ~/tls/certs/ca-chain.cert.pem
~/tls/certs/logstash.local.flex.cert.pem
~/tls/certs/logstash.local.flex.cert.pem: OK
```

You should now have the keys and a signed certificate for Logstash.

Directory Preparation

Now you can start using Logstash with TLS settings in its inputs. First, change directories into your ~/*Downloads* folder. (Create this directory if it doesn't exist already.) Download the 64-bit Logstash package from Elastic's website using **wget**, substituting the most recent version for *X.Y.Z*. Then, extract the file using **tar**:

```
$ mkdir ~/Downloads
$ cd ~/Downloads
$ wget https://artifacts.elastic.co/downloads/logstash/logstash-X.Y.Z-linux-x86_64.tar.gz
$ tar xvzf logstash-X.Y.Z-linux-x86_64.tar.gz
```

If you wish to save some typing when you reference this directory in the future, rename the resulting versioned directory to just *logstash*, change into it, and make two new directories to hold certificates and pipeline configurations:

```
$ mv logstash-X.Y.Z logstash
$ cd logstash
$ mkdir {certs,conf.d}
```

Copy the Logstash signed certificate, key, and CA chain into the Logstash folder:

```
$ cp ~/tls/certs/ca-chain.cert.pem ~/Downloads/logstash/certs/
$ cp ~/tls/certs/logstash.local.flex.cert.pem ~/Downloads/logstash/certs/
$ cp ~/tls/keys/logstash.local.flex.key.pem ~/Downloads/logstash/certs/
```

Next, you'll create a short configuration for Logstash.

Logstash Configuration

Beats is a family of data shipper tools created by Elastic that includes Filebeat and Winlogbeat. We'll cover them in Chapters 4 and 5. The following Logstash configuration accepts data from Beats over TLS. Create the configuration *conf.d/beats-mtls.conf* using your text editor of choice and add the following code; ensure that you change the username from *j* to your own:

```
input {
    beats {
        port => 5044
        ssl_enabled => true
        ssl_client_authentication => "required"
        ssl_certificate => "/home/j/Downloads/logstash/certs/logstash.local.flex.cert.pem"
        ssl_key => "/home/j/Downloads/logstash/certs/logstash.local.flex.key.pem"
        ssl_key_passphrase => "abcd1234"
        ssl_certificate_authorities => [ "/home/j/Downloads/logstash/certs/ca-chain.cert.pem" ]
    }
    syslog {
        port => 5514
    }
}
filter {
    # We'll transform data here later.
}
output {
    stdout { codec => rubydebug {metadata => true}}
}
```

This configuration uses TLS connections to display Beats and syslog data on screen. It starts with an input block that contains two types of inputs: beats and syslog. Within the beats section, we specify the default Beats TCP port 5044 and enable SSL/TLS. We force mutual TLS client authentication, then specify our signed certificate, key, key passphrase, and CA chain file. Within the syslog section, we specify port 5514.

The filter block is where we'll rename fields to the Elastic Common Schema and perform many other transformations in Chapter 9. Next is the output block, which here pretty-prints JSON output using the Ruby Debug output codec. In Chapter 6, you'll include an output to send data from Logstash to a database called Elasticsearch. You'll also explore Logstash inputs and outputs in greater detail in Chapter 8.

Firewall Ports

We need to open some firewall ports to allow Logstash traffic. Use the following commands for Ubuntu's Uncomplicated Firewall (UFW):

```
$ sudo ufw allow 5044/tcp
$ sudo ufw allow 5514/tcp
```

Open the ports with Firewalld using Rocky Linux, CentOS, or RHEL:

```
$ sudo firewall-cmd --zone=public --add-port={5044,5514}/tcp --permanent
$ sudo firewall-cmd --reload
```

Test the Logstash configuration. The following command will alert us to any syntax errors or other issues:

```
$ bin/logstash -f conf.d/beats-mtls.conf --config.test_and_exit
```

Open a new terminal, then navigate to the Logstash directory. Using two terminals allows you to view standard output in one terminal, while still being able to control Logstash in the other terminal. The argument `config` `.reload.automatic` means any changes made to the running configuration will kick in immediately, without having to restart Logstash:

```
$ bin/logstash -f conf.d/beats-mtls.conf --config.reload.automatic
```

Logstash should now be running, and you can stream data to it using encrypted Beats and plaintext syslog. You'll use Logstash extensively in the following chapters to receive, send, request, transform, display, and load data into a database.

SSH

The Secure Shell protocol establishes encrypted connections between two systems. These connections allow administrators and automated processes to open remote terminal sessions, conduct file transfers, or create secure tunnels between networks with untrusted connections. Like TLS, SSH uses asymmetric key pairs to establish communications, but unlike TLS, there are no certificates and no CAs.

Ansible, a tool covered in Chapters 11 and 12, relies on SSH to perform automated remote administration. SSH is also a great security wrapper for tunneling data from programs that don't support encryption on their own or between remote networks.

A *forward SSH tunnel* binds a tunnel to a local port so that any local data sent to that port will be sent to the IP address and port on the distant end. A *reverse tunnel* connects to a distant address and then allows distant services to send data back through the tunnel to the originating host. SSH can serve as a SOCKS proxy to securely ship data through these tunnels to any number of distant IP addresses and ports accessible by the distant host. If you encounter situations where TLS connections aren't feasible or supported, SSH tunnels still allow you to encrypt otherwise unprotected data.

Enabling SSH

OpenSSH is a collection of tools that implement the SSH protocol to create secure connections, including a tool that allows servers to listen for incoming connections. We'll use SSH throughout this book, so let's install OpenSSH now.

Run the following commands on Ubuntu to install OpenSSH Server, allow SSH through the firewall, and restart the SSH service:

```
$ sudo apt install openssh-server
$ sudo ufw allow ssh
$ sudo systemctl restart ssh
```

These commands perform the same tasks on Red Hat Enterprise Linux (RHEL), Rocky Linux, and CentOS; take note that on these systems, the service name is sshd, not just ssh:

```
$ sudo dnf install openssh-server
$ sudo firewall-cmd --zone=public --add-service=ssh --permanent
$ sudo firewall-cmd --reload
$ sudo systemctl restart sshd
```

Now your servers are ready to receive connections from users who supply their usernames and passwords. Next, you'll create SSH key pairs so that users don't have to enter a username and password every time they access the system.

Creating SSH Keys

Key pairs prevent brute-force attacks against passwords and improve user experience. Specify a bit size of 4,096 and a filename inside *~/.ssh*. I like to include my username, *j*, in the filename, although it's best to use an SSH configuration to manage multiple key names:

```
$ ssh-keygen -b 4096 -f ~/.ssh/j_id_rsa
```

You'll be prompted to set a passphrase, and it's a security best practice to do so. As with the TLS files, use the passphrase *abcd1234*; everything in this book that needs a password will use this one, but you'll be reminded to use it when necessary. Next, you'll start the SSH agent to hold your key in memory, so you don't have to enter a passphrase every time you use it.

Starting the Agent

The *SSH agent* keeps a private key in memory and allows you to skip the step of entering the key's passphrase every time you log in to a server with it. This feature comes in handy when you're remotely accessing multiple servers at a time, such as when using Ansible, covered in Chapters 11 and 12.

Before starting the agent, load variables set by the agent into your current shell's environment variables, which you'll need to interact with the agent, by using **eval** with the output from **ssh-agent**:

```
$ eval $(ssh-agent -s)
Agent pid 4604
```

You should now have a process ID you could use to terminate the agent, if needed, with the command `kill -9 ProcessId`. Load the private key into the agent:

```
$ ssh-add ~/.ssh/j_id_rsa
Enter passphrase for /home/j/.ssh/j_id_rsa: your passphrase
```

You can create an *alias*, or shortcut command, that combines these commands into a single simpler one by adding the following line to the file *~/.bashrc*:

```
alias start-ssh='eval "$(ssh-agent -s)" && ssh-add /home/j/.ssh/j_id_rsa'
```

The SSH agent isn't persistent, and you'll need to restart it after a reboot or when opening a new terminal.

Creating Configuration Files

SSH configuration files map keys to servers and define connection-specific information for each server, such as port numbers, usernames, and other details that are beyond the scope of this chapter. They save you from having to juggle multiple keys and authentication options in cases where you have development, production, and other network servers.

OpenSSH uses two types of configuration files: one that affects the whole system, called a *global* configuration, and individual configurations for each user on a system. The global configuration is located at */etc/ssh/ssh_config*, or */etc/sshd/sshd_config* for a server configuration that accepts incoming connections. The user configuration files take precedence over the global file and are in each user's home directory in the hidden *.ssh* directory. Command line arguments take precedence over both global and user configurations.

Create a new SSH user configuration file at *~/.ssh/config* (note the period before *ssh*):

```
$ nano ~/.ssh/config
```

Next, add the following lines; substitute the username on the remote host that you want to connect to for *j*:

```
Host 10.*.*.* 192.168.*.* *.local *.internal
Port 22
User j
IdentityFile ~/.ssh/j_id_rsa
```

The Host statement uses wildcards (*) to apply to broad or dynamic values, including the 10.0.0.0/8 and 192.168.0.0/16 network blocks and anything on the *.local* or *.internal* domains, which you'll use throughout this book. Port 22 is the standard SSH port, but you could use another port here if the service is listening elsewhere. I've specified the connecting username *j*, but you should specify different usernames here as needed. IdentityFile specifies which private key to use. Save and exit the file.

SSH configurations can have multiple sections formatted, like the previous snippet that might list development and production servers with different keys, allowing administrators to use the same commands to access each server. You can also list specific IP addresses or hostnames for one-off connections, such as for jump boxes or demilitarized zone (DMZ) bastions. In Chapter 3, you'll back up this file using Git.

Distributing Public Keys

You must distribute SSH public keys to the hosts you want to access. The following command copies the new SSH public key onto the remote server *192.168.2.20* as the remote user *j*. Substitute your own IP address and username, or use *localhost* if you're running a single virtual machine:

```
$ ssh-copy-id -i ~/.ssh/j_id_rsa.pub j@192.168.2.20
```

After you enter your username and password, the key becomes available for use. If you've never before connected to this server, respond **yes** when asked if you trust the host fingerprint, a unique identifier that helps keep track of known hosts you've connected to.

If you need to update SSH keys in the future for any reason, repeat the process described here and then update your configuration file to point to the new key before shredding the old one. (Yes, there is a shred command in Linux.)

Verifying Connectivity

Now that you've created SSH keys and a configuration file, started the agent, and copied the public key to the remote servers, test the secure connection by entering the following command. Substitute the following IP address with the one you're connecting to:

```
$ ssh 192.168.2.20
```

This command should load you straight into the remote client without issue, as you've already specified a user, an IP address range, a private key in the configuration file, and the private key loaded in the SSH agent. If your local username differs from that of the remote one but you forgot to set or update the User entry in your SSH configuration, use the syntax ssh *user@ip*.

An equivalent command without an SSH configuration file would look like the following:

```
$ ssh -i ~/.ssh/j_id_rsa j@192.168.2.20
```

Take some time to explore the many useful SSH hardening guides online. Some easy steps to take include mandating keys for remote access, denying remote root logins, rate-limiting connection attempts, and blocking a user after a certain number of failed login attempts.

Summary

TLS and SSH are critical to ensuring that data traveling through our pipelines remains confidential. In this chapter, we created root and intermediate CAs, private keys, and signed certificates so our tools can communicate using TLS. Then, we started Logstash using a configuration that accepts Beats over TLS. We also created SSH keys and a configuration file to make remote access more convenient.

This is a great time to snapshot your virtual machines! In the next chapter, you'll install Git and use it to manage the configurations in this book and then back them up to a remote location.

3

SOURCE AND CONFIGURATION MANAGEMENT

When managing a data pipeline, you'll find it helpful to keep track of edits to your configuration files, collaborate with team members to alter them, and roll back any breaking changes made to a known-good version. In this chapter, we'll explore Git, a free version control tool, then practice using it to keep track of the configurations you'll create throughout this book. You'll start a project, use branches to develop code without affecting production releases, and synchronize your code with a remote repository.

In Chapters 11 and 12, we'll cover Ansible, which you can use with Git to deploy tools using an *infrastructure as code* approach; Git will store working copies of your configurations and tool layouts, and Ansible can dynamically install and configure the tools. Git makes this possible by centralizing working copies of configurations to prevent discrepancies between different servers or environments.

The Git Version Control Workflow

Version control systems allow organizations to track changes to code and see who authored them. They let you reverse changes if a new feature breaks something, which occurs frequently in development releases. Git is free, and two major websites, GitHub and GitLab, use their own versions of Git under the surface to host projects online. Both GitHub and GitLab have their own spins on project terminology, but the underlying Git language is the same.

In a Git-based workflow, a production project typically resides in a remote *repository*, or storage location, accessible to the whole world, the company, or the development team and users only. The production copy of the project resides in a *branch* of the repository, or a development space, typically called *main*.

To make changes to the project, the author *clones*, or downloads, a copy of the main branch from the remote repository into a local repository on their machine. The author may also *pull* updates from the remote repository to their local repository instead of downloading the whole project via a clone. Next, they create a new branch in which to make their changes. Once changes have been made, the author *adds*, or tracks, all changes, then *commits* the changes along with a message describing the changes to the branch. Think of a commit as a point-in-time snapshot; you may revert from one snapshot to a previous one to undo changes to a project.

Next, the author *pushes*, or uploads, the branch back to the project's remote repository. Once reviewed and approved, the new branch *merges* into the production branch. The author may also choose to merge their code into the main branch locally and push it directly to production, although this is discouraged on teams of more than one person.

Installation

On Red Hat and similar flavors of Linux, use dnf to install Git. On Ubuntu and Debian, use apt:

```
$ sudo apt install git
```

On Windows, an installer package available at *https://gitforwindows.org* integrates with the command shell environment. Those with winget installed on their Windows system can retrieve Git using the following command:

```
PS> C:\Users\James\> winget install --id Git.Git -e --source winget
```

Now let's configure Git to work with SSH and GitHub or GitLab.

Setting Up GitHub or GitLab

Accounts on GitHub (*https://www.github.com*) and GitLab (*https://gitlab.com*) are free to make and use, and both offer the option to create private repositories. Pick one, follow the steps they provide to create an account, then make a new private repository (on GitHub) or private project (on GitLab) named *my-repository*. Be sure to select the option to initialize the project with a README file.

Next, add your SSH public keys to your account. On GitHub, click your profile picture in the top-right corner, select **Settings ▸ SSH keys**, and click **New SSH key**. Add your public key as an authentication key and give it a title. On GitLab, click your profile picture in the top-left corner, then select **Preferences ▸ SSH Keys** on the left side of the menu and click **Add new key**. Add the public key, give it a title, and opt to use it for authentication. You can also choose to set an expiration date.

Now that you have new SSH destinations, add the following lines to the SSH configuration file you created in Chapter 2. This will make pushing and pulling code require fewer command line options:

```
Host github.com
PreferredAuthentications publickey
IdentityFile ~/.ssh/j_id_rsa

Host gitlab.com
PreferredAuthentications publickey
IdentityFile ~/.ssh/j_id_rsa
```

If you created both GitHub and GitLab accounts, this configuration shows what separate entries for each website should look like. I specify new hosts for GitHub and GitLab and specify a preferred authentication method of publickey to use this key instead of a password to access the account. Edit the IdentityFile lines with your filepaths. If you created only one account, you don't need to specify the other account.

Next, we'll configure three global Git options to accompany all commits we'll make. These will apply identifying information to all commits and create a new default branch name in new repositories. Provide your email and desired username, which can be anything you want. (It doesn't have to match your GitHub or GitLab account name.) We'll also specify any new repositories we make locally to use the industry standard name main instead of the older name master as the default:

```
$ git config --global user.email "your-email@domain.com"
$ git config --global user.name "your-username"
$ git config --global init.defaultBranch main
```

Now start the SSH agent if it's not already running after following the instructions in Chapter 2. You could also use the start-ssh alias in that same chapter, which expands to the following:

```
$ eval "$(ssh-agent -s)" && ssh-add ~/.ssh/j_id_rsa
```

The SSH agent should now be running, so you shouldn't be prompted for a passphrase before running any remote Git commands.

Creating New Directories

Since you probably don't want to work entirely from your home directory, make a *projects* directory to hold your work, and change directories into it:

```
$ mkdir ~/projects
$ cd ~/projects
```

There are two main ways to link a local repository on your computer with your online repository. The first is to make a new local directory and initialize the project files, then point the directory to the online repository. The second option is to clone the online repository to the local system. Let's do both for practice.

Before continuing, you must copy the remote address of your new online repositories. On GitHub, click **Code** in your repository and retrieve the address from the SSH text box. On GitLab, click **Clone** inside your project and copy the address from the Clone with SSH text box. The SSH address should be something like *git@github.com:bonifield/my-repository.git*, with your account name in place of *bonifield*.

Initializing Locally

Let's start with the manual initialization option. First, make a local directory named *my-repository*, then change into it. This will serve as your local repository:

```
$ mkdir my-repository
$ cd my-repository
```

Now initialize the local directory as a Git repository by running the following:

```
$ git init
Initialized empty Git repository in /home/j/projects/my-repository/.git/
```

To link this local repository with your remote one, use the SSH address you copied previously; substitute your own account name for *bonifield*:

```
$ git remote add origin git@github.com:bonifield/my-repository.git
```

To add some content to the new repository, create a *README.md* file to fill in later:

```
$ echo "# my-repository" > README.md
```

Now we need to track and commit the file in the new repo. I'll cover each of these steps in more detail shortly, but for now, run the following commands:

```
$ git add .
$ git commit -m "initialized with readme"
```

Finally, push this repository and its new *README.md* file to the remote one. This will forcibly sync the two, and you should be able to use it in the following examples. Since the new remote repo likely has its own empty *README.md* file, you must overwrite it with your own:

```
$ git push --set-upstream origin main
```

As you just witnessed, setting up a new blank repository and mapping it to a new one hosted online involves many steps. Let's cover how to jump-start a local repo using a remote one.

Cloning the Remote Repository

By running git clone right away, we can skip most of the initialization steps covered in the previous section. This command will initialize the project for us locally and set most of the tracking variables we had to use in the previous, manual initialization method. Clone the repository using the Git address you copied, changing your account name as necessary:

```
$ git clone git@github.com:bonifield/my-repository.git
```

Finally, change into the new directory:

```
$ cd my-repository
```

You're now ready to work on your project.

Updating README.md

For our first example of working with Git, let's update the *README.md* file. In a Git project, this file serves as both the welcome page and documentation. Run the following to open the file in your local repository:

```
$ nano README.md
```

This file uses Markdown syntax to communicate formatting information; for example, the leading hash mark (#) before the repository name indicates that you should use the largest font available when the file is displayed. Below this repository title, add some text of your choosing:

```
# my-repository
Hello, world!
```

Then save and exit the file. Now that you've made changes, you should verify that Git is aware of them. Use the following command to display the current branch, as well as any untracked changes:

```
$ git status
```

The status command is likely the most common Git command you'll enter. The output should show the modified *README.md* in red, since it now differs from the state it was in when pulled. I've bolded it here:

```
On branch main
Your branch is up to date with 'origin/main'.
Changes not staged for commit:
  (use "git add <file>..." to update what will be committed)
  (use "git restore <file>..." to discard changes in working directory)
modified:   README.md
no changes added to commit (use "git add" and/or "git commit -a")
```

This output tells us several important details about the project. You're on the main branch, which is the default, as you didn't specify anything else to the command. You're also up to date with the remote repository, or *origin*, and its main branch, which may seem counterintuitive, as you modified *README.md*. The reason for this is that you haven't staged or committed the changes yet. Finally, you can see the name of the modified file.

Let's stage the changes so Git can track them. We'll use a period to indicate that we want to stage all files in the present directory, although we could also explicitly name *README.md*:

```
$ git add .
```

Run another status check. This time, the changes should be shown as staged and the modified files should be green to indicate they're ready for committing. I've bolded the file here:

```
$ git status
--snip--
Changes to be committed:
  (use "git restore --staged <file>..." to unstage)
modified:   README.md
```

You can add --short to the command to get a slimmed-down output that is still color-coded:

```
$ git status --short
M  README.md
```

Next, commit the changes, which is akin to saving them, and include a message using -m about what you did:

```
$ git commit -m "modified README with demo text"
[main 64f16fe] modified README with demo text
 1 file changed, 2 insertions(+), 1 deletion(-)
```

One more status check should reveal that you're now *ahead* of the remote origin, meaning your local code is more recent than the remote code. You are ready to push:

```
$ git status
On branch main
Your branch is ahead of 'origin/main' by 1 commit.
  (use "git push" to publish your local commits)
nothing to commit, working tree clean
```

Now all you need to do is push the changes back to the remote repository with the **push** command:

```
$ git push
Enumerating objects: 5, done.
Counting objects: 100% (5/5), done.
Writing objects: 100% (3/3), 291 bytes | 72.00 KiB/s, done.
Total 3 (delta 0), reused 0 (delta 0), pack-reused 0
To github.com:bonifield/my-repository.git
   a1e4315..64f16fe  main -> main
```

Refresh your browser, and your changes should appear! Note that the timestamp shown online (and when using git log) is the commit time, not the push time, reflecting the point-in-time save state and not the time at which you shipped the code to the web.

Creating a New File

We just modified a file, but what if we want to add a new one? Use the echo command to add some new text to a file:

```
$ echo "Don't forget to bring a towel!" > advice.txt
```

Now that you have a new file, view its status:

```
$ git status
--snip--
Untracked files:
  (use "git add <file>..." to include in what will be committed)
advice.txt
```

The file is untracked, since we still need to stage the changes and make Git aware that the new file exists. Untracked files in a short status check should have two question marks in red (shown in bold here):

```
$ git status --short
?? advice.txt
```

Stage the changes, then ensure that the status command shows the filename in green (shown in bold here):

```
$ git add .
$ git status
--snip--
Changes to be committed:
  (use "git restore --staged <file>..." to unstage)
new file:   advice.txt
```

Commit the changes with a message, and once again check the status:

```
$ git commit -m "created advice.txt"
[main 519cdfa] created advice.txt
  1 file changed, 1 insertion(+)
  create mode 100644 advice.txt
$ git status
--snip--
Your branch is ahead of 'origin/main' by 1 commit.
```

Now push the changes to the remote repository:

```
$ git push
--snip--
Writing objects: 100% (3/3), 313 bytes | 104.00 KiB/s, done.
--snip--
```

Refresh the browser to see that the new file has been added.

Ignoring Files

What if you don't want Git to track a certain file at all? The *.gitignore* file is a list of files, directories, and wildcards that prevents Git from revealing your private files, such as sensitive configurations or private keys, to the whole world.

To practice using this feature, make a blank file named *sensitive.conf* in your project directory:

```
$ touch sensitive.conf
```

Now add *.conf to the *.gitignore* file, indicating we don't want any configuration files tracked or pushed:

```
$ echo "*.conf" >> .gitignore
```

Check the status of the project, and note that the configuration file isn't listed but that *.gitignore* is. Add the directory again and check the status one more time:

```
$ git status
--snip--
Untracked files:
  (use "git add <file>..." to include in what will be committed)
.gitignore
$ git add .
$ git status
--snip--
Changes to be committed:
  (use "git restore --staged <file>..." to unstage)
new file:   .gitignore
```

Commit these changes, then push the code:

```
$ git commit -m "added config and .gitignore"
[main 51e5bd1] added config and .gitignore
  1 file changed, 1 insertion(+)
  create mode 100644 .gitignore
$ git push
--snip--
Writing objects: 100% (3/3), 330 bytes | 110.00 KiB/s, done.
```

Now only *.gitignore* should appear on the page, as *sensitive.conf* is located only on your personal machine.

GitHub offers a great collection of standard *.gitignore* files hosted at *https://github.com/github/gitignore*, with examples for common programming and tool projects.

Creating a Development Branch

So far, we've committed changes directly to the project's main branch. Let's practice creating separate branches for development and testing. By using separate branches, you can avoid messing with production code every time you add a new feature with potential bugs.

Adding the Branch

First, use **branch** to create a new dev branch, then run **checkout** to move into it:

```
$ git branch dev
$ git checkout dev
On branch dev
```

You could also have used git checkout -b dev to create the new branch in one command. A status check should show that you're on the new branch:

```
$ git status
On branch dev
nothing to commit, working tree clean
```

The branch command shows an asterisk next to the active branch. Adding -a shows all remote branches:

```
$ git branch
* dev
  main
$ git branch -a
* dev
  main
  remotes/origin/HEAD -> origin/main
  remotes/origin/main
```

Now that you've confirmed you're on the new branch (three times), add new files to it.

Creating a New File

Let's pretend you've added a new feature that introduced some bugs to your code. Create a new empty file:

```
$ touch buggy-feature.txt
```

By now, checking the project's status should be muscle memory, but do it again, then track the new file:

```
$ git status
On branch dev
Untracked files:
  (use "git add <file>"... to include in what will be committed)
buggy-feature.txt
$ git add .
```

Next, commit the changes to generate a snapshot of them:

```
$ git commit -m "created new project file"
[dev 7bfb810] created new project file
  1 file changed, 0 insertions(+), 0 deletions(-)
  create mode 100644 buggy-feature.txt
```

Now compare the files in your two branches. List your dev branch's directory contents, where the new, buggy feature is stored:

```
$ ls
advice.txt  buggy-feature.txt  README.md  sensitive.conf
```

Switch to the main branch, list the files again, and then switch back to dev:

```
$ git checkout main
Switched to branch 'main'
Your branch is up to date with 'origin/main'.
$ ls
advice.txt  README.md  sensitive.conf
$ git checkout dev
Switched to branch dev
```

You just verified that *buggy-feature.txt* exists only on the dev branch.

Setting the Branch's Remote Origin

If you try to push your code to the remote repository, however, you'll get an error, as you haven't set the remote-origin version of the dev branch:

```
$ git push
The current branch dev has no upstream branch.
To push the current branch and set the remote as upstream, use
    git push --set-upstream origin dev
```

Run the following command, which will simultaneously create the dev branch and trigger an update notification if you're logged in to your remote repository in your browser:

```
$ git push --set-upstream origin dev
Enumerating objects: 4, done.
--snip--
Writing objects: 100% (3/3), 285 bytes | 95.00 KiB/s, done.
--snip--
Branch 'dev' set up to track remote branch 'dev' from 'origin'.
```

You've just modified the local dev branch so that it pushes to the remote dev branch. You can see these relationships using the following command:

```
$ git remote show origin
* remote origin
  Fetch URL: git@github.com:bonifield/my-repository.git
  Push  URL: git@github.com:bonifield/my-repository.git
  HEAD branch: main
  Remote branches:
    dev  tracked
    main tracked
  Local branches configured for 'git pull':
    dev  merges with remote dev
    main merges with remote main
  Local refs configured for 'git push':
    dev  pushes to dev  (up to date)
    main pushes to main (up to date)
```

Refresh your browser, and click **main** to see a drop-down menu with the new dev branch you just pushed.

Merging the Branch into main

Suppose you fixed your buggy code file and are ready to merge it into a production release. Switch to the main branch:

```
$ git checkout main
```

The following (intuitively named) command merges the dev branch into the current local main branch:

```
$ git merge dev
Updating 51e5bd1..7bfb810
Fast-forward
  buggy-feature.txt | 0
  1 file changed, 0 insertions(+), 0 deletions(-)
  create mode 100644 buggy-feature.txt
$ ls
advice.txt  buggy-feature.txt  README.md  sensitive.conf
```

A quick status check shows you are now ahead of the remote main branch:

```
$ git status
On branch main
Your branch is ahead of 'origin/main' by 1 commit.
  (use "git push" to publish your local commits)

nothing to commit, working tree clean
```

To change this, push the code to the remote repository:

```
$ git push
Total 0 (delta 0), reused 0 (delta 0), pack-reused 0
To github.com:bonifield/my-repository.git
  51e5bd1..7bfb810  main -> main
```

You're now hosting the new file for the whole world to see.

Performing Optional Cleanup

If you decide to delete the development branches after you're done, make sure to delete the remote branch using a push operation:

```
$ git push -d origin dev
Deleted branch dev (was 7bfb810).
```

Then delete the local branch to remove your copy of it:

```
$ git branch -D dev
To github.com:bonifield/my-repository.git
  - [deleted]        dev
```

The dev branch should no longer exist.

Rebasing and Resetting Your Code

Suppose one of your co-workers made a change to the main repository while you were at the vending machine. Now your working base is slightly off from the production version, causing a problem: deviating code. You can fix this problem by *rebasing* your code, or aligning it with the commits made to the remote main branch, before you push your changes.

WARNING *There are potentially destructive components to this action. Rebasing or resetting code may delete or overwrite the contents of your local repository. Back up any files you don't want to lose outside of the repository, or use* git stash, *which we'll cover shortly, to temporarily keep files safe from being deleted.*

Creating a New Test Branch

Let's make a test branch and add some files we want to later merge into the main branch. Track the *testfeature.txt* file and commit the changes. We'll add -a to the commit command to ensure we commit all files Git knows about (noting, however, that if we had untracked changes and used this command, it would cause an error):

```
$ git checkout -b test
Switched to a new branch 'test'
$ touch testfeature.txt
$ git add .
$ git commit -a -m "added test feature"
[test 63d1b41] added test feature
  1 file changed, 0 insertions(+), 0 deletions(-)
  create mode 100644 testfeature.txt
```

Since you've made your changes, merge the test branch back into your local main branch:

```
$ git checkout main
Switched to branch 'main'
Your branch is up to date with 'origin/main'.
$ git merge test
Updating 7bfb810..63d1b41
Fast-forward
  testfeature.txt | 0
  1 file changed, 0 insertions(+), 0 deletions(-)
  create mode 100644 testfeature.txt
```

Now let's alter the remote main branch to simulate a change we aren't aware of.

Modifying the Remote main Branch

We'll make a remote change that your local repository does not know about. Go to the remote repository in the main branch and create an empty file named *someoneelsewashere.txt* using the website's **Add file** button. Commit the changes and add a message about simulating a new change.

Back in your local main repository, attempt to push your changes to the remote branch:

```
$ git push
! [rejected]        main -> main (fetch first)
error: failed to push some refs to 'github.com:bonifield/test.git'
hint: Updates were rejected because the remote contains work that you do
hint: not have locally.
--snip--
```

Uh oh; your code was rejected! The error message provides some insight into what happened: Essentially, the local copy of the main branch is out of date and also has a new file compared to the remote one, and locally Git doesn't know how to reconcile that difference.

You could always force an update to the remote main branch, but unless you simultaneously want to update your resume, you should probably consult your team before doing so.

Let's correct this issue by pulling the remote main branch into our local branch. First, make sure you're in your local main branch:

```
$ git branch
* main
test
```

Now use a **pull** operation:

```
$ git pull origin main
To github.com:bonifield/my-repository.git
  ! [rejected]        main -> main (fetch first)
From github.com:bonifield/my-repository
  * branch            main       -> FETCH_HEAD
hint: You have divergent branches and need to specify how to reconcile them.
--snip--
hint:   git config pull.rebase false  # Merge (the default strategy)
hint:   git config pull.rebase true   # Rebase
hint:   git config pull.ff only       # Fast-forward only
--snip--
fatal: Need to specify how to reconcile divergent branches.
```

Normally, this operation syncs changes from the remote repository into the local repository. However, the local code is still divergent from the remote repository, and the default code-merging strategy is false to avoid overwriting local files. Try executing a fast-forward pull, as mentioned in the error messages, in an attempt to skip to the most recent state:

```
$ git pull --ff-only
fatal: Not possible to fast-forward, aborting.
```

A fatal error is the sure sign of something problematic. You must take one of two actions: rebase your main repository, which means merging any prior commits into a new baseline so you can remerge the test branch, or obliterate what you have locally and start anew with the remote version.

The first option is to specify a rebase to pull remote changes while preserving the merged test branch contents. A status check still shows your local branch is ahead of the remote branch, as the pull shouldn't affect the new files you merged previously. Run the following commands:

```
$ git pull --rebase
$ git status
On branch main
Your branch is ahead of 'origin/main' by 1 commit.
  (use "git push" to publish your local commits)
$ git push
--snip--
To github.com:bonifield/my-repository.git
   ef366a9..6938a47  main -> main
```

Both local and remote main branches are now synchronized.

Let's perform a hard reset, which forcibly synchronizes your local repository with the remote version. Re-create the previous conundrum by making *testfeature2.txt* in your local test branch and committing it and then creating *someoneelsewashere2.txt* in the remote main branch. Merge your local test into main and attempt to push, which should produce an error.

Fetch any changes from the remote (origin) branch, then issue a **git reset** command:

```
$ git fetch origin
$ git reset --hard origin/main
HEAD is now at fa5f628 Create someoneelsewashere2.txt
```

The local repository commit is now synced with the remote one. Had you made any further changes to the local main branch, those also would have been destroyed during the reset.

Now that you're synced with the remote version, merge your local test branch into the local main branch and push it to the remote repository. Immediately after running the merge command, an editor should open to prompt you for your commit message explaining the merge; edit the message if desired and then save and exit:

```
$ git merge test
Merge branch 'test'
# Please enter a commit message to explain why this merge is necessary,
# especially if it merges an updated upstream into a topic branch.
--snip--
```

Push the code to the remote repository, which shouldn't generate errors this time:

```
$ git push
--snip--
To github.com:bonifield/my-repository.git
  fa5f628..0804e9f  main -> main
```

Viewing the remote repository, you should see the file you added and the one your simulated "co-worker" added.

Temporarily Stashing Changes

Suppose you're working on a branch, but your team needs an emergency fix pushed right away. You don't want to remove changes and have your hard work go to waste, nor do you want to store them outside the repository in a random untracked folder. The git stash command lets you set aside your current files temporarily, so you can pull and push updates without worrying about pushing any unfinished code.

On your remote repository, add some random text to an existing file, or add a new empty file, and then commit the changes. Make a new local file, *testfeature99.txt*, but don't commit yet. Track the files, then run **git stash** to set aside your working files:

```
$ touch testfeature99.txt
$ git add .
$ git stash
Saved working directory and index state WIP on main: f5e81c8 Update
file testfeature99.txt
```

Next, pull the remote changes, and you should see the changes you made to the remote file, not the local one. You may commit and push code as needed without affecting your stashed files. Finally, restore your stashed files:

```
$ git stash pop
On branch main
Your branch is up to date with 'origin/main'.
Changes to be committed:
  (use "git restore --staged <file>..." to unstage)
    new file:   testfeature99.txt
```

Your stashed files are restored and still tracked, so you don't need to git add them.

Cleanup

With your code pushed to the main branch, you may delete your local testing branch if you desire. If you got ahead of yourself and deleted the local test branch before rebasing, you would lose your work:

```
$ git branch -D test
```

With the code disseminated and repository cleaned up, you can consider this project finished . . . until someone changes it again.

Now that we've covered the basics of Git, create a new repository to store your data pipeline configurations throughout this book.

Creating a Repository for the Book's Project Code

You'll need to safely store the code you write in this book in a repository. Let's start by saving the Transport Layer Security (TLS) files created in Chapter 2. On GitHub or GitLab, make a new private repository named *book-data-pipelines* and initialize it with a *README.md* file. On your local virtual machine, clone down the repository and change directories into it; be sure to change your username in the Git address:

```
$ git clone git@github.com:your-username/book-data-pipelines.git
$ cd book-data-pipelines
```

Make a *.gitignore* file for TLS files you don't want to publish:

```
$ nano .gitignore
```

Add the following lines, then save and exit:

```
*.attr
*.old
*.csr
*index-*
*serial-*
*.pem
*.pass
*.pkcs12
```

You don't want to accidentally publish any certificates or keys from this directory or any subdirectories, and this *.gitignore* should ensure that you don't do so. Now make a directory named *tls* and copy the TLS configurations and any notes you made in Chapter 2 into it. Substitute *your-tls-config-location* with the path at which you saved them:

```
$ mkdir tls
$ cp -r /your-tls-config-location/ ./tls/
```

Track your new files and check the repository status:

```
$ git add .
$ git status
On branch main
Your branch is up to date with 'origin/main'.
Changes to be committed:
  (use "git restore --staged <file>..." to unstage)
    new file:   tls/configs/openssl-rootca.cnf
    new file:   tls/configs/openssl-intermediateca.cnf
--snip--
```

Commit the changes with a message stating you're pushing new TLS files and then push the changes:

```
$ git commit -a -m "added TLS configs and command notes"
--snip--
$ git push
```

You've now backed up your TLS configurations and notes to your private remote repository.

Summary

Git is a powerful version management tool that we'll use throughout the remainder of this book to store configurations. In this chapter, you learned how to pull and push repository code, create and modify files, and fix issues that may arise when working with others. The ability to modify code for testing without breaking the rest of your working project is a core benefit of using Git and will save you hours of heartache when something goes wrong.

There are Git capabilities well beyond the scope of this chapter, so I recommend learning about the tool and becoming comfortable with what Git can do for your team. Version-controlled code can help your organization recover after a disaster, especially when combined with automation tools like Ansible and offsite backups. We'll use Git in the following chapters to store our working backups, and eventually you can call them using Ansible to automate your entire tool chain's deployment.

PART II

LOG EXTRACTION
AND MANAGEMENT

Data engineers must often figure out how to get data from remote hosts and into the security information event manager (SIEM). In this part of the book, we'll cover tools that can run on the endpoints in your environment, collect logs from them, and forward these logs to a central location for storage or further processing. In Chapter 4, we'll focus on the extraction of logs from an organization's endpoints and network using a tool called Filebeat. In Chapter 5, we'll discuss the Windows event log and how you can mine this critical data source with Winlogbeat, a companion tool to Filebeat. To centrally manage the log collection agents running on devices across your environment, you might choose to use Elastic Agent, covered in Chapter 6. Lastly, in Chapter 7, we'll explore the syslog logging format and collect syslog data using Rsyslog.

4

ENDPOINT AND NETWORK DATA

All effective monitoring and security infrastructures rely on the ability to collect data from diverse sources across an organization. We'll begin our discussion of log collection with Elastic Filebeat, which can extract dozens of log types from endpoints and the network.

You'll discover how to harvest local logfiles and listen to the network for incoming data. Then, you'll use Filebeat's modules and processors to convert data to the Elastic Common Schema (ECS) naming convention, extract relevant fields from a filestream, apply tags to events to aid later analysis, and read custom logs that Filebeat's modules don't support.

Once you've collected logs from endpoints, you'll likely want to transmit them to another tool. We'll explore ways of outputting data to tools covered in later chapters, including Kafka, Redis, Logstash, and text files.

Collecting Logs with Filebeat

You can install Filebeat on any device running Linux, Windows, or macOS to collect data from it. Filebeat reads logs on the host machine or from the network; converts them into JSON; uses its internal processors to add, modify, or delete the content of events; and then sends the logs downstream to Logstash, Kafka, Elasticsearch, or other tools. Its many modules allow it to interpret events from various vendor technologies, including commercial tools like Cisco and Palo Alto Networks and open source tools like Zeek.

Filebeat can also rename log values using the ECS naming convention, which is helpful because different tools use distinct names to label the same information. For example, they might include destination IP address fields called `dst_ip` or `dip`; ECS would convert both names into `destination.ip`, making searching for data from multiple sources much easier.

The tool provides several advantages over other log collectors we'll discuss later in this book, such as Elastic Agent and Rsyslog, covered in Chapters 6 and 7, respectively. Unlike Rsyslog, it automatically converts many log varieties into JSON and ECS by default, although Filebeat needs Elasticsearch or Logstash for complex ECS conversions. Filebeat can also prune and privatize data, and it requires relatively few configuration settings to do so. Additionally, Filebeat can output logs to more destinations than Elastic Agent can, including Redis and text files, and offers a lower barrier to entry than Elastic Agent.

Another advantage of Filebeat over other traditional logfile collectors is that it provides *backpressure support* when outputting events directly to Logstash and Elasticsearch. This means that if Logstash experiences a spike in data that it needs time to process, it can notify Filebeat to slow things down so it can catch up. Alternatives to Filebeat would continue to firehose data, causing queue backups or potential data loss.

Filebeat could even replace the need for Logstash in environments running technologies supported by Filebeat and Winlogbeat that consume JSON downstream. Written in Golang, Filebeat is more lightweight than Logstash, which is written in Java and Ruby. However, Filebeat supports only one output destination at a time, whereas Logstash can send data to any of several destinations by using conditional statements. Logstash also has a much more robust filtering capability than Filebeat, but if an organization needs only the features Filebeat can provide, Filebeat is the better option.

One downside to Filebeat is that it acts as a stand-alone agent rather than a centrally managed one. Operators must manually upgrade and reconfigure Filebeat, whereas they can modify and upgrade Elastic Agent from a central server. We'll explore Elastic Agent in Chapter 6 and compare its functions to those of Filebeat. We'll also use Ansible in Chapters 11 and 12 to demonstrate deploying Filebeat on multiple servers.

Another challenge is that Filebeat requires a unique socket for each enabled module when receiving events from other tools. For instance, it might receive some traffic on port 514/TCP, with the Cisco module listening on 5514/TCP for router and switch events and the Palo Alto module listening on 55514/TCP. If not managed properly, this can certainly lead to configuration clutter and a multitude of firewall holes across the network.

Installation

The majority of this chapter will focus on reading logs from Linux hosts. You can download Filebeat from the Elastic website in several file formats, including DEB, RPM, Apt, Yum, Windows, and macOS and Linux tarballs. Let's use the tarball package, which makes it easier to start and stop Filebeat frequently. The configurations you'll make for the tarball package are compatible with Apt and Yum installations.

On your Linux host, navigate to your user's home *Downloads* directory and download the *Linux x86_64* tarball from Elastic's Filebeat downloads web page. Replace the version number in the filename as appropriate:

```
$ cd ~/Downloads/
$ wget https://artifacts.elastic.co/downloads/
beats/filebeat/filebeat-X.Y.Z-linux-x86_64.tar.gz
$ tar xvzf filebeat-X.Y.Z-linux-x86_64.tar.gz
$ cd filebeat-X.Y.Z-linux-x86_64
```

We'll cover Windows installation and configuration instructions in "Filebeat for Windows" on page 78.

Enabling TLS

To protect our data, we need to create a TLS certificate for Filebeat so we can encrypt the data it sends. In Chapter 2, we created root and intermediate CAs. Let's use the intermediate CA to sign a new flex certificate request.

Creating a Configuration File

We'll use OpenSSL to create a new TLS flex certificate. Store this file, *openssl-flex-filebeat.local.cnf*, in the TLS configuration directory (*~/tls/configs*) you created in Chapter 2. Open your preferred text editor and enter the following:

```
##############################################################
[ req ]
prompt              = no
default_bits        = 4096
default_md          = sha512
❶ default_keyfile    = tls/keys/filebeat.local.flex.key.pem
distinguished_name  = flex_distinguished_name
req_extensions      = flex_cert
##############################################################
❷ [ flex_distinguished_name ]
countryName                 = US
stateOrProvinceName         = MO
```

```
         localityName                = St. Louis
         organizationName            = Business, Inc.
         organizationalUnitName      = Information Technology
      ❸ commonName                   = Filebeat Flex
         emailAddress                = none@localhost
         ##############################################################
         [ flex_cert ]
      ❹ nsComment                    = OpenSSL Certificate for Clients or Servers
      ❺ subjectAltName               = @alternate_names
         ##############################################################
         [ alternate_names ]
      ❻ DNS.1  = filebeat
      ❼ DNS.2  = filebeat.local
```

OpenSSL will use this configuration to create a new private key ❶ in the *tls/keys* directory. Replace the location information in flex_distinguished _name with your own ❷ (unless you, like me, come from the land of toasted ravioli and pork steaks). We'll use the commonName ❸ and nsComment ❹ statements to indicate that this is a client certificate for initiating and receiving encrypted connections, although please note commercial certificate providers require an FQDN as the commonName value for backward browser compatibility. The subject alternative names ❺ include the base name ❻ and fully qualified domain name ❼ of the server running Filebeat.

If you haven't already done so, be sure to add your Filebeat IP address, hostname, and Logstash information to your DNS server or to */etc/hosts* so that the hostnames resolve to the proper destinations. These entries should look like the following; substitute your IP addresses as necessary:

```
--snip--
192.168.8.133  filebeat
192.168.8.133  filebeat.local
192.168.8.133  logstash
192.168.8.133  logstash.local
--snip--
```

Without the ability to resolve hostnames, Filebeat won't be able to establish TLS connections, since the certificate's subject alternative name doesn't include IP addresses. Next, we'll generate the private key and signing request.

Generating Certificate Signing Requests

Let's create the key pair and a certificate signing request. We'll also include the key passphrase on the command line to skip being prompted for it, but you shouldn't type passwords on the command line in production:

```
$ openssl req -config tls/configs/openssl-flex-filebeat.local.cnf -new
-out tls/csr/filebeat.local.flex.csr -outform PEM -passout pass:abcd1234
```

Next, let's use the intermediate CA from Chapter 2 to create the signed certificate. Pass in the private key's passphrase and specify the CA's signing_policy and flex_cert extensions:

```
$ openssl ca -batch -notext -config tls/configs/openssl-intermediateca.cnf -passin
pass:abcd1234 -policy signing_policy -extensions flex_cert -out
tls/certs/filebeat.local.flex.cert.pem -infiles tls/csr/filebeat.local.flex.csr
```

You should now have the signed certificate, *filebeat.local.flex.cert.pem*. View it to check its extensions:

```
$ openssl x509 -in tls/certs/filebeat.local.flex.cert.pem -text -noout
--snip--
    X509v3 Extended Key Usage:
    ❶ TLS Web Client Authentication, TLS Web Server Authentication
    X509v3 Subject Alternative Name:
    ❷ DNS:filebeat, DNS:filebeat.local
--snip--
```

The certificate indicates that it's for client and server connections ❶, and the DNS entries ❷ show both the base name and the fully qualified domain name (FQDN) we specified. Check that the certificate can be authenticated using the CA chain file:

```
$ openssl verify -CAfile tls/certs/ca-chain.cert.pem tls/certs/filebeat.local.flex.cert.pem
tls/certs/filebeat.local.flex.cert.pem: OK
```

As we have a valid certificate with both the *clientAuth* and *serverAuth* extensions, we can begin configuring Filebeat.

Configuration

Filebeat uses the *filebeat.yml* configuration file to centralize core settings. This is where you'll configure inputs, transformations not found in modules, and outputs, along with other settings.

The default outputs in *filebeat.yml* immediately try to connect to local Elasticsearch and Kibana instances. So, instead of using the file as provided, we'll slim it down and then fill it in over the course of this chapter to better understand how it works.

For the purposes of this example, let's say we used Project Discovery's network reconnaissance tools Subfinder and Httpx to acquire subdomain information about *https://owasp.org*, resulting in JSON output files. We'll edit *filebeat.yml* to provide a path to these files and an ID for troubleshooting, then explicitly enable the input.

First, copy the original file into a backup:

```
$ cp filebeat.yml filebeat.yml.original
```

Then, edit the filestream input statement in the file to match the following slimmed-down version, substituting your username for *j* as needed:

```
filebeat.inputs:

# Input that reads local files from custom recon tooling
❶ - type: filestream
❷   id: recon-logs
    enabled: true
❸   paths:
      - /home/j/example-logs/subfinder*.json
      - /home/j/example-logs/httpx*.json

# Module location
❹ filebeat.config.modules:
    path: ${path.config}/modules.d/*.yml
❺ tags: [ "tags-for-everybody", "you-get-a-tag", "and-you-get-a-tag" ]

❻ output.logstash:
    enabled: true
    hosts: [ "logstash.local:5044" ]
❼ ssl.enabled: true
❽ ssl.verification_mode: full
❾ ssl.certificate: "/home/j/tls/certs/filebeat.local.flex.cert.pem"
    ssl.key: "/home/j/tls/keys/filebeat.local.flex.key.pem"
    ssl.key_passphrase: abcd1234
    ssl.certificate_authorities:
      - /home/j/tls/certs/ca-chain.cert.pem
```

The filebeat.inputs section contains one input, filestream ❶. Adding an id statement ❷ is a best practice for troubleshooting missing or unexpectedly high-volume logs, as it allows us to easily identify a problematic configuration block.

The paths statement ❸ provides the locations of the files containing the input. We've specified newline-delimited JSON (NDJSON) files that use wildcards to match any file beginning with *subfinder* or *httpx* and ending in the *.json* extension. This should let us read logs generated by the reconnaissance tools Subfinder and Httpx.

The filebeat.config.modules section ❹ tells Filebeat where to find its processing modules. We've left this section unchanged because these modules are part of the downloaded tarball. We add custom tags ❺ to every event to categorize them for later analysis. Finally, output.logstash ❻ describes where to send the data it outputs. Be sure that the IP address in the output statement matches that of the Logstash instance you configured in Chapter 2.

We enable TLS ❼ and set the verification mode to full ❽, requiring Filebeat to verify the downstream server's certificate against the CA and match the domain name against the one listed in the downstream certificate. We also specify the signed client certificate ❾, key file and passphrase, and our CA chain.

Let's copy this new *filebeat.yml* to its own backup, which we'll save in our remote Git repository at the end of this chapter:

```
$ cp filebeat.yml filebeat.yml.backup
```

Next, open a new terminal in which to run Logstash so it can receive data from Filebeat. Load the *beats-mtls.conf* Logstash pipeline we created in Chapter 2 in another terminal and keep the Logstash instance running to monitor the output on screen:

```
$ bin/logstash -f conf.d/beats-mtls.conf --config.reload.automatic
```

You can now view any output sent to Logstash on the screen in real time. But while this is ideal for testing purposes, it probably won't be useful in production unless you can read at *Matrix* speeds. Let's explore input and output types and use Logstash to view the data processed by Filebeat.

Input Sources

Filebeat extracts data by reading files on the host, listening to the network, or reaching out to external systems like Redis or Kafka. We configure these input sources in *filebeat.yml*, as shown in the previous section, or inside the individual module configuration files. Multiple inputs can run at once (though Filebeat can output data to only one location).

Reading Local Files

Filebeat will use the filestream inputs you configured in *filebeat.yml* to vacuum up local logs and send them downstream. If you're migrating to Filebeat from tools like Rsyslog and Syslog-ng, this process should look familiar; Filebeat reads the logs, parses them loosely into JSON and ECS when able, and ships them off.

The tool also keeps track of where it left off in each file using a registry of *offsets*, or byte positions. For the sake of testing, let's write a short bash script in the Filebeat directory, named *clean-and-reload-filebeat.sh*, that will delete this registry so we can reread the same logs multiple times, which will make it easier to generate test data. Open your editor of choice:

```
$ vim clean-and-reload-filebeat.sh
```

Add these lines and then save and close the file:

```
#!/bin/bash
rm -rf data/
./filebeat -e
```

Note that if you installed Filebeat using the DEB or RPM packages, you'll find your */data* directory in */var/lib/filebeat*, and you'll need sudo privileges to delete it.

The script will remove the cached positions and then restart Filebeat. Make the script executable:

```
$ chmod +x clean-and-reload-filebeat.sh
```

Invoke Filebeat for the first time by running the following command in its own terminal window. It should read the NDJSON files we listed as inputs during configuration:

```
$ ./filebeat -e
```

The -e option sends all output to the standard error stream. Also note the leading period before the slash.

NOTE   *You might find it helpful to create a split terminal window using tools like Tmux or Terminator. By placing Filebeat on the left side of the screen and Logstash on the right side, you can watch both tools in action without navigating between terminals.*

As a result of running the command, Filebeat will process the logs configured earlier.

Applying Parsers and New Fields

Parsers interpret or translate an input format into another format, typically JSON unless otherwise specified. This may include reading a string containing JSON data and converting it into usable key-value pairs. Note that the NDJSON we read as input in the previous section appeared in the Logstash terminal as a giant blob in the message field:

```
{
          "log" => {
         "file" => {
         "path" => "/home/j/example-logs/httpx_owasp.org.json"
         },
       "offset" => 134706
         },
   "@timestamp" => 2040-04-28T20:29:57.884Z,
     "@version" => "1",
      "message" => "{\"timestamp\":\"2040-04-27T15:23:03.636525891-
                    05:00\",\"csp\":{\"domains\":[\"https://
--snip--
```

To properly format these key-value fields, let's add a parser inside of the *filebeat.yml* file's filestream statement. In this case, we'll use a parser called ndjson:

```
filebeat.inputs:
- type: filestream
  id: recon-logs
  enabled: true
  paths:
    - /home/j/example-logs/subfinder*.json
    - /home/j/example-logs/httpx*.json
❶ parsers:
  ❷ - ndjson:
    ❸ target: "processed"
    ❹ add_error_key: true
  fields_under_root: true
❺ fields:
    threat.tactic.name: "Reconnaissance"
    threat.tactic.id: "TA0043"
    threat.technique.name: "Gather Victim Network Information"
    threat.technique.id: "T1590"
```

We nest the parser under the `type: filestream` section ❶. We specify that it will read NDJSON from the event ❷, nest the new JSON under the `processed` key ❸, and add an error message ❹ if something unexpected happens.

We also add ECS-aligned custom fields ❺ to describe MITRE ATT&CK framework values present in these logfiles. MITRE ATT&CK is a popular system used to describe adversary behavior during threat modeling and analysis. You could use these fields downstream to categorize these logs as network reconnaissance activity.

Filebeat expects a dotted field name representing nested JSON objects, meaning a field named `abc.123.xyz` would have a top-level key of `abc` and a value of `123`, which itself is a key containing the final string value `xyz`.

Now that we can parse NDJSON into a nested field of its own, run the handy Filebeat cleaner script to wipe out the registry and reingest the files:

```
$ ./clean-and-reload-filebeat.sh
```

Much better! Filebeat can now parse the JSON fields, so other tools can reference them later. We'll also be able to use the custom threat fields for filtering or analysis:

```
{
  ❶ "@timestamp" => 2040-05-08T09:00:47.133Z,
         "log" => {
        "file" => {
        "path" => "/home/j/example-logs/httpx_owasp.org.json"
      },
      "offset" => 134706
    },
      "threat" => {
         "technique" => {
               "id" => "T1590",
             "name" => "Gather Victim Network Information"
```

```
            },
            "tactic" => {
                "id" => "TA0043",
              "name" => "Reconnaissance"
            }
          }
        },
    ❷ "processed" => {
                "timestamp" => "2040-04-27T15:23:03.636525891-05:00",
                   "method" => "GET",
           "content_length" => 74814,
                "webserver" => "Server",
                   "scheme" => "https",
              "status_code" => 200,
                     "host" => "...
--snip--
```

ECS uses @timestamp to label the time an event occurred, although additional time-related fields, such as event.start and event.end, can provide more granular time information.

Notice a problem in this example: The @timestamp value ❶ shows the time at which the logs were read by Filebeat, instead of the value in processed .timestamp ❷ representing the time of the actual event. The value is notably wrapped in quotes when displayed, as Filebeat treats it as a string object, not a date object. This is because we didn't tell Filebeat to use processed .timestamp. We'll discuss modifying this behavior in the "Processors" section on page 65.

Let's add another filestream input to ingest events from local files in */var/log*:

```
- type: filestream
❶ id: local-syslog-files
  enabled: true
  paths:
    - /var/log/*.log
❷ exclude_lines: ['.*UFW.*']
  parsers:
❸ - syslog:
      format: auto
      add_error_key: true
```

We set a new input ID ❶ and exclude lines ❷ that contain UFW, which stands for Uncomplicated Firewall, the default firewall on Ubuntu. We also use the syslog parser ❸ with the auto format to detect both RFC 3164 and 5424 formats. Note that Filebeat also has a system module for reading files in */var/log*.

For the remainder of this chapter, whenever we enable a new input, we'll disable the previous one. This will allow us to become familiar with the outputs from each new input without getting lost in the flow from other inputs.

Listening to the Network

Filebeat has a variety of network inputs that allow it to receive data from remote systems over TCP, User Datagram Protocol (UDP), and Unix sockets. It can also act as an HTTP application programming interface endpoint that accepts requests and sends HTTP requests at specified intervals.

To listen for incoming syslog messages over the network using a plaintext (unencrypted) listener, add a new input type to *filebeat.yml* below the filestream section:

```
❶ - type: syslog
    id: syslog-tcp-5514
    enabled: true
    # Can also specify rfc3164 and rfc5424
❷ format: auto
❸ tags: [ "forwarded" ]
❹ protocol.tcp:
  ❺ host: "localhost:5514"
    exclude_lines: ['.*UFW.*']
```

The syslog input type ❶ used with the auto format ❷ will detect both RFC 3164 and RFC 5424 syslog messages. Add the tag forwarded ❸ to indicate that the messages originated elsewhere. Filebeat will listen for TCP ❹ connections on localhost port 5514 ❺ because ports below 1024 (including the standard syslog port 514/TCP) require elevated permissions. Exclude all lines containing the string UFW, as it's best to track firewall logs separately due to the volume of traffic they generate.

We'll configure Rsyslog in Chapter 7, but if you already have it running, you can add the following line to a new configuration at */etc/rsyslog.d/send-to-filebeat.conf* and then restart Rsyslog to output logs to Filebeat:

```
*.*     @@localhost:5514
```

The double at sign (@@) represents TCP. (To represent UDP, use a single at sign.) Now run Filebeat again, and notice the forwarded tag present in the streaming data:

```
$ ./filebeat -e
--snip--
    "message" => "pam_unix(sudo:session): session closed for user root",
      "tags" => [
    [0] "tags-for-everybody",
    [1] "you-get-a-tag",
    [2] "and-you-get-a-tag",
    [3] "forwarded",
    [4] "beats_input_codec_plain_applied"
  ],
      "log" => {
    "source" => {
    "address" => "127.0.0.1:46474"
```

```
        }
    },
      "@version" => "1",
      "process" => {
      "program" => "sudo"
    },
        "syslog" => {
        "facility_label" => "security/authorization",
              "facility" => 10,
              "priority" => 86,
        "severity_label" => "Informational"
--snip--
```

Filebeat is now parsing events from a remote system and forwarding them.

You may have noticed that the process name sudo is now nested under process.program and that the filestream input puts it under syslog.appname. This is worth paying attention to, as you might want to copy the name into the preferred process.name field using Logstash or a Filebeat processor. Most modules in *filebeat/modules.d* that extract process information will correctly place its name in process.name, but inputs defined in *filebeat.yml* don't always align all fields to ECS.

Connecting to External Systems

Filebeat can reach out to external systems to pull data from them, which becomes useful when working with systems that cannot initiate the sending of data, as well as systems that need a middleman to cross network boundaries. For example, event stores such as Kafka don't send data to other systems directly; instead, producers send data into Kafka and consumers pull data out. Filebeat performs both functions, as you'll see shortly. We'll discuss Kafka in much greater depth in Chapter 10.

Filebeat's Kafka input needs a few settings for the connection to succeed. Add the following to *filebeat.yml*:

```
- type: kafka
  enabled: true
❶ hosts:
    - kafka01:9093
    - kafka02:9093
❷ topics: [ "filebeat" ]
❸ group_id: "filebeat"
❹ tags: [ "from-kafka" ]
  parsers:
  ❺ - ndjson:
      message_key: "message"
      target: "processed"
      overwrite_keys: true
      add_error_key: true
```

The hosts array ❶ contains two Kafka *brokers*, which are server nodes that process messages. Curiously, these might not represent the actual destinations to which Filebeat will send data. Instead, they're often hosts called *bootstrap servers*, which return metadata about the nodes inside of the Kafka cluster, describing where Filebeat will ultimately send data. Filebeat will read this metadata and then send data to the actual brokers.

Next, we specify the *topic*, which is a stream of events we want to subscribe to so we can read data from them. We define topics as an array of strings ❷. In this example, we include a single topic, named `filebeat`, containing data previously pushed into the cluster using the Kafka output we'll explore later in this chapter.

We set the consumer group using a group ID ❸. A *consumer group* is a collection of one or more subscribers that read the data in a topic as a single unit. This allows Kafka to load-balance the data it sends out, increasing total throughput. More importantly, it can avoid sending the same message more than once to a given group.

In this example, we use the group ID `filebeat`, which specifies a unique set of consumers that should receive data from a topic. If three Filebeat instances belong to one consumer group, Kafka will load-balance outgoing data by distributing it evenly among the instances. In this case, however, the single Filebeat will receive all the data from the topic, as it's the only group member.

We also specify a parser ❺ to read the `message` field and output the JSON structure into the `processed` field, as before. Note that the `from-kafka` tag ❹ exists only at the top level of the JSON structure and not inside of the nested `processed` fields we want to use downstream.

When Filebeat is running, the terminal should show output like the following:

```
--snip--
    "processed" => {
            "tags" => [
            [0] "tags-for-everybody",
            [1] "you-get-a-tag",
            [2] "and-you-get-a-tag",
            [3] "forwarded"
        ],
            "process" => {
            "program" => "sudo"
        },
            "message" => "pam_unix(sudo:session): session closed for user root",
            "syslog" => {
--snip--
```

You can see the tool sending the log to Kafka and then Logstash retrieving it and displaying it on the screen, including the `message` field containing the *sudo* event. Next, let's a new tag to the `processed` field.

Processors

Like parsers, processors modify incoming events, yet they offer more horsepower than parsers. For example, the processors enabled by default in *filebeat.yml* add host- or cloud-related data, such as machine type or instance ID, to events. Other processors might add details about the network direction, decode base64 strings, perform DNS lookups, or parse XML. A list of processors is available on Elastic's website at *https://www.elastic.co/guide/en/ beats/filebeat/current/filtering-and-enhancing-data.html.*

Let's use a small add_tags processor to demonstrate adding a new array field inside a nested structure. This might come in handy if you eventually prune similar events down to just the processed fields, so you don't lose the array. The processor might look like this:

```
❶ processors:
❷ - add_tags:
❸   tags: [ "from-kafka" ]
❹   target: "processed.tags"
```

Under the processors level ❶, we use the add_tags processor ❷ to include a tag that indicates that the log came from Kafka ❸. We then nest the new field inside of processed.tags ❹.

Earlier in this chapter, we discussed another opportunity to use a processor: modifying the processed.timestamp field so that Filebeat can use it as an event's timestamp. To create such a processor, however, we'll have to write conditional statements.

Controlling Processors with Conditionals

Conditional statements allow us to specify the conditions in which to run processors. For example, we can use them to check whether a field contains a certain value (or explicitly doesn't contain it) and whether multiple fields are equal; then we can run a processor only if the condition is met.

We nest conditional statements under a processor's when statement and define them using operators such as and, or, and not. Table 4-1 lists Filebeat's conditional operators. You can use a single conditional statement or nest the statements to support complex comparisons.

Table 4-1: Filebeat's Conditional Operators

Conditional operator	Purpose
equals	Compares strings or integer equality
and	Meets all conditions in a list
or	Meets one or more conditions in a list
contains	Checks for a match in a string
regexp	Uses regular expression statements
network	Validates IP address membership in a network
range	Checks a number in upper/lower bounds
has_fields	Checks whether a field exists
not	Negates the following comparison

Let's use these conditionals to add processors that alter the processed .timestamp field from the custom JSON logs. Though we can read the field, we need to change its formatting so that Filebeat can understand its layout and use it as the event's timestamp:

```
2040-04-27T15:23:03.636525891-05:00
```

We must do two things to this value. First, we'll truncate the timestamp to millisecond resolution (the most granular resolution Logstash can handle). Then, we'll overwrite the top-level @timestamp field with this truncated timestamp.

We'll use the script processor to run custom JavaScript code that extracts the date, time, and time zone. (The script processor uses an implementation of ECMAScript written purely in Go.) Then we'll use the timestamp processor to overwrite the @timestamp field at the top of the JSON structure, making the event ready for database entry.

Add these lines to *filebeat.yml* inside of the processor block:

```
- script:
    lang: javascript
    # Example:
    # 2040-04-27T22:37:12.463504006-05:00
    #           | 10         |23    |29
    source: >
      function process(event) {
    ❶ var t = event.Get("processed.timestamp")
    ❷ var front = t.slice(0, 23)
      var back = t.slice(29)
    ❸ var combined = front+back
      event.Put("processed.timestamp_fixed", combined)
      }
  ❹ when:
      has_fields: [ "processed.timestamp" ]
```

First, we fetch the timestamp from the nested data ❶ and save it as the variable t. Next, we create slices of it up to and including the 23rd character ❷ (counting from position zero), saving it as front, and make a second slice from character 29 onward to capture the time zone offset, saving it as back.

Now that we've removed characters 24 through 28, we combine front and back into a single string named combined ❸, which we add to a new field, process.timestamp_fixed, for the timestamp processor to pick up. This processor runs only if the when conditional is met and the processed.timestamp field exists ❹. Note that I've intentionally written this code in a contrived manner to demonstrate running a code block inside of a processor; you might find more efficient ways to perform this example.

The following snippet shows the timestamp value before and after using the script processor to create the new `timestamp_fixed` field:

```
--snip--
    "processed" => {
    "timestamp" => "2040-04-27T15:23:03.636525891-05:00",
"timestamp_fixed" => "2040-04-27T15:23:03.636-05:00",
--snip--
```

The `timestamp` processor uses a reference time layout from the underlying Go `time` package to recognize timestamps:

```
01/02 03:04:05PM '06 -0700'
# Converted to the Filebeat-preferred layout
2006-01-02T15:04:05.999-07:00
```

Using this layout, it can understand the new string we just created with the script processor. It can also test whether the conversion will work and exit if it fails. The following snippet shows the processor in action:

```
- timestamp:
❶ field: "processed.timestamp_fixed"
❷ layouts:
    - '2006-01-02T15:04:05.999-07:00'
❸ test:
    - '2040-04-27T22:37:12.463-05:00'
❹ when:
    has_fields: [ "processed.timestamp_fixed" ]
```

The processor runs on the defined field we created (`process.timestamp_fixed`) ❶ only when the field exists ❹. The layout statement ❷ forms a template for the reference timestamp, and the unit test ❸ will force the module to exit if it fails during testing with an error message. Now Filebeat will overwrite the timestamp value with the one extracted from the nested JSON. You should see this output after running the *timestamp* processor:

```
--snip--
    "timestamp" => "2040-04-27T15:23:03.636525891-05:00",
"timestamp_fixed" => "2040-04-27T15:23:03.636-05:00",
    ...
    "@timestamp" => 2040-04-27T20:23:03.636Z
--snip--
```

We've updated the event timestamp to properly reflect the nested data, and Filebeat has converted it to the Greenwich Mean Time (GMT) time zone.

Screening Out Data

We can also use processors to screen out data, preventing unnecessary bytes from flowing across the network and eating up storage. One way to drop fields we don't need is by using multiple conditional statements:

```
processors:
  - drop_fields:
❶ fields: ["ecs", "agent.ephemeral_id"]
    when:
❷ or:
        - contains:
          log.file.path: "/home/j/example-logs/"
        - equals:
          input.type: "syslog"
        - contains:
          tags: "from-kafka"
```

We list fields to be dropped in an array ❶ and nest the required conditional logic ❷ to specify when to drop the fields. Here, we use the equals statement to match a field example, and we use contains to specify a portion of a name, allowing us to match multiple fields or names that might change.

Note that you can't drop the field event.original or any metadata fields beginning with @ using the drop_fields processor. One way to remove these fields is to set them to an empty string or to another desired value using Filebeat processors or Logstash filters.

Modules

The true strength of Filebeat lies in its modules. Dozens of modules provide powerful transformation and parsing capabilities, such as reading complex firewall or cloud logs, and many of them contain submodules, or *filesets*, related to multiple technologies by the same vendor. Modules handle their own inputs; some can read files and network sockets, while others connect outbound to an API and request logs. You define processors directly in the module YML file to compartmentalize configurations and add tags where necessary.

NOTE *Many modules use Elasticsearch ingest pipelines to rename fields to ECS. We'll touch on ingest pipelines in Chapter 6 when we discuss Elasticsearch and Elastic Agent integrations.*

To explore Filebeat's modules, let's work with Zeek, a popular network traffic analyzer formerly known as Bro. Zeek provides metadata about happenings on the wire, and Filebeat's Zeek module converts local logs into ECS if Zeek is configured to write JSON data. Here is a Zeek log in raw JSON form:

```
{"ts":1688955554.952633,"uid":"CDYUvz2iep4cP5GKI6","id.orig_h":
"192.168.28.32","id.orig_p":62299,"id.resp_h":"239.255.255.250",
"id.resp_p":1900,"proto":"udp",
--snip--
```

To convert these hard-to-read logs into JSON and ECS, first enable the Zeek module:

```
$ ./filebeat modules enable zeek
```

Next, open the module configuration file, *modules.d/zeek.yml*. Zeek creates individual logs for its dozens of supported protocol analyzers, and Filebeat breaks them into individual statements that we can turn on or off:

```
- module: zeek
  capture_loss:
❶ enabled: true
❷ var.paths: ["/opt/zeek/spool/zeek/capture_loss.log"]
  connection:
    enabled: true
    var.paths: ["/opt/zeek/spool/zeek/conn.log"]
  dce_rpc:
    enabled: true
    var.paths: ["/opt/zeek/spool/zeek/dce_rpc.log"]
--snip--
```

We toggle each supported log type on or off by setting `enabled` to either true or false ❶. Also note that the configuration file specifies file-name paths inside arrays ❷ in case Filebeat is running on a landing pad or middleman server and needs to read from multiple sources for the same log type.

Zeek requires elevated privileges to listen to the network interface, and it protects its logs accordingly. Add your username to the zeek group. The following adds my account, *j*:

```
$ sudo usermod -aG zeek j
```

Log out and back in for the change to take effect. If the change doesn't kick in for some reason, run the command **groups** and check the contents of */etc/group* to make sure your username is in the zeek group. Try the `newgrp` command if your username isn't there:

```
$ groups
$ grep zeek /etc/group
$ newgrp zeek
```

Now test and start Filebeat again, then watch the converted log populate in the Logstash terminal:

```
$ ./filebeat test config
$ ./filebeat test output
$ ./filebeat -e
```

The module converts the logs into lovely JSON, with most of the key fields converted to ECS:

```
    "source" => {
        "mac" => "11:50:56:c4:00:a2",
      "bytes" => 812,
    "packets" => 4,
       "port" => 62299,
    "address" => "192.168.28.32",
         "ip" => "192.168.28.32"
},
  "@timestamp" => 2040-07-10T02:20:22.191Z,
--snip--
```

Modules typically do a great job of converting fields to ECS, but there are gaps in what Filebeat converts locally versus downstream. For example, some Filebeat modules for technologies like Cisco and Palo Alto push ECS conversions to Elasticsearch ingest pipelines if they're deemed too complex for Filebeat.

We can use processors within each fileset so that the global configurations won't bloat to dozens or hundreds of lines. These module-based processors sit at the same level as the `enabled` and `var.*` statements and will run alongside the processors defined globally in *filebeat.yml*. If needed, we can add tags directly in the fileset using `var.tags`:

```
# modules.d/zeek.yml
❶ connection:
    enabled: true
    var.paths: ["/opt/zeek/spool/zeek/conn.log"]
  ❷ input:
      processors:
        - add_tags:
            tags: ["tag-in-connection-log"]
--snip--
```

Within the connection fileset ❶, we add an `input` field ❷ at the same level as the other options, then define a processor within it. As expected, this processor adds a tag to the output:

```
--snip--
       "tags" => [
     [0] "you-get-a-tag",
     [1] "zeek.connection",
     [2] "tag-in-connection-log",
--snip--
```

Here we see the new tag applied to this connection event using the `add_tags` processor, alongside tags you added earlier in the chapter.

Sending Outputs

Filebeat can define only one output at a time, leaving very little wiggle room for modifications after you've established a pipeline. In most cases, Filebeat sends data to Logstash or directly to Elasticsearch, but sending data to message brokers such as Kafka and Redis is common, too.

Publishing to Kafka

Sending output to Kafka works similarly to reading input from it: We rely on topics to determine where and how data gets pushed out.

We previously used consumer groups inside of *filebeat.yml* to define our identity when reading data from Kafka:

```
group_id: "filebeat"
```

For servers sending data to Kafka, set the `client_id` value to the hostname of the server running Filebeat or to some other value that will make troubleshooting easier if things go sideways. (This setting defaults to `beats`, which is unhelpful when you need to troubleshoot more than one server running Filebeat!)

Kafka stores JSON fields in a single string field. Logstash needs to decode the string back into usable JSON fields. Let's add a *conf.d/plain-kafka-consumer .conf* file in the Logstash directory to consume messages and display them on standard output:

```
# plain-kafka-consumer.conf
input {
    kafka {
      ❶ bootstrap_servers => "kafka01:9092,kafka02:9092"
      ❷ group_id => "logstash"
      ❸ topics => [ "filebeat" ]
    }
}

filter {
    # convert data back into JSON
  ❹ json {
        source => "[event][original]"
    }
}

output {
    stdout { codec => rubydebug { metadata => true }}
}
```

Note that we send this data in plaintext; we'll discuss configuring TLS for Kafka in Chapter 10.

The Kafka input for Logstash lists bootstrap servers ❶ used to acquire cluster metadata in a comma-separated string, the consumer group ID ❷, and the topic ❸ Logstash will pull from. The filter ❹ will expand the `event.original` field containing the string pulled from Kafka into the proper JSON structure.

Navigate to the Logstash directory in another terminal and run the Logstash pipeline:

```
$ bin/logstash -f conf.d/plain-kafka-consumer.conf --config.reload.automatic
```

Inside of *filebeat.yml*, define the new Kafka output and then restart Filebeat:

```
output.kafka:
  enabled: true
  hosts: [ "kafka01:9092", "kafka02:9092" ]
  topic: "filebeat"
❶ client_id: "my-awesome-server-running-filebeat"
❷ headers:
    - key: "category"
      value: "remoteaccess"
      when:
        equals:
          event.dataset: "zeek.ssh"
    - key: "category"
      value: "web"
      when:
        equals:
          event.dataset: "zeek.tls"
```

Like in the Kafka input, we define the bootstrap servers in an array, the topic to write to, the unique client identifier of the server running Filebeat ❶, and conditionally applied optional headers for Kafka ❷.

Kafka headers are key-value pairs that provide extra metadata for the purposes of routing data and analyzing performance. They're analogous to the HTTP headers that track the details of who sent a message, what was sent, when it was sent, and so on. You can add them to the outgoing message, and their syntax supports conditional logic. You can also specify multiple keys with the same name, as they don't need to be unique.

Specifying an array of hosts returns metadata about the cluster itself, and Filebeat uses this information to connect to the actual addresses where messages are sent. Kafka will do its best to load-balance itself by telling producers and consumers where to connect.

Unlike inputs, outputs don't directly support tags, which get applied globally in *filebeat.yml* or using modules. You might find it useful to add directional tagging in *filebeat.yml* when transmitting data in and out of Kafka. If Filebeat writes to a topic and then Logstash consumes and enriches that data before sending to a different topic, you might tag each step to capture this lineage. The following is just one tag you may add:

```
tags: [ "to-kafka-filebeat" ]
```

After you start Filebeat, data should flow, appearing as usable JSON fields:

```
--snip--
  "process" => {
  "program" => "sudo"
},
    "tags" => [
    [0] "tags-for-everybody",
    [1] "you-get-a-tag",
    [2] "and-you-get-a-tag",
    [3] "to-kafka-filebeat",
    [4] "forwarded"
],
  "message" => "pam_unix(sudo:session): session closed for user root",
    "input" => {
    "type" => "syslog"
},
--snip--
```

Logstash should display these JSON fields on the screen.

Publishing to Redis

Redis is an in-memory message broker that we can use as an intermediary between Filebeat and another system. Sending logs to Redis functions mostly the same way as sending them to Kafka: We specify a key, which will then store the values sent to it in a queue structure, along with a password and network details.

The key statement in the Redis output block supports conditional statements such as when, which is useful for routing per module or input type. The following example uses nested subconditionals to check for the Zeek module and either the SSH or the Telnet dataset:

```
output.redis:
  enabled: true
  hosts: ["localhost"]
  password: "YOUR-REDIS-PASSWORD"
❶ key: "filebeat"
❷ keys:
    - key: "remoteaccess"
    ❸ when:
        ❹ or:
          ❺ - contains:
              event.dataset: "zeek.ssh"
            - contains:
              event.dataset: "zeek.telnet"
          and:
            - equals:
              event.module: "zeek"
  ssl.enabled: true
  ssl.verification_mode: full
  ssl.certificate: "/home/j/tls/certs/filebeat.local.flex.cert.pem"
```

```
  ssl.key: "/home/j/tls/keys/filebeat.local.flex.key.pem"
  ssl.certificate_authorities:
    - /home/j/tls/certs/ca-chain.cert.pem
--snip--
```

In this statement, we funnel Zeek SSH and Telnet events to a Redis list named remoteaccess using the keys (plural) statement ❷ and conditionals, with a fallback to the filebeat list when key (singular) ❶ is also specified for logs that don't meet the conditional statements. The when ❸ conditional contains multiple checks ❹, which also have subconditions ❺ defined.

Simply checking event.module is a slimmed-down approach to data routing, as it pushes routing complexity downstream, away from endpoints. In the following snippet, we apply this approach using a single conditional:

```
output.redis:
  enabled: true
  hosts: ["localhost"]
  password: "YOUR-REDIS-PASSWORD"
  key: "filebeat"
  keys:
    - key: "zeek"
      when:
      ❶ equals:
          event.module: "zeek"
--snip--
```

Notice that the YML syntax changes when equals moves up a level ❶, as we don't use the hyphenated list structure. Here, Filebeat will send this network data to the Redis key zeek only when the event.module field is also zeek; everything else will go to the filebeat key.

Writing Output Data to a File

One straightforward way to output processed data is to write it to a file on disk that Filebeat has write access to. Unless we specify otherwise, Filebeat will name this file using the mandatory path value, followed by the program name and a timestamp, potentially with trailing numbers that increment, such as */var/log/filebeat-20400501-1.ndjson*. By default, files rotate every 10MB and roll over every seven files, or every time the Filebeat process starts. The default file permission mode is 0600, meaning that only the owner of the Filebeat process can read or write to the file.

For example, the following output section would write 10 files that are approximately 100MB each before rotating, for a total of about 1GB:

```
output.file:
  enabled: true
  path: /var/log/filebeat/
  rotate_every_kb: 100000
  number_of_files: 10
```

Start Filebeat so we can monitor the creation of new output files by running the `watch` command. The following will list the new logfiles every second and will highlight where byte sizes change or new files appear:

```
$ watch -n 1 -d ls -l /var/log/filebeat/
-rw------- 1 j    j      33M May  1 22:53 filebeat-20400501-1.ndjson
-rw------- 1 j    j      49M May  1 22:52 filebeat-20400501.ndjson
```

We can watch files being written to, and aged off, in real time. Cancel the updating terminal with CTRL-C.

Sending Data to Logstash

Another output option is to send data to Logstash. Filebeat can receive status checks from Logstash telling it to slow down to reduce congestion or to apply *backpressure*, which results in smaller peaks and valleys in traffic volume across the network. Filebeat can also ramp up the level of compression when sending traffic to Logstash to reduce load on the network, but at the cost of slightly higher CPU usage by Logstash.

In this example, let's use two worker threads with no load balancing and crank the compression to 9 (the maximum). Use these lines for the Logstash output in *filebeat.yml*:

```
output.logstash:
  enabled: true
  hosts: ["192.168.8.132:5044"]
  workers: 2
  compression_level: 9
--snip--
```

Filebeat and other Beats add metadata fields that aren't typically displayed using the Logstash `stdout` output. To see this data in action, let's modify the *beats-mtls.conf* Logstash configuration by copying the invisible `@metadata` field into a new one named `metadata`:

```
--snip--
filter {
    mutate {
      ❶ copy => { "@metadata" => "metadata" }
    }
}
--snip--
```

The `mutate` filter copies the `@metadata` field, which we can't normally see, into a `metadata` field we can see ❶. The configuration should reload automatically, since Logstash is still running in another terminal.

You may also set `metadata => true` in the output, which we'll configure later in the book. For now, let's copy the metadata to get comfortable using filters. Downstream, Elasticsearch will use the `@metadata.beat` and `@metadata.version` to direct the indexing, or storage, of data in the database.

Although Filebeat sets fields such as `agent.name`, I've found that including the static IP address of the host at that point in time also helps troubleshoot issues, as seen in `metadata.beats.host.ip`:

```
--snip--
  "metadata" => {
        "beat" => "filebeat",
     "version" => "8.7.0",
   "truncated" => false,
        "type" => "_doc",
       "input" => {
       "beats" => {
           "host" => {
             ❶ "ip" => "192.168.8.134"
    --snip--
    "message" => "pam_unix(sudo:session): session closed for
                  user root",
      "input" => {
       "type" => "syslog"
},
    "process" => {
    "program" => "sudo"
     --snip--
```

Having the IP address ❶ of the node running Filebeat provides insight if something in the pipeline goes awry.

Pruning and Privatizing Data

At some point, you'll need to privatize or remove unnecessary data from your logs. Perhaps an auditor is reviewing your company's logs for compliance reasons, or maybe a machine learning algorithm requires only certain fields and nothing more.

Earlier in this chapter, we covered the `drop_fields` and script processors. Let's now use these to remove sensitive data. Say an auditor needs to review metadata from a bank's servers; we could replace all `user.name` values with a generic term, such as `BankUser`. We could also drop everything irrelevant to the auditor, such as tags and agent names:

```
processors:
❶ - drop_fields:
    fields: ["agent", "ecs", "event.severity", "host",
      "input", "log", "syslog", "tags"]

❷ - script:
    lang: javascript
    source: >
      function process(event) {
      ❸ event.Put("user.name", "BankUser")
      }
    when:
      has_fields: [ "user.name" ]
```

First, we drop the fields we don't need to send ❶. Next, a short script overwrites all usernames ❷ with a single value ❸.

This results in an extremely truncated log (minus the otherwise invisible @metadata fields) to send downstream:

```
{
    "process" => {
    "program" => "sudo"
},
        "user" => {
        "name" => "BankUser"
},
    "@version" => "1",
    "message" => "pam_unix(sudo:session): session opened for
                  user root by (uid=0)",
  "@timestamp" => 2040-04-30T05:04:19.000Z,
    "hostname" => "server01"
}
```

This log meets the minimum requirements in our hypothetical audit situation. It may also be ideal for your daily needs; keep in mind that the bytes you store on disks come out of your budget!

Filebeat for Windows

Filebeat can read any logfile on Windows that isn't part of the Windows Event Log. (To read events from the Windows Event Log, we use Winlogbeat, discussed in Chapter 5.)

The fantastic web request tool cURL is now built into Windows, so you can download the Filebeat ZIP file for Windows directly using *curl.exe*. Don't skip the *.exe* portion, as plain curl is an alias for the Invoke-WebRequest PowerShell command. Download the latest version of Filebeat, substituting *X.Y.Z* for a version number:

```
PS> curl.exe -O https://artifacts.elastic.co/downloads/
beats/filebeat/filebeat-X.Y.Z-windows-x86_64.zip
```

Extract the ZIP somewhere and copy it into *C:\Program Files\Filebeat* using an administrator PowerShell prompt. Then, change directories into that path:

```
PS> copy -r .\filebeat-8.x.x-windows-x86_64\ "C:\Program Files\Filebeat"
PS> cd "C:\Program Files\Filebeat"
```

Next, run the provided install script to create a Windows service:

```
PS>.\install-service-filebeat.ps1
```

If you receive an error while running the script stating that running scripts is disabled on the system, change the PowerShell execution policy temporarily:

```
PS> Get-ExecutionPolicy
PS> Set-ExecutionPolicy Bypass
```

Run the install script and then set the execution policy back to the previous value identified with Get-ExecutionPolicy.

This script should install the Windows service with the startup type Automatic (Delayed Start), which means it may take around a minute to start. The Filebeat service will wait for other Windows services marked as Automatic to fully load after the next reboot. For now, don't manually start the service or execute *filebeat.exe*.

You should also use this *filebeat.yml* instead of the ones shown earlier in this chapter, as it contains a useful logfile for testing data found on most versions of Windows 10 and 11:

```
filebeat.inputs:

# Input that reads Edge update logs
- type: filestream
  enabled: true
  id: edgeupdate-logs
  paths:
    - C:/ProgramData/Microsoft/EdgeUpdate/Log/*.log
❶ encoding: utf-16le-bom

# Module locations
filebeat.config.modules:
  path: ${path.config}/modules.d/*.yml

tags: ["windows", "tags-for-everybody", "you-get-a-tag", "and-you-get-a-tag"]

output.logstash:
  enabled: true
  hosts: ["logstash.local:5044"]
--snip--
```

We use little-endian UTF-16 encoding with a required byte order mark ❶ to accurately read text files generated by Windows.

NOTE *Keep the following filepath handy for testing Filebeat on a Windows system: C:/ ProgramData/Microsoft/EdgeUpdate/Log/*.log. When the Edge browser checks for or performs an update, it appends an entry to this log, making it an ideal data source when testing Filebeat on Windows.*

Before we wrap up, let's store our configurations in our Git repository.

Summary

Filebeat is a simple yet powerful tool for extracting data, transforming it into something useful, and shipping it elsewhere. It formats data into JSON early in the data pipeline, then offloads further complex processing downstream. Filebeat's processors can also format, drop, or privatize data if needed, and its modules provide standardized field names by producing output in the ECS. Filebeat also supports industry-standard, enterprise-scale data engineering tools such as Kafka, Redis, and Logstash. In the next chapter, we'll use Elastic Winlogbeat to collect event logs from Windows systems.

5

WINDOWS LOGS

For decades, Windows servers and workstations have written logs to a centralized location: the event log. A mature feature of Windows, the event log exists on every instance of the operating system, but its event logs are *circular* by design, meaning their initial entries get deleted after the file size reaches a limit. Winlogbeat, the Elastic log collector for Windows, can read these binary logs and then ship them downstream so you won't lose them before they're rotated out.

In this chapter, we begin by examining the various types of Windows event logs, including Application, System, Security, and Sysmon. Understanding these different data sources and where to find them is crucial for effectively performing incident response in Windows environments.

Then, you'll use Winlogbeat to collect event logs on Windows and send them to other tools. You'll install and use Sysmon to gather new security events, then enable PowerShell script-block logging to capture detailed system behaviors, track script execution, and monitor PowerShell module activities. Through practical examples, you'll learn to navigate the Windows event logging system efficiently and extract useful information from these rich data sources.

Collecting Logs with Winlogbeat

Winlogbeat reads the Windows event log, formats events into JSON, and sends them to a single specified output. Winlogbeat and Filebeat share a common code base, so Winlogbeat supports all processors and outputs that Filebeat uses. It doesn't have vendor input modules or network listeners, however, since it reads solely from the event log.

There are two common options for deploying Winlogbeat. You could run it on all Windows servers and workstations as a service or install it on a special type of server called a *Windows Event Collector (WEC)*. WECs receive logs forwarded from other hosts according to domain subscription policy settings, reducing the number of agents to manage. Configuring a WEC server in a Windows domain is beyond the scope of this chapter, but the process of installing Winlogbeat is the same whether it's running on a laptop or a server.

Winlogbeat performs only minor Elastic Common Schema conversions, as it assumes its data will eventually reach Logstash or an Elasticsearch database, which would perform the rest of the conversions. Instead, it renames fields using a naming convention based on the XML events retrieved from the event log, such as `winlog.event_data.ProcessId`. You'll use Logstash extensively in Chapters 8 and 9.

Event Log Types

Windows has hundreds of event logs to support thousands of applications. These event logs could contain evidence of security issues, crash reports, hard drive performance data, CPU temperature warnings, and more. Windows stores the binary logfiles in *C:\Windows\System32\winevt\Logs*. Let's cover the most common logs by volume, as well as some uncommon ones that provide immense security value.

Application and System Logs

The Application log includes details about application errors, resource utilization, and some update events. This information is helpful for assisting users with troubleshooting application issues. While it could be useful in a database for long-term storage and trend analysis since it does capture certain application login events, it may not provide enough value to justify storing in your SIEM.

The System log contains kernel events, update statuses, service starts and failures, Domain Name System (DNS) and Network Time Protocol (NTP) issues, system crashes or power changes, and similar host-critical events. This information could help you understand a system's behavior during or after a security incident. Unfortunately, the System log can generate more events than the Application and Security logs combined, vastly increasing your storage usage if not tuned. While it provides insight into system activities that other logs don't, its data may prove difficult to store in the long term.

The Security Log and Sysmon

The Security log tracks events like failed and successful logons, process executions, user and group events, and permission changes. It provides reliable telemetry about enterprise activities and is a critical source for log correlation. Security log events can help you detect rare or never-before-seen processes, brute-force logins, and illicit file transfers.

Sysmon, an enhanced security logging tool from Microsoft, isn't built into Windows by default. When running, it can track parent and child process relationships, network connections and DNS requests, registry and file changes, named pipe activity, new executables, and much more. Sysmon is a critical source of Windows security information, and Microsoft recommends it for monitoring systems. You'll install Sysmon on your Windows host in "Sysmon" on page 90.

You should consider collecting both Security and Sysmon logs to be a mandatory part of your security monitoring program.

Other Log Sources

There are a few additional log types you should collect with Winlogbeat. First, *Windows Defender* is Microsoft's built-in security tool. Defender logs provide information about detected threats, quarantine actions taken, and failed or successful updates. You should consider collecting these logs even if you are running third-party security agents.

Windows also has robust PowerShell logging capabilities, some of which are disabled by default. For example, Windows can log PowerShell commands and screen output transcripts as displayed to the user. Because malicious actors widely use PowerShell, you should consider these logs to be a high priority for collection.

In the classic Windows PowerShell event log, we'll capture the following event codes, which we'll configure in "Configuration" on page 87:

400 – Engine state is changed from None to Available   Indicates that PowerShell has started running a command and may include the invoked command

403 – Engine state is changed from Available to Stopped   Indicates that the PowerShell command from event ID 400 has ended and may include the invoked command

600 – Provider is started   Indicates that PowerShell is using a .NET object called a *provider* to access various specialized internal data stores

800 – Pipeline execution details for the command line   Shows a command's pipeline execution and the parameters invoked

In the PowerShell/Operational log, we'll log event IDs 4103 and 4104:

4103 – Module logging   Captures command pipeline execution; however, doesn't yet include user data and parameters like event ID 800

4104 – Script block logging   Captures original commands as provided to PowerShell before execution, including encoded or otherwise obfuscated commands, and all output as it appears onscreen

We won't enable the following events due to the volume of logs they create, but we'll keep the entries in *winlogbeat.yml* for convenience in case you decide to test them on your own:

4105 – Command started   Performs additional script block logging when commands start

4106 – Command ended   Performs additional script block logging when commands end

Another potential source of logs is the Background Intelligent Transfer Service (BITS), a downloader and uploader built into Windows. Though it's meant for developer and programmatic use, adversaries commonly employ it to download files as part of a living-off-the-land strategy. BITS generates an HTTP HEAD request to determine the size of a file to download, then follows this with an HTTP GET request to fetch the file. Both actions generate logs with forensic value, but because Windows uses BITS frequently and adversary actions are exceedingly rare, BITS logs need extensive tuning to provide value.

Installation

Winlogbeat is available as ZIP and Microsoft Software Installer (MSI) packages from Elastic. You'll download the ZIP file, then edit the main configuration *winlogbeat.yml* to specify the event logs you want to collect and send to Logstash.

The Winlogbeat ZIP file is available from the Elastic website at *https://www.elastic.co/downloads/beats/winlogbeat*. Download it to your Windows user's *Downloads* directory. Extract the files and rename the resulting directory to just *Winlogbeat*, removing the version numbers from the directory name. Enter the *Winlogbeat* folder to locate its configuration files.

Enabling TLS

Let's follow the same process we used for Filebeat in Chapter 4 to make a TLS client certificate for initiating connections only. On your Linux host, create a client OpenSSL configuration, generate keys and a certificate signing request, then sign the request using the intermediate CA to create the signed certificate. Alternatively, you may use the wildcard certificate and key from Chapter 6.

Elasticsearch, which we'll cover in Chapter 6, comes bundled with tools to generate a CA and sign certificates for various Elastic tools. As many organizations require following a certificate management process, we'll continue creating certificates manually using the CA from Chapter 2.

Creating a Configuration File

The following OpenSSL client configuration (not flex configuration) is identical to the one in Chapter 4, except we've changed instances of filebeat to winlogbeat and instances of flex to client, and we won't include serverAuth, as Winlogbeat won't receive network connections. Store it in the TLS configurations directory on your Linux host as ~/tls/configs/openssl-client-winlogbeat .local.cnf:

```
############################################################
[ req ]
prompt               = no
default_bits         = 4096
default_md           = sha512
❶ default_keyfile      = tls/keys/winlogbeat.local.client.key.pem
  distinguished_name = client_distinguished_name
  req_extensions       = client_cert
############################################################
[ client_distinguished_name ]
countryName                 = US
stateOrProvinceName         = MO
localityName                = St. Louis
organizationName            = Business, Inc.
organizationalUnitName      = Information Technology
❷ commonName                = Winlogbeat Client
  emailAddress              = none@localhost
############################################################
[ client_cert ]
nsComment                  = OpenSSL Certificate for Clients
subjectAltName             = @alternate_names
############################################################
[ alternate_names ]
❸ DNS.1  = winlogbeat
❹ DNS.2  = winlogbeat.local
```

OpenSSL will create Winlogbeat's private key ❶ in the *tls/keys* directory. The commonName ❷ indicates that this is a Winlogbeat client certificate, only useful for initiating TLS connections; as mentioned previously in

Chapter 2, you may also put a domain name here. The subject alternative names include the base `winlogbeat` ❸ and fully qualified domain name `winlogbeat.local` ❹.

Generating a Key Pair and Client Certificate

Create a 4,096-bit key pair and a certificate signing request:

```
$ openssl req -config tls/configs/openssl-client-winlogbeat.local.cnf -new -out
tls/csr/winlogbeat.local.client.csr -outform PEM -passout
pass:abcd1234
```

Next, use the intermediate CA from Chapter 2 to create the signed certificate. As with Filebeat, pass in the private key's passphrase and specify the intermediate CA's `signing_policy` and `client_cert` extensions:

```
$ openssl ca -batch -notext -config tls/configs/openssl-intermediateca.cnf
-passin pass:abcd1234 -policy signing_policy -extensions client_cert -out
tls/certs/winlogbeat.local.client.cert.pem -infiles
tls/csr/winlogbeat.local.client.csr
```

This should have created the signed certificate *winlogbeat.local.client.cert.pem*. Check that the certificate's extensions are correct:

```
$ openssl x509 -in certs/winlogbeat.local.client.cert.pem -text -noout
--snip--
    X509v3 Extended Key Usage:
        TLS Web Client Authentication
    X509v3 Subject Alternative Name:
        DNS:winlogbeat, DNS:winlogbeat.local
--snip--
```

The certificate is for client use only, and the DNS entries show both the base name and the fully qualified domain name. Verify that you can authenticate the certificate with the CA chain file:

```
$ openssl verify -CAfile tls/certs/ca-chain.cert.pem tls/certs/winlogbeat.local.client.cert.pem
certs/winlogbeat.local.client.cert.pem: OK
```

The new key file is now ready for Winlogbeat to use. Be sure to save the OpenSSL commands you just ran so you can back them up using Git at the conclusion of this chapter.

Let's also update the *hosts* file on your Windows system so it knows Logstash's IP address; this will allow Winlogbeat to connect to Logstash using the hostname only. (This step is unnecessary if you have a DNS server in your environment.) Launch *notepad* as an administrator and add the following to your *C:\Windows\System32\drivers\etc\hosts* file, specifying your Logstash instance's IP address:

```
--snip--
192.168.65.131  logstash
192.168.65.131  logstash.local
```

Save and close the administrator text editor.

On your Windows host, use WinSCP or another file transfer client to connect over Secure Shell to the Linux host that made the TLS files. Locate Winlogbeat's public and private keys and signed certificate, then copy them to the *Winlogbeat* folder on Windows. Exit WinSCP once finished.

If you don't have WinSCP, start a Python web server on your Linux host in the directory with the TLS files:

```
$ python3 -m http.server 8080
```

Then, on Windows, use curl.exe (which is now built into Windows) to download Winlogbeat, as in the following example (substituting your own IP address as necessary):

```
PS> curl.exe -O http://192.168.8.133:8080/tls/certs/ca-chain.cert.pem
PS> curl.exe -O http://192.168.8.133:8080/tls/certs/
winlogbeat.local.client.cert.pem
PS> curl.exe -O http://192.168.8.133:8080/tls/keys/
winlogbeat.local.client.key.pem
```

Next, you'll configure Winlogbeat and verify that its settings work.

Configuration

We'll configure and test Winlogbeat before copying it to a location accessible only to administrators, where making changes would be tedious. Copy the primary configuration file, *winlogbeat.yml*, to a backup copy named *winlogbeat.yml.original* so you can restore it if needed. Then, open *winlogbeat .yml* using your editor of choice and replace its contents with the following:

```
winlogbeat.event_logs:
❶ - name: Application
  ❷ ignore_older: 72h
   - name: System
   - name: Security
   - name: Microsoft-Windows-Sysmon/Operational
   - name: Windows PowerShell
   ❸ event_id: 400, 403, 600, 800
   - name: Microsoft-Windows-PowerShell/Operational
     event_id: 4103, 4104, 4105, 4106

output.logstash:
  enabled: true
  #hosts: [ "LOGSTASH-IP:5044" ] # Causes TLS errors due to lack of IP SANs
❹ hosts: [ "logstash.local:5044" ]
❺ ssl.enabled: true
```

```
ssl.verification_mode: full
ssl.certificate: "C:\\Users\\j\\Downloads\\
Winlogbeat\\winlogbeat.local.client.cert.pem"
ssl.key: "C:\\Users\\j\\Downloads\\
Winlogbeat\\winlogbeat.local.client.key.pem"
ssl.key_passphrase: "abcd1234"
ssl.certificate_authorities: [ "C:\\Users\\j\\Downloads\\Winlogbeat\\
ca-chain.cert.pem" ]
```

Winlogbeat reads the event logs specified in the `winlogbeat.event_log` heading. For the purposes of this example, include the Application event log ❶, but ignore any logs older than three days ❷. Next, add a few other logs, such as Sysmon, which you'll install shortly, and two kinds of PowerShell logs. You'll monitor only the specific event codes from each PowerShell event log recommended by Elastic ❸ in the default configuration. For more information on finding these event log names, see "Exploring Available Event Logs" on page 93.

To configure Logstash as an output, specify the Logstash hostname and port, but not the IP address, as you used hostnames in the Logstash certificate's Subject Alternative Name (SAN) ❹. Enable SSL/TLS ❺ and specify full verification mode, as you did for Filebeat. This means Winlogbeat won't connect to Logstash unless the Logstash certificate is signed by a trusted CA (specified in *ca-chain.cert.pem*) and lists the network hostname. Also specify the signed certificate, the private key and its passphrase, and the CA chain file. The TLS settings need full filepaths with escaped backslashes (\\) or single forward slashes (/).

Save and exit the configuration. Next, test it to ensure the formatting is correct and there are no typos:

```
PS> .\winlogbeat.exe test config
Config OK
```

The configuration is formatted correctly. Now test the network connectivity between Winlogbeat and Logstash:

```
PS> .\winlogbeat.exe test output
```

A series of `OK` messages should appear, indicating the connection works. If you get the following error, you might have specified an IP address for Logstash instead of its domain name:

```
x509: cannot validate certificate for <your Logstash IP address>
because it doesn't contain any IP SANs
```

Next, change the TLS filepaths from your *Downloads* directory to their ultimate destination, *C:\Program Files\Winlogbeat*, as you've successfully tested connectivity:

```
--snip--
ssl.certificate: "C:\\Program Files\\Winlogbeat\\winlogbeat.local.client.cert.pem"
ssl.key: "C:\\Program Files\\Winlogbeat\\winlogbeat.local.client.key.pem"
ssl.certificate_authorities: [ "C:\\Program Files\\Winlogbeat\\ca-chain.cert.pem" ]
```

Finally, you need to copy the *Winlogbeat* directory to its production location. Copying the files to *C:\Program Files* shouldn't preserve user permissions to the destination directory, so users shouldn't have write access to any destination files.

Open an administrator PowerShell terminal and navigate to the user *Downloads* directory one level above the *Winlogbeat* directory. Copy the *Winlogbeat* directory to *C:\Program Files*. Substitute your username for *j*:

```
PS> copy -recurse "C:\Users\j\Downloads\Winlogbeat" "C:\Program Files\"
```

Next, you'll install the Winlogbeat service and start it.

Starting the Service

Elastic includes a PowerShell script to install the Winlogbeat service inside the *Winlogbeat* directory. However, your local PowerShell execution policy is likely the default of restricted, meaning you can't run scripts until you change the policy to something more permissive. Verify the current execution policy:

```
PS> Get-ExecutionPolicy
Restricted
```

Take note of the policy, as you'll restore it at the end of this chapter. For now, change the policy to bypass, which allows PowerShell to run the Winlogbeat installer script. Read the security warning, then enter Y or A when prompted to allow the policy change:

```
PS> Set-ExecutionPolicy bypass
--snip--
[Y] Yes  [A] Yes to All  [N] No
```

The installer script checks for an existing Winlogbeat installation, runs the New-Service PowerShell command, and uses the sc command to set the service to delayed start. Run the script, then check the Winlogbeat service's status:

```
PS> .\install-service-winlogbeat.ps1
PS> Get-Service -name Winlogbeat
Status    Name                 DisplayName
------    ----                 -----------
Stopped   winlogbeat           Winlogbeat
```

Once you've finished performing the steps in this chapter, remember to change the execution policy back to restricted by running Set-ExecutionPolicy restricted. While the execution policy itself isn't a security boundary, it does prevent unintended changes when working on the command line or with scripts.

Start the Winlogbeat service to begin streaming logs to Logstash, and check its status again to verify that it's running:

```
PS> Start-Service -name Winlogbeat
PS> Get-Service -name Winlogbeat
Status    Name                DisplayName
------    ----                -----------
Running   winlogbeat          Winlogbeat
```

On the Linux host running Logstash, verify that Windows logs are streaming in. You should see events like the following:

```
--snip--
"computer_name" => "LabBox",
   "event_data" => {
                "ProcessName" => "C:\\Windows\\System32\\services.exe",
           "TargetDomainName" => "NT AUTHORITY",
             "SubjectUserSid" => "S-1-5-18",
                  "ProcessId" => "0x24c",
--snip--
```

This output means Winlogbeat is sending event logs to Logstash.

Collecting Logs from Sysmon and PowerShell

Now that Winlogbeat is running, let's configure several essential Windows log sources—Sysmon and PowerShell events—so we can forward them to other tools in our data pipeline. As discussed in "Event Log Types" on page 82, collecting these log types should be a high priority.

Sysmon

Sysmon provides critical insight into system and user activity. In this section, you'll download Sysmon and an XML configuration file, then install Sysmon as a service.

The latest version of Sysmon is available in a ZIP file from Microsoft's SysInternals website at *https://learn.microsoft.com/en-us/sysinternals/downloads/sysmon*. The ZIP file contains both 32-bit and 64-bit versions of the executable. Download the latest version to your user *downloads* directory, then extract it.

Sysmon requires an XML configuration file for its advanced features, like DNS query logging, so let's use a preconfigured one from GitHub. Olaf Hartong, a Netherlands-based security researcher, created and maintains a comprehensive and noise-balanced configuration for Sysmon. Download the "default+" *sysmonconfig-with-filedelete.xml* file from *https://github.com/ olafhartong/sysmon-modular* into the Sysmon directory you just extracted. Review the contents of the file to become familiar with its layout, inclusions, and exclusions.

Using the administrative PowerShell terminal, copy the *Sysmon* directory to *Program Files*, the default software installation directory for Windows (replacing *j* with your username):

```
PS> copy -recurse C:\Users\j\Downloads\sysmon "C:\Program Files\Sysmon"
```

Navigate to the new location in your PowerShell terminal. Then run the following command to install Sysmon with Olaf's configuration on your Windows host:

```
PS> .\sysmon64.exe -i -c sysmonconfig-with-filedelete.xml -accepteula
```

Sysmon should now be running on your system. You don't need to reconfigure or restart Winlogbeat to include Sysmon data because you already included the line `Microsoft-Windows-Sysmon/Operational` in *winlogbeat.yml*. On the Linux host running Logstash, verify that Sysmon logs are streaming:

```
--snip--
"event_data" => {
  "TargetFilename" => "C:\\ProgramData\\winlogbeat\\.winlogbeat.yml.new",
 "CreationUtcTime" => "2040-09-12 19:37:37.405",
         "UtcTime" => "2040-09-12 19:59:38.166",
      "ProcessGuid" => "{a76dbf58-2807-6551-9a5e-000000003300}",
        "ProcessId" => "15372",
            "Image" => "C:\\Program Files\\Winlogbeat\\winlogbeat.exe",
             "User" => "NT AUTHORITY\\SYSTEM",
         "RuleName" => "-"
--snip--
```

Configuring Sysmon for an entire domain is beyond the scope of this book, but keep in mind that Sysmon is easily accessible at the enterprise level. You can install Sysmon remotely on a Windows domain using Group Policy and a Windows Server's System Volume (SYSVOL), or add it to a gold image for provisioning cloud or virtual desktop system images. Alternatively, Windows endpoints can remotely execute *sysmon64.exe* with the XML configuration so the files don't have to be pushed to every host on your network.

PowerShell Script Blocks

PowerShell *script block logging* captures PowerShell code as deobfuscated for execution. This means that if an attacker attempts to run base64-encoded commands to hide their activity, some of the decoded content will appear in the event log, providing defenders with a better view of what the command is doing.

By default, Windows only partially enables script block logging to capture commands it thinks are suspicious, so let's fully enable it. The "About Logging Windows" article on Microsoft Learn contains a PowerShell function for this purpose: *https://learn.microsoft.com/en-us/powershell/module/microsoft.powershell.core/about/about_logging_windows*. Copy this function into your administrative PowerShell terminal, then execute it:

```
PS> function Enable-PSScriptBlockLogging {
❶ $basePath = @(
        'HKLM:\Software\Policies\Microsoft'
        'PowerShellCore\ScriptBlockLogging'
❷ ) -join '\'

❸ if (-not (Test-Path $basePath)) {
        $null = New-Item $basePath -Force
    }

❹ Set-ItemProperty $basePath -Name EnableScriptBlockLogging -Value "1"
}
❺ PS> Enable-PSScriptBlockLogging
```

This code first establishes a new function, `Enable-PSScriptBlockLogging`. Here, we create a long registry path ❶ by linking two strings in an array with a backslash ❷, but you could combine the strings into a single line if desired. The registry path must exist before you can define a value ❸, and the function ends by setting the new registry path's value to 1 ❹. Finally, we invoke the function by its name ❺.

You can also enable script block logging via the registry. Run the following commands from the administrator PowerShell terminal to create the registry key and value needed to enable it:

```
PS> New-Item -Path "HKLM:\SOFTWARE\Wow6432Node\Policies\Microsoft\
Windows\PowerShell\ScriptBlockLogging" -Force
PS> Set-ItemProperty -Path "HKLM:\SOFTWARE\Wow6432Node\Policies\Microsoft\
Windows\PowerShell\ScriptBlockLogging" -Name "EnableScriptBlockLogging"
-Value 1
```

Group Policy enables script block logging in Windows domains. In the Group Policy editor, navigate to **Computer Configuration ▸ Policies** (if linking via Group Policy Management Editor) ▸ **Administrative Templates ▸ Windows Components ▸ Windows PowerShell ▸ Turn On PowerShell Script Block Logging**.

Toggle the radio button to **Enabled**. Don't check the box labeled "Log script block invocation start/stop events"; this prevents event IDs 4105 (command started) and 4106 (command ended) from being created every time a PowerShell script block log is created.

Because you already specified both the `Windows PowerShell` and `Microsoft-Windows-PowerShell/Operational` input sources in *winlogbeat.yml*, PowerShell script block logs should now be flowing to your Logstash host. If nothing appears, try restarting the Winlogbeat service or your Windows host or updating Group Policy. For more information about how script block logging works, read BC Security's blog post about it at *https://bc-security.org/powershell-logging-obfuscation-and-some-newish-bypasses-part-1*.

PowerShell Modules

Module logging captures the PowerShell command, functions, or modules as they're invoked. Module logging also captures obfuscated commands and potentially suspicious or noteworthy command parameters and module names in the log. Both event ID 800 and event ID 4103 contain similar information; however, the newer 4103 code sometimes misses the full obfuscated command line that can be found in 800.

Module logging produces a high volume of events, so carefully consider storage requirements before enabling it. Further module logging details can be found on Microsoft Learn under "About Eventlogs."

Similar to script blocks, module logging is enabled via the registry or Group Policy. Enter the following commands to enable it via the registry:

```
PS> New-Item -Path "HKLM:\SOFTWARE\Wow6432Node\Policies\Microsoft\Windows\
PowerShell" -Name ModuleLogging -Force
PS> Set-Itemproperty -path 'HKLM:\SOFTWARE\Wow6432Node\Policies\Microsoft\
Windows\PowerShell\ModuleLogging' -Name 'EnableModuleLogging' -Value '1'
PS> New-Item -Path "HKLM:\SOFTWARE\Wow6432Node\Policies\Microsoft\Windows\
PowerShell\ModuleLogging" -Name ModuleNames -Force
PS> Set-Itemproperty -path 'HKLM:\SOFTWARE\Wow6432Node\Policies\Microsoft\
Windows\PowerShell\ModuleLogging\ModuleNames' -Name '*' -Value '*'
```

To enable module logging via Group Policy, open the policy editor. Navigate to **Computer Configuration ▸ Policies** (if linking via Group Policy Management Editor) ▸ **Administrative Templates ▸ Windows Components ▸ Windows PowerShell ▸ Turn On Module Logging**. Toggle the radio button to **Enabled**, set Modules Names to **Show**, and set the text box value to ***=***.

Run the following command to enable module logging for the current session only, which is useful for testing:

```
PS> Get-Module | foreach { $_.LogPipelineExecutionDetails = $true }
```

Now that we've enabled PowerShell script block and module logging, let's explore additional Windows event logs.

Exploring Available Event Logs

Winlogbeat can read any source in the event log, adding flexibility to your logging strategy and collection requirements. This includes third-party antivirus event logs, Dynamic Host Configuration Protocol (DHCP) events, Server Message Block (SMB) client activity, and more. Let's examine additional event logs Winlogbeat can read.

Use the following two PowerShell commands to view all available log sources and all log sources with more than zero events, sorted by size:

```
PS> Get-WinEvent -ListLog *
--snip--
PS> Get-WinEvent -ListLog * | where RecordCount -gt 0 | sort -descending -property RecordCount
--snip--
LogMode    MaximumSizeInBytes RecordCount LogName
-------    ------------------ ----------- -------
Circular        67108864        59022     Microsoft-Windows-Sysmon/Operational
Circular        20971520        41110     System
Circular        20000000        27175     Microsoft-Windows-Store/Operational
Circular        20971520        26654     Security
Circular        20971520        22128     Application
Circular        33554432        15217     Microsoft-Windows-Ntfs/Operational
--snip--
Circular         1052672         1299     Microsoft-Windows-Bits-Client/Operational
--snip--
Circular         1052672          291     Microsoft-Windows-Windows Defender/Operational
--snip--
```

This system has 409 available log sources, but only 123 of them have events. Take some time to explore the available logs and their contents. For example, try including Defender and BITS logs in the Winlogbeat configuration. Add the following lines to *winlogbeat.yml* under the `winlog.event` data section:

```
--snip--
  - name: Microsoft-Windows-Windows Defender/Operational
  - name: Microsoft-Windows-Bits-Client/Operational
```

Restart the Winlogbeat service for the changes to take effect.

Working with Processors

Winlogbeat, Filebeat, Elastic Agent, and other Beats use the same underlying Golang library, *libbeat*, to handle inputs, processors, and outputs. This uniform approach allows you to easily copy the Logstash output from a Filebeat configuration to Winlogbeat, changing only the filenames for the TLS components. Similarly, you can copy custom processors from Filebeat to Winlogbeat if needed.

Processors can add tags, add or drop fields, run scripts, redact fields, and more, as we discussed in Chapter 4. This provides your pipeline with the flexibility to handle enterprise data across multiple operating systems.

Let's add a processor to *winlogbeat.yml* that drops BITS events destined for an official Microsoft URL. BITS frequently connects to Microsoft domains, so deciding to exclude trusted domains will save you storage space (but at the expense of losing telemetry, of course):

```
processors:
--snip--
  - drop_event:
    when:
      or:
        - contains:
          winlog.event_data.url: "https://g.live.com/"
        - equals:
          event.code: 12345
        - range:
          event.code.gte: 0
          event.code.lte: 999
```

There are two spaces preceding the hyphen (-) before drop_event. This processor drops events where the field winlog.event_data.url contains the specified Microsoft URL. It also drops event codes equal to 12345 and event codes greater than or equal to (gte) 0 and less than (lt) 999 (both 999 and 12345 are just example codes). The range statement uses field names with .gte and .lte appended, respectively.

Because we've modified *winlogbeat.yml*, restart the Winlogbeat service for the changes to take effect.

SAVING CONFIGURATIONS WITH GIT

Let's back up the Winlogbeat TLS configuration and *winlogbeat.yml* configuration file in the Git repository you created in Chapter 3. On your Linux host, in your local project repository, make a folder for Winlogbeat:

```
$ mkdir winlogbeat
```

Use WinSCP or another file transfer client to connect your Windows Winlogbeat directory with the new one on your Linux host. Drag and drop *winlogbeat.yml* from Windows to Linux, or simply copy the file's contents to your Linux host. Copy any command notes and redact passphrases as desired.

Next, track the changes to the repository and check the status:

```
PS> git add .
PS> git status
On branch main
Your branch is up to date with 'origin/main'.
Changes to be committed:
  (use "git restore --staged <file>..." to unstage)
    new file:   winlogbeat/winlogbeat.yml
--snip--
```

(continued)

Commit the changes and push them to the project's remote repository:

```
PS> git commit -a -m "added Winlogbeat files"
PS> git push
```

Your Winlogbeat configurations are now stored in the remote repository.

Summary

Winlogbeat is a straightforward approach to collecting logs from Windows hosts and servers: it reads event logs, formats them into JSON, and ships them off the host. In this chapter, you configured Winlogbeat, installed the useful Sysmon logging tool, and enabled PowerShell script block and module logging to provide better insight into security events. You also located new sources of event logs on your Windows system, such as Defender and BITS, and added them to your Winlogbeat input configuration. In the next chapter, we'll explore Elastic Agent for collecting a variety of host and network logs.

6

INTEGRATING AND STORING DATA

Chapters 3 and 4 covered examples of agents able to collect logs from devices and ship them elsewhere. Many other log-collecting agents exist, however. When an organization's logging infrastructure becomes complex, it can be hard to manage the multitude of agents hosted on devices across an enterprise. Security data engineers may face challenges with version management, interrupted installs and upgrades, or *agent bloat* (having too much security software installed).

One way to simplify the collection of logs from endpoints is to replace the multitude of manually installed and managed agents with Elastic Agent, a tool that bundles and manages other Elastic log collectors, such as Filebeat and Winlogbeat discussed in the previous two chapters, and Packetbeat, a tool we'll discuss shortly. Elastic Agent also offers its own features beyond those that Beats provide. For instance, Elastic Agent allows you to define a central policy that all agents will receive after installation, enabling you to easily manage log collection across your environment and update it as necessary.

You'll use Elastic Agent to pick which agent features to use; for example, you might collect firewall logs with Filebeat and capture network logs with Packetbeat. You'll also install the Elasticsearch database to store events from Elastic Agent, then learn how to query the Kibana web graphical user interface (GUI) to view individual events and manage your configuration.

Lastly, you'll walk through two configuration examples: separate Elastic Agents able to send data directly to Elasticsearch using the central policy manager and a stand-alone policy able to run on endpoints that are separated from Elasticsearch and Kibana by a firewall.

An Elastic Agent Architecture

Elastic Agent runs on endpoints and servers and can operate either as stand-alone, unmanaged log-and-metrics collectors or as members of a centrally managed *fleet*: a group of agents that can receive policy updates. The Agent package includes all of the Beats software, such as Filebeat and Packetbeat, and utilizes them through a series of *integrations*, or data collection policies.

As shown in Figure 6-1, an Elastic Agent architecture comprises several components.

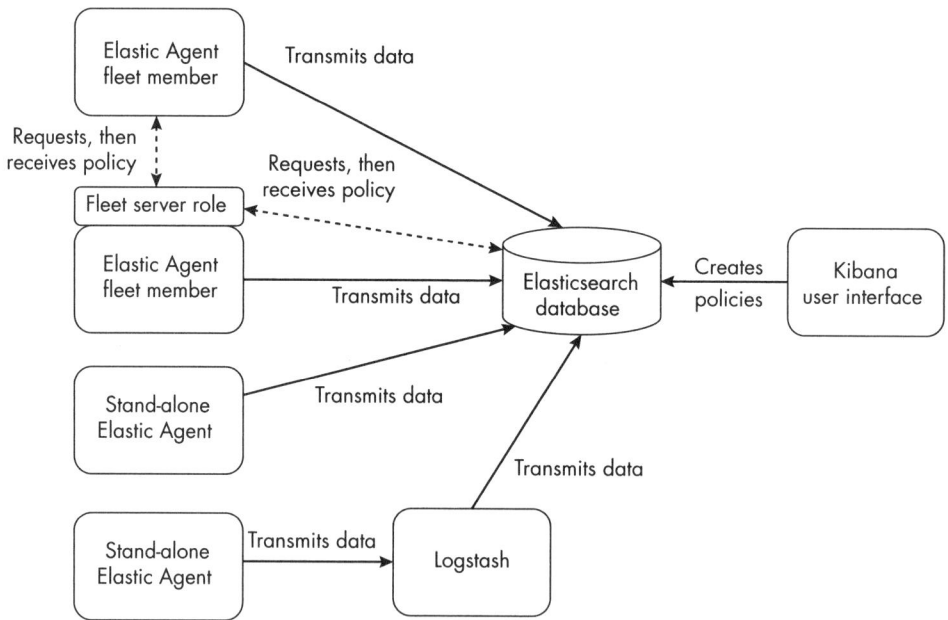

Figure 6-1: Data collection with Elastic Agent

In this diagram, agents and Kibana interact with *Elasticsearch*, a database that the agent relies on for storing configuration information and events. *Kibana* provides a visual, browser-based experience for administering Elasticsearch, performing data analysis, and managing agents. We'll configure and use Elasticsearch and Kibana in this chapter to store and work with agent and Beats data.

The agent also relies on a *fleet server* to coordinate a fleet's policies, enrollment, unenrollment, and data collection. The fleet server itself is simply a special role in which Elastic Agents can run. In Figure 6-1, the fleet server role is depicted as attached to one of the Elastic Agents. Agents request policies, new or updated, from the fleet server, which then requests them from Elasticsearch. Elasticsearch provides policies to the fleet server, which distributes them to all members of the fleet. Users configure policies via Kibana's GUI or via the API. In this chapter, you'll use Kibana to create and update policies, which then update on Agent hosts.

The figure also depicts stand-alone agents, which aren't enrolled in the fleet, meaning they don't communicate with the fleet server. These agents instead run configurations provided during installation that tell them how to operate. You'll configure a stand-alone agent later in this chapter, in addition to the one acting as a fleet server and the one running as a general fleet-enrolled data collector.

You might wonder when to use Elastic Agent and when to use a stand-alone tool like Filebeat. Although Elastic Agent uses Beats under the hood, it has several configuration requirements that make it more challenging to work with than Beats, such as requiring a direct connection to a fleet manager server if not running in stand-alone mode. Elastic Agent can send data to Elasticsearch or to Logstash and Kafka, while Filebeat and the rest of Beats support additional options, including Redis, writing to files, and console output. Beats also have simpler setup steps for stand-alone or air-gapped networks.

The agent includes integrations that Beats doesn't support, however. For example, it can perform AWS cloud monitoring via APIs, fetch performance statistics from Apache Airflow, and make use of a growing endpoint detection and response capability following Elastic's acquisition of Endgame. Because it includes all the Beats, you could use a single policy to collect operating system and application logs, performance metrics, and host-level network traffic metadata.

Setting Up the Environment

In this section, we'll install the components described in the previous section. Be sure to copy the commands you execute into a file for your own reference so you can store them using Git at the end of this chapter.

Enabling TLS

You'll use Elasticsearch, Kibana, and two different Elastic Agents in this chapter. You may use one certificate per tool if you desire, but for practice, we'll use a wildcard TLS certificate to encrypt communications between these tools. Wildcard certificates use asterisks as placeholders rather than specifying a specific tool's name, letting you use the certificate on multiple servers at once.

Wildcard certificates may pose a slightly elevated risk to your security posture, because anyone with a copy of the key can host their own trusted services on the network. While this can alleviate managing dozens or hundreds of certificates internally, if you're opposed to accepting this risk in your environment, consider using different wildcard certificates that contain only clientAuth or serverAuth extensions, but not both. If one key becomes compromised but not the other, at least the attacker is restricted to only initiating *or* only receiving connections using your certificates. You may also use certificates with multiple subject alternative names, which would list only a specific set of hostnames, instead of using a wildcard that covers a whole subdomain. Generally, wildcard certificates are more than adequate to protect a lab or small development network, but consult your organization's encryption policies before putting anything in production.

The Configuration File

The following OpenSSL configuration uses a wildcard (*) in the alternate _names section to match anything in the *.local* domain, along with a long list of DNS names for tool servers used in this book. Save the file as *~/tls/configs/openssl-flex-wildcard.local.cnf*:

```
##################################################################
[ req ]
prompt               = no
default_bits         = 4096
default_md           = sha512
default_keyfile      = tls/keys/wildcard.local.flex.key.pem
distinguished_name   = flex_distinguished_name
req_extensions       = flex_cert
##################################################################
[ flex_distinguished_name ]
countryName                    = US
stateOrProvinceName            = MO
localityName                   = St. Louis
organizationName               = Business, Inc.
organizationalUnitName         = Information Technology
commonName                     = Wildcard Flex
emailAddress                   = none@localhost
##################################################################
[ flex_cert ]
nsComment                  = OpenSSL Wildcard Certificate for Clients and Servers
subjectAltName             = @alternate_names
##################################################################
[ alternate_names ]
DNS.1   = *.local
```

```
DNS.2   = localhost
DNS.3   = elasticsearch01.local
DNS.4   = elasticsearch01
DNS.5   = kibana.local
DNS.6   = kibana
DNS.7   = fleet.local
DNS.8   = fleet
DNS.9   = elasticagent.local
DNS.10  = elasticagent
--snip--
DNS.39  = logstash03.local
DNS.40  = elasticsearch03.local
```

I've bolded the word Wildcard to emphasize changing the key name, common name, and comment. Using a wildcard means you may use the certificate with any server or tool name in the local domain, such as mail.local or filebeat.local. The alternate_names section also includes localhost and the names of tools explored in this chapter.

Consider also adding the names of tools explored in later chapters, such as logstash, minio, rsyslog, kafka01 through kafka03, threatintel, redisleader, and redisreplica01 through redisreplica03, and tools from previous chapters, such as filebeat and winlogbeat. As some cybersecurity tools may outright reject a wildcard in favor of an explicit DNS name match, adding the tool names with and without the domain to the list of SANs errs on the side of connectivity.

If you choose to experiment on your own with multiple Elasticsearch and Logstash nodes, add numbers to the tool names, like elasticsearch02 and logstash01, and so forth. Be sure to increment the numbers in each DNS statement in the alternate_names section accordingly, and add both a base hostname and an entry with the .local domain for each tool name.

The Certificate and Key

Create the wildcard certificate signing request with this command:

```
$ openssl req -config tls/configs/openssl-flex-wildcard.local.cnf -new -out
tls/csr/wildcard.local.flex.csr -outform PEM -passout pass:abcd1234
```

Next, sign the certificate signing request using the intermediate certificate authority:

```
$ openssl ca -batch -notext -config tls/configs/openssl-intermediateca.cnf
-passin pass:abcd1234 -policy signing_policy -extensions flex_cert
-out tls/certs/wildcard.local.flex.cert.pem -infiles
tls/csr/wildcard.local.flex.csr
```

Check that OpenSSL copied the extensions from the certificate signing request into the signed certificate and that the wildcard and tools in your SAN look good:

```
$ openssl x509 -in tls/certs/wildcard.local.flex.cert.pem -text -noout
--snip--
    X509v3 Extended Key Usage:
        TLS Web Client Authentication, TLS Web Server Authentication
    X509v3 Subject Alternative Name:
        DNS:*.local, DNS:elasticsearch.local, DNS:elasticsearch
--snip--
```

Finally, verify the certificate against the CA chain file:

```
$ openssl verify -CAfile tls/certs/ca-chain.cert.pem tls/certs/wildcard.local.flex.cert.pem
certs/wildcard.local.flex.cert.pem: OK
```

Let's make an unencrypted private key for the wildcard certificate, as some tool options don't support encrypted private keys:

```
$ openssl rsa -in wildcard.local.flex.key.pem -out
wildcard.local.flex.key.nopass.pem
```

Elasticsearch supports a combined keystore file that can contain both a signed certificate and its matching private key, so let's make that file now.

The Keystore File

Elasticsearch supports individual PEM key and certificate files, combined Java Keystore files, and PKCS#12 container files. For simplicity, let's combine the private key and certificate into one PKCS#12 file:

```
$ openssl pkcs12 -export -inkey tls/keys/wildcard.local.flex.key.pem -in
tls/certs/wildcard.local.flex.cert.pem -passin pass:abcd1234 -out
tls/certs/wildcard.local.flex.pkcs12 -passout pass:abcd1234
```

The combined PKCS#12 file is now ready for Elasticsearch. Save the OpenSSL configuration and any notes in your Git repository.

Configuring DNS and Firewall Rules

Let's add firewall rules so the services can communicate with each other. On systems that use Uncomplicated Firewall, add the following allow rules. Note that if you've already added the SSH port (22) rule, this command will skip over it:

```
$ sudo ufw allow 22,9200,5044,5601,8220,8221/tcp
```

On systems that use Firewalld, use brace expansion to run a single command for all ports (although you may instead add as many --add-port arguments as you want):

```
$ sudo firewall-cmd --permanent --add-port={22,9200,5044,5601,8220,8221}/tcp
```

You may recognize 5044 as the Logstash port used for Beats and Elastic Agent. Port 9200 is for Elasticsearch connections, 5601 is the default port for the Kibana web GUI, and both 8220 and 8221 are for Elastic Agent.

Let's also update the *hosts* file on your Linux and Windows systems so the hostnames can resolve to IP addresses properly. Substitute your own IP addresses in the following snippet. On Windows, the *hosts* file is located at *C:\Windows\System32\drivers\etc\hosts*, and on Linux, it's at */etc/hosts*. You'll need superuser privileges to change either file:

```
--snip--
192.168.8.130    elasticsearch01
192.168.8.130    elasticsearch01.local
192.168.8.130    kibana
192.168.8.130    kibana.local
192.168.8.130    elasticagent
192.168.8.130    elasticagent.local
192.168.8.131    fleet
192.168.8.131    fleet.local
192.168.8.131    logstash
192.168.8.131    logstash.local
```

Save and close the administrator text editor. Now that you've completed this setup, you can download and install the tools.

Installing Tools on Multiple Servers

I recommend using two Ubuntu virtual machines in addition to your primary workstation. We'll refer to these as the first and second Elastic virtual machines. The first Elastic virtual machine will host Elasticsearch, Kibana, and an Elastic Agent instance running a data collection policy, which we'll explore later in this chapter. The second Elastic virtual machine will run another Elastic Agent instance, which will act as the fleet server, and Logstash.

Feel free to instead run some of the tools on your main workstation virtual machine if you don't have the resources to run three virtual machines. You'll need at least two virtual machines, however, as two instances of Elastic Agents can't run on the same host. Alternatively, if you want to use one virtual machine per tool (and have the resources to do so), you can host Elasticsearch, Kibana, Logstash, and each Elastic Agent instance separately.

By dividing the tools in this chapter between different virtual machines, you mimic the spreading of services across multiple servers in a production environment. You'll gain familiarity with connecting Elasticsearch, Kibana, and multiple agents using DNS hostnames and TLS, instead of routing connections locally on a single host.

Elasticsearch

You'll find many guides on the internet for installing Elasticsearch using its own self-signed certificate generator. These quick setup steps don't use the custom CAs and certificates you'll need in production environments, however. Follow the instructions in this section to run the tool using mutual TLS right from the start.

On your first Elastic virtual machine, download Elastic's GNU Privacy Guard (GPG) key, which ensures that Elastic has approved the packages you download next. Then, configure the official Elastic repository that Ubuntu's apt command uses to find and download packages. Substitute *x.y* with the software version number you're downloading:

```
$ wget -qO - https://artifacts.elastic.co/GPG-KEY-elasticsearch | sudo gpg
--dearmor -o /usr/share/keyrings/elasticsearch-keyring.gpg

$ echo "deb [signed-by=/usr/share/keyrings/elasticsearch-keyring.gpg]
https://artifacts.elastic.co/packages/x.y/apt stable main" | sudo tee
/etc/apt/sources.list.d/elastic-x.y.list
```

The first command downloads and converts the ASCII-encoded GPG key to bytes, and the second command specifies that Elastic must have signed the packages using the GPG key.

Next, update the system's cache of available packages and install both Elasticsearch and Kibana:

```
$ sudo apt update
$ sudo apt install elasticsearch kibana
```

Now you need the TLS wildcard files. On the host where you made the TLS files, navigate to the level above the *tls* directory (likely your home directory, if you followed along in Chapter 2), and launch a web server using Python:

```
$ python3 -m http.server 8080
```

Return to your Elasticsearch host. When Elasticsearch and Kibana run, the root user kickstarts those tools' processes but drops permissions to the *elasticsearch* and *kibana* users, respectively. In a new terminal, become the root user locally for the following installation steps:

```
$ sudo su -
```

Your terminal prompt might change from a dollar sign ($) to a hash mark (#). Next, download the wildcard certificates to the */etc/elasticsearch/ certs* directory:

```
$ cd /etc/elasticsearch/certs
$ wget 192.168.8.133:8080/tls/certs/wildcard.local.flex.pkcs12
$ wget 192.168.8.133:8080/tls/certs/ca-chain.cert.pem
$ chown -R root:elasticsearch *
$ chmod 0640 *
```

These commands download the TLS files, change file ownership to the *elasticsearch* group, and change the file access mode. As a result, only root should be able to both read and write to the files; the *elasticsearch* group should only be able to read them. Next, navigate up one level to */etc/elasticsearch*, back up the main configuration file *elasticsearch.yml*, then open a new configuration:

```
$ cd /etc/elasticsearch
$ mv elasticsearch.yml elasticsearch.yml.original
$ nano elasticsearch.yml
```

Add the following lines to your new *elasticsearch.yml*:

```
❶ node.name: "elasticsearch01.local"
  node.roles: [ "master", "data", "ingest", "transform" ]
❷ cluster.name: "es"
  path.data: /var/lib/elasticsearch
  path.logs: /var/log/elasticsearch
  xpack.security.enabled: true
  xpack.security.enrollment.enabled: true
❸ xpack.security.http.ssl:
    enabled: true
    verification_mode: full
    keystore.path: "certs/wildcard.local.flex.pkcs12"
    certificate_authorities: "certs/ca-chain.cert.pem"
❹ xpack.security.transport.ssl:
    enabled: true
    verification_mode: full
    keystore.path: "certs/wildcard.local.flex.pkcs12"
    certificate_authorities: "certs/ca-chain.cert.pem"
❺ network.host: ["elasticsearch01.local"]
  bootstrap.memory_lock: true
❻ cluster.initial_master_nodes: ["elasticsearch01.local"]
  discovery.seed_hosts: ["elasticsearch01.local"]
```

These lines tell Elasticsearch what its own name is ❶, as well as the name of the cluster ❷ and TLS settings. The http SSL options ❸ are for client connections to Elasticsearch, whether they're made using a custom Python script or the Kibana frontend GUI you'll configure shortly. The transport SSL options ❹ are for an Elasticsearch-only internal communication protocol it uses to send data between nodes. The network.host option ❺ is the listener where Elasticsearch accepts incoming HTTP or transport connections. Both cluster.initial_master_nodes and discovery.seed_hosts ❻ help Elasticsearch discover *itself* as a single node; they also help new nodes discover an existing cluster, if you decide to add more nodes on your own.

Instead of storing the private key's password in *elasticsearch.yml*, let's add it to a *keystore*, a file Elasticsearch can privately access to retrieve secret values. Set both passwords to *abcd1234*:

```
$ /usr/share/elasticsearch/bin/elasticsearch-keystore add
xpack.security.http.ssl.keystore.secure_password
$ /usr/share/elasticsearch/bin/elasticsearch-keystore add
xpack.security.transport.ssl.keystore.secure_password
```

Please note that Logstash and Beats support using keystores as well. Elasticsearch is based on Java and includes the necessary self-contained code to run when you install it. As this isn't a production deployment, let's severely limit the Java Virtual Machine (JVM) heap size, where certain values are held in memory. These heap changes prevent Elasticsearch from consuming all available resources on your virtual machine. Create */etc/elasticsearch/jvm.options.d/heap.options* and add the following lines:

```
$ nano /etc/elasticsearch/jvm.options.d/heap.options
-Xms1g
-Xmx1g
```

These lines set the minimum and maximum values for the heap size to 1GB, which you can increase if desired; Elastic recommends setting these values to no more than 50 percent of available RAM and keeping both minimum (Xms) and maximum (Xmx) heap values equal to each other.

Next, start Elasticsearch, then follow its logs to check its startup status:

```
$ systemctl start elasticsearch
$ tail -f /var/log/elasticsearch/es.log
```

The systemctl command may take some time to finish. Note that you defined the filename *es.log* in the cluster.name value you set in *elasticsearch .yml*. If for some reason you didn't change that value, this log may instead be named *elasticsearch.log*.

Let's change certain system passwords Elasticsearch and Kibana use to interact with one another. Change both the *elastic* and *kibana_system* accounts to use the password *abcd1234*:

```
$ /usr/share/elasticsearch/bin/elasticsearch-reset-password -u elastic
-i --url https://elasticsearch01.local:9200
$ /usr/share/elasticsearch/bin/elasticsearch-reset-password -u kibana_system
-i --url https://elasticsearch01.local:9200
```

The *elastic* user is a built-in superuser for performing administrator tasks in Elasticsearch. The *kibana_system* user links Kibana to Elasticsearch, allowing you to perform administrative tasks in the GUI. Now let's use three curl commands to test the status of the new database using the *elastic* account; you may run these from your first Elastic virtual machine or your main workstation, as Elasticsearch should be network accessible now:

```
$ curl -sku "elastic:abcd1234" https://elasticsearch01.local:9200
{
  "name" : "elasticsearch01.local",
  "cluster_name" : "es",
  "cluster_uuid" : "ufZj38auRLyoV1kQW71A6A",
  "version" : {
    "number" : "X.YY.Z",
    "build_flavor" : "default",
    "build_type" : "deb",
    "build_hash" : "1a77947f34deddb41af25e6f0ddb8e830159c179",
    "build_date" : "2040-01-01T12:34:56.546347365Z",
    "build_snapshot" : false,
    "lucene_version" : "X.YY.Z",
    "minimum_wire_compatibility_version" : "X.YY.Z",
    "minimum_index_compatibility_version" : "X.YY.Z"
  },
  "tagline" : "You Know, for Search"
}

$ curl -sku "elastic:abcd1234" https://elasticsearch01.local:9200/
_cat/health
1999817015 03:50:15 elasticsearch green 1 1 54 54 0 0 0 0 - 100.0%

$ curl -sku "elastic:abcd1234" "https://elasticsearch.local:9200/
_cluster/health?pretty&filter_path=cluster_name,status"
{
  "cluster_name" : "es",
  "status" : "green"
}
```

The first command sends a request using basic authentication (username and password) to the Elasticsearch server, which responds with a JSON message stating simple information about the server. The second command calls an API for health status, which, among other details, shows the status as green. The third command calls a different health API, and the filters in the URL path show only the JSON keys we're interested in: the cluster name and status, which is also green. These responses mean Elasticsearch installed successfully.

To add more Elasticsearch nodes to your single-node cluster, repeat the installation steps described in this section with a few minor changes:

- Change node.name and network.host to each new host's values.
- Update keystore passwords for TLS files on each new host.

- Add at least one existing master node to `discovery.seed_hosts` in *elasticsearch.yml*.

- Do not change the *elastic* and *kibana_system* passwords, as this change will happen automatically.

With a working Elasticsearch in place, let's install Kibana, the frontend GUI for Elasticsearch, which lets us manage Elastic Agent deployments.

Kibana

In the root terminal on your first Elastic virtual machine, run the following commands to create a certificate directory for Kibana and download the TLS wildcard files:

```
$ mkdir -p /etc/kibana/certs
$ cd /etc/kibana/certs
$ wget 192.168.8.133:8080/tls/certs/wildcard.local.flex.pkcs12
$ wget 192.168.8.133:8080/tls/certs/ca-chain.cert.pem
$ chown -R root:kibana *
$ chmod 0640 *
```

Next, generate encryption keys for Kibana. These keys encrypt various saved settings and reports inside Kibana. Run the following command, and copy the last three lines of output:

```
$ /usr/share/kibana/bin/kibana-encryption-keys generate
xpack.encryptedSavedObjects.encryptionKey: 3bb719...
xpack.reporting.encryptionKey: ab54f0...
xpack.security.encryptionKey: 5b6ff5...
```

The first key protects saved objects, such as graphs and dashboards, as well as settings that may contain passwords to other systems. The second key encrypts saved reports, and the third key encrypts connection session and cookie information.

Now let's add the main configuration file, */etc/kibana/kibana.yml*. Change directories to */etc/kibana*, back up the original *kibana.yml* file, and open a new blank one:

```
$ cd /etc/kibana
$ mv kibana.yml kibana.yml.original
$ nano kibana.yml
```

Add the following lines to *kibana.yml*:

```
❶ server.publicBaseUrl: "https://kibana.local:5601"
  pid.file: /run/kibana/kibana.pid
❷ server.host: "kibana.local"
  server.port: "5601"
❸ elasticsearch.hosts: ["https://elasticsearch01.local:9200"]
❹ elasticsearch.username: "kibana_system"
❺ elasticsearch.ssl.verificationMode: "full"
```

```
  elasticsearch.ssl.keystore.path:
  "/etc/kibana/certs/wildcard.local.flex.pkcs12"
  elasticsearch.ssl.certificateAuthorities:
  ["/etc/kibana/certs/ca-chain.cert.pem"]
  server.ssl.enabled: true
❻ server.ssl.clientAuthentication: none
  server.ssl.keystore.path:
  "/etc/kibana/certs/wildcard.local.flex.pkcs12"
  server.ssl.certificateAuthorities: ["/etc/kibana/certs/ca-chain.cert.pem"]
  logging:
    appenders:
      file:
        type: file
        fileName: /var/log/kibana/kibana.log
        layout:
          type: json
    root:
      appenders:
        - default
        - file
  xpack.encryptedSavedObjects.encryptionKey: 3bb719...
  xpack.reporting.encryptionKey: ab54f0...
  xpack.security.encryptionKey: 5b6ff5...
```

The first options define the URL that users will visit to access Kibana ❶ and the DNS name on which to expect incoming connections ❷. Include all of your Elasticsearch nodes, if you made more than one, in the array elasticsearch.hosts ❸. The elasticsearch.username ❹ option has no corresponding password value, since that's kept safely in a keystore you'll configure shortly. Require mutual TLS for all connections with Elasticsearch ❺, then configure filepaths. The server SSL settings are for client connections to Kibana. The default client authentication setting is none ❻, but you may change it to required if users will install signed certificates in their browsers.

Next, let's add necessary secrets to the keystore; set all values to *abcd1234*:

```
$ /usr/share/kibana/bin/kibana-keystore add elasticsearch.password
$ /usr/share/kibana/bin/kibana-keystore add elasticsearch.ssl.keystore.password
$ /usr/share/kibana/bin/kibana-keystore add server.ssl.keystore.password
```

The first value is the password corresponding to the Elasticsearch username. The next two values both specify the password for the private key in the PKCS#12 file, as we use the same key to connect to Elasticsearch and listen for Kibana web connections. With the secrets in place, start Kibana:

```
$ systemctl start kibana
$ tail -f /var/log/kibana/kibana.log | jq '.["message"]'
```

The second command shows Kibana's JSON log and uses jq, a tool you can install in this book's introduction, to display only the message field. Kibana's JSON logs include several fields, such as timestamps and other metrics, but the message field contains useful status details.

To access the Kibana GUI, navigate to *https://kibana.local:5601* in a web browser. Log in with the username *elastic* and the password *abcd1234*. The interface should look similar to Figure 6-2.

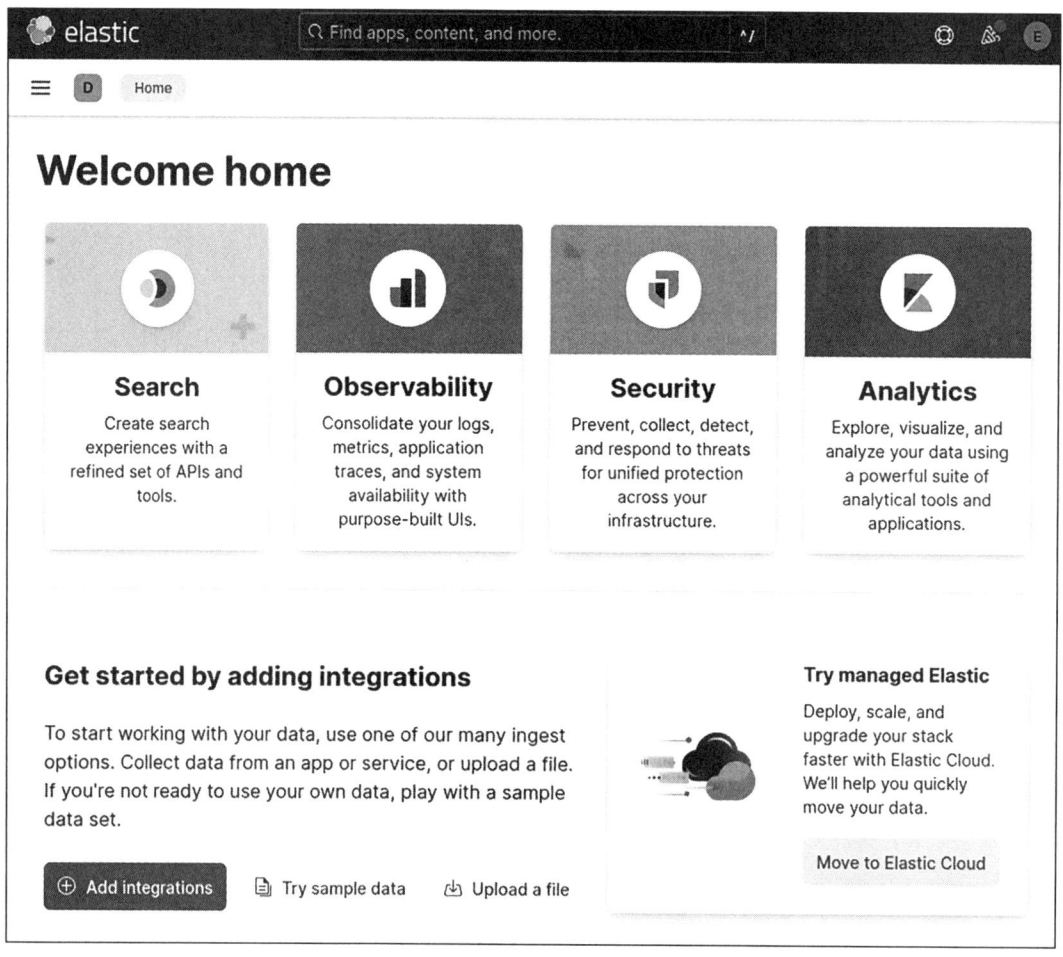

Figure 6-2: The Kibana home page

With Elasticsearch and Kibana up and running, let's configure the fleet server to manage the Elastic Agent.

NOTE *If you're like me and want to use a darker visual theme that is easier on the eyes, turn on Dark Mode by clicking the hamburger menu (the icon with three horizontal lines) in the top-left corner. Navigate to **Stack Management ▸ Advanced Settings**, then search for **dark** in the text box. Toggle Dark mode to **Enabled**, then click the **Reload page** pop-up button that appears.*

The Fleet Server

The fleet server receives periodic check-ins from endpoint Elastic Agent instances and distributes policy changes to tell the agents what data to collect and where to send it. The fleet server is just a dedicated agent given the fleet-server integration.

Let's first configure the fleet server's output settings so that the agents send data to Elasticsearch. From the Kibana hamburger menu, navigate to **Fleet ▸ Settings ▸ Add output**. Set **My Elasticsearch** as the output's new name. Leave the type as Elasticsearch, and set the Hosts field to **https://elasticsearch01.local:9200**. You could add more Elasticsearch nodes to this field in the future, such as *https://elasticsearch02.local:9200*. Toggle on both radio buttons to make this output the default for both agent integrations and monitoring.

Let's add our CA chain so it's included in policies and so the agent doesn't need to read certificate files after installing. In the Advanced YAML section, paste the contents of the CA chain. Be sure to copy the root CA and intermediate CA into the following bulleted-list format, with the proper indentation:

```
ssl:
  certificate_authorities:
  - |
    -----BEGIN CERTIFICATE-----
    MIIGVzCCBD...
    --snip--
  - |
    -----BEGIN CERTIFICATE-----
    MIIINjCCBh6g...
    --snip--
```

This entry embeds the CA chain into the policy configurations that each agent loads once connected to the fleet server. Click **Save and apply settings**.

Now let's add the fleet-server integration, which will distribute initial policies and any policy updates to agents as they periodically check in. Navigate to **Fleet** in the hamburger menu, then click **Add Fleet Server** and select the **Advanced** tab.

For Step 1, "Select a policy for Fleet Server," leave the name "Fleet Server policy 1" populated, then click **Create policy**. For Step 2, "Choose a deployment mode for security," toggle **Production** so you can use your own certificates. For Step 3, "Add your Fleet Server host," set the name to **My Fleet** and the URL to *https://fleet.local:8220*. Click **Add Host**.

Next, click **Generate a service token** under Step 4. This token lets the fleet server authenticate to the Agent cluster to begin filling the fleet server role. If you accidentally turn off the menu and lose the token, the fastest way to get a new one is to click the **Add Fleet Server** button again to generate a new one. The token should be a long string of alphanumeric characters, like the following:

```
AAEAAWVsYXNOaWMvZmx...
```

Kibana should also show you the agent installation commands for Linux, macOS, Kubernetes, and Windows. Copy the Linux commands into a separate document, and note the placeholders, as we'll update these shortly.

Let's begin installing the fleet server. First, start a Python webserver on the host with your TLS files. From a root terminal on your second Elastic virtual machine, create the */opt/Elastic/Agent/certs/* directory and download the wildcard files and CA chain there. Then, change directories back to the root user's home:

```
$ mkdir -p /opt/Elastic/Agent/certs/
$ cd /opt/Elastic/Agent/certs/
$ wget 192.168.8.133:8080/tls/certs/wildcard.local.flex.cert.pem
$ wget 192.168.8.133:8080/tls/keys/wildcard.local.flex.key.nopass.pem
$ wget 192.168.8.133:8080/tls/certs/ca-chain.cert.pem
$ chmod 0640 *
$ cd
```

Using the curl, tar, and cd commands that you saved in a separate file, download and extract the Elastic Agent tarball, then change directories into the extracted folder. Note that the X.YY.Z placeholders indicate version numbers in the following snippet; you should replace these with the versions listed in Kibana:

```
$ curl -L -O https://artifacts.elastic.co/downloads/beats
/elastic-agent/elastic-agent-X.YY.Z-linux-x86_64.tar.gz
$ tar xzvf elastic-agent-X.YY.Z-linux-x86_64.tar.gz
$ cd elastic-agent-X.YY.Z-linux-x86_64
```

Finally, run the installation command with the URL and filename placeholders appropriately updated:

```
$ ./elastic-agent install \
  --force \
  --url=https://fleet.local:8220 \
  --fleet-server-port=8220 \
  --fleet-server-es=https://elasticsearch01.local:9200 \
  --fleet-server-service-token=AAEAAWVsYXNOaWMvZmx... \
  --fleet-server-policy=fleet-server-policy \
  --certificate-authorities=/opt/Elastic/Agent/certs/ca-chain.cert.pem \
  --fleet-server-es-ca=/opt/Elastic/Agent/certs/ca-chain.cert.pem \
  --fleet-server-cert=/opt/Elastic/Agent/certs/wildcard.local.flex.cert.pem \
  --fleet-server-cert-key=
/opt/Elastic/Agent/certs/wildcard.local.flex.key.nopass.pem \
  --elastic-agent-cert=/opt/Elastic/Agent/certs/wildcard.local.flex.cert.pem \
  --elastic-agent-cert-key=
```

```
/opt/Elastic/Agent/certs/wildcard.local.flex.key.nopass.pem \
   --fleet-server-client-auth=required
```

This command specifies the fleet server, the fleet port, the authorization token and policy names, and the CAs for connecting to Elasticsearch and for the fleet server itself. It also includes the key and certificate for connecting to Elasticsearch. The force option bypasses a yes/no confirmation prompt, which is useful when installing multiple agents using Ansible (a topic discussed in Chapter 11).

Note the fleet-server* TLS options are for the agent connecting to Elasticsearch and the elastic-agent* TLS options are for the agent connecting to itself (a local fleet server process). Subsequent agent installations will use the same elastic-agent* TLS options. The default client authentication is none, but let's change it to required to use mutual TLS, as done elsewhere in this book. This setting will require new agents to provide a certificate and key upon setup.

You should see output like the following, indicating success:

```
[    ] Service Started  [7s] Elastic Agent successfully installed,
starting enrollment.
--snip--
Successfully enrolled the Elastic Agent.
--snip--
[=== ] Done  [17s]
Elastic Agent has been successfully installed.
```

If the installation fails for any reason, the Agent installer will remove all files in */opt/Elastic/*, so you'll need to re-create the nested *certs* subdirectory and download the TLS files again.

Back inside Kibana, the message under Step 6 should turn green and read "Fleet Server connected." If you refresh the fleet page, you should see your new server listed, along with its CPU and memory usage.

The Elastic Agents

To add an agent to your fleet, repeat the agent setup process on your first Elastic virtual machine host. Because you won't configure this agent to be a fleet server, you can skip certain steps. Create a directory for TLS files and download them:

```
$ mkdir -p /opt/Elastic/Agent/certs/
$ cd /opt/Elastic/Agent/certs/
$ wget 192.168.8.133:8080/tls/certs/wildcard.local.flex.cert.pem
$ wget 192.168.8.133:8080/tls/keys/wildcard.local.flex.key.nopass.pem
$ wget 192.168.8.133:8080/tls/certs/ca-chain.cert.pem
$ chmod 0640 *
```

Inside Kibana, navigate to **Fleet** and click **Add agent**. For Step 1, "What type of host do you want to monitor," leave "Agent policy 1" populated and click **Create policy**. For Step 2, "Enroll in Fleet," leave the option toggled on. Step 3 shows more installation commands for Elastic Agent, but more importantly, it shows an *enrollment token*, which authorizes your agent to join the fleet; copy it somewhere temporarily.

To install the agent, download and extract the Elastic Agent tarball, as you did previously; substitute *X.YY.Z* for your version numbers as necessary:

```
$ curl -L -O https://artifacts.elastic.co/downloads/beats/
elastic-agent/elastic-agent-X.YY.Z-linux-x86_64.tar.gz
$ tar xzvf elastic-agent-X.YY.Z-linux-x86_64.tar.gz
$ cd elastic-agent-X.YY.Z-linux-x86_64
```

In a root terminal or using sudo, run the following command to install the agent:

```
$ ./elastic-agent install \
  --force \
  --url=https://fleet.local:8220 \
  --enrollment-token=ZUVrVWt... \
  --elastic-agent-cert=
/opt/Elastic/Agent/certs/wildcard.local.flex.cert.pem \
  --elastic-agent-cert-key=
/opt/Elastic/Agent/certs/wildcard.local.flex.key.nopass.pem \
  --certificate-authorities=/opt/Elastic/Agent/certs/ca-chain.cert.pem
```

As with the previous fleet agent, you should see output indicating success. Back in Kibana, Step 4 should turn green and say "Agent enrollment confirmed." You now have a full Elasticsearch, Kibana, Fleet, and Agent software stack installed.

Logstash

We'll use Logstash in "Stand-Alone Agents" on page 118 to receive data from an Elastic Agent instance that isn't connected to a fleet. On your second Elastic VM, follow the same steps as you did in Chapter 2 to run Logstash from the tarball downloaded from Elastic's website. Be sure to create both *certs* and *conf.d* directories inside the extracted Logstash directory if they aren't present. Use the wildcard flex certificate you generated previously in this chapter.

Alternatively, you could use the Logstash instance that you made in Chapter 2; if you do, I recommend updating that configuration to use the new wildcard flex certificate, too.

Viewing Events in Kibana

You can view individual event log messages from your hosts and network devices within the Analytics context using Kibana's Discover feature. Discover lets you see individual events, called *documents* in Elastic parlance, and export them as CSVs or PDFs. Click the hamburger menu, then click

Discover under the Analytics drop-down menu. This should take you to the screen shown in Figure 6-3.

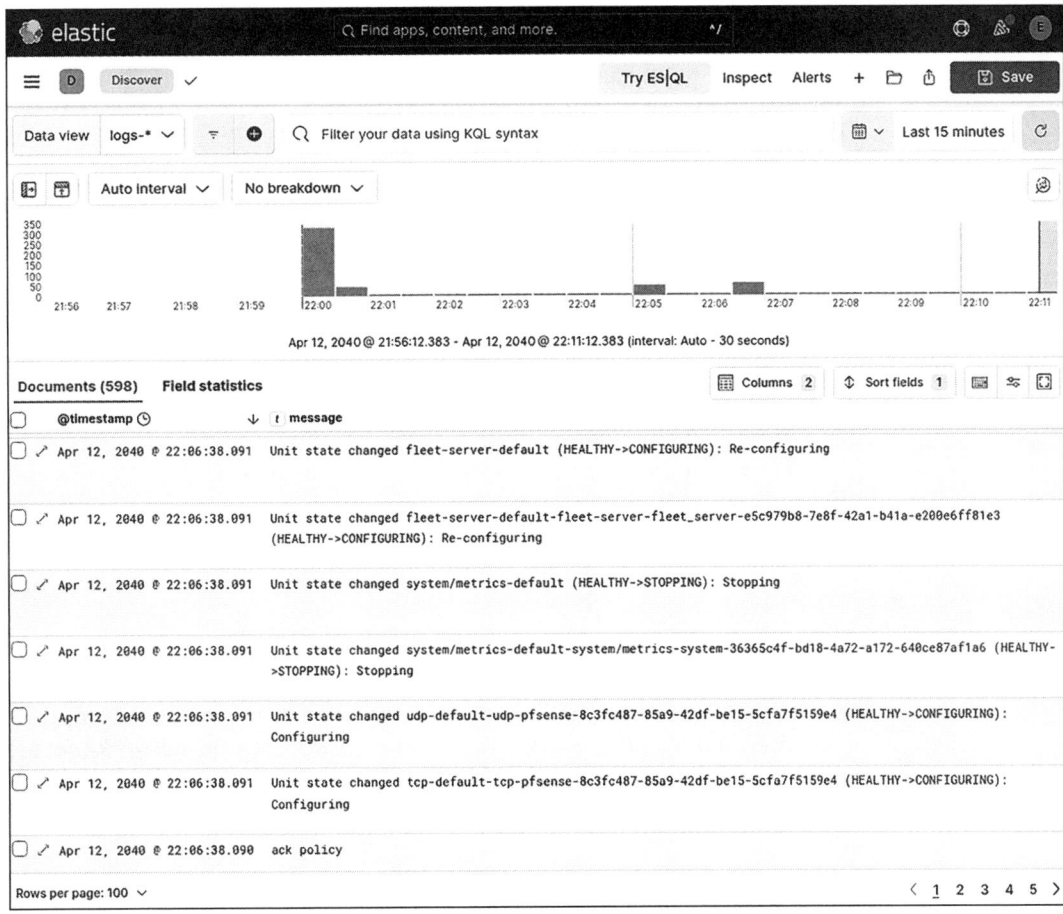

Figure 6-3: Viewing events in Kibana's Discover interface

The Discover interface includes a search bar, a time picker, a drop-down menu for selecting various available datasets, and rows of individual events. The only logs coming into Elasticsearch should be system metrics and a handful of host events generated by your Elastic Agents.

To search for events in Kibana, use the syntax *field*:*value*. For example, the search term source.ip:192.168.8.130 would find events originating from the specified IP address. You can use parentheses, quotations, OR, and AND statements to craft more complex queries, as in this example:

```
destination.domain:("fleet.local" OR "kibana.local") AND destination.ip:"192.168.8.0/24"
```

You can search for both single IP addresses and Classless Inter-Domain Routing network blocks (CIDRs) in IP address fields (such as destination.ip), as shown in this snippet. You can also negate terms using the NOT operator to exclude results you don't want. To learn more about searching Kibana, consult the many free Kibana references available in Elastic's official Kibana documentation.

Now is a great time to shut down your virtual machines and take a snapshot. As Elasticsearch and Kibana likely aren't set to start automatically, you may need to run `sudo systemctl start elasticsearch kibana` once your reboot is complete and you've logged back in to the first Elastic virtual machine.

Next, let's explore Elastic Agent features for data collection.

Configuring Different Technology Integrations

Integrations are specialized data collection policies that let Elastic Agent collect local logs, retrieve logs from commercial tools or APIs, and act as a log receiver. The available integrations allow agents to connect to hundreds of technologies to receive and retrieve data, such as cloud services, routers and switches, and host-level network metadata.

Let's add an integration that will run Packetbeat behind the scenes to capture network traffic for each process emanating from the host. We'll also add the *Iptables* integration to capture firewall logs from your first Elastic virtual machine. Ubuntu uses UFW, which is a streamlined interface for Iptables.

Network Metadata

The Network Packet Capture integration won't perform full packet captures or log the contents of network traffic; rather, it will capture network metadata, such as process names, source and destination IP addresses and ports, network protocols, timestamps, and much more. It's akin to Zeek but operates at the host level.

In Kibana's Fleet screen, click the **Agent policies** tab, then click **Agent policy 1**. You should have the *System* integration by default. To add a new one, click **Add integration**. You should arrive at a menu containing several hundred integrations you could add.

Under the Network option, click **Network Packet Capture**, then click the **Settings** tab. Click **Install Network Packet Capture assets** to configure Kibana and Elasticsearch with preconfigured items like dashboards and ingest pipelines. Once that process completes, take a moment to explore the other tabs. Notice that the Configs tab shows you settings you could add to a custom *elastic-agent.yml* configuration file to create your own standalone policy.

Next, click **Add Network Packet Capture** at the top-right to visit the integration's setup page. You could accept the defaults, but let's expand the **Change defaults** menu, which lets you pick which network protocols to include or exclude.

Importantly, this menu lets you toggle the Monitor Processes button for various protocols to add process names to each network event, which is incredibly helpful for linking suspicious network traffic logs to the host process that created it. Toggle on as many or as few of the protocols and process name settings as you want, although I recommend enabling them all. This way, you can see the host process behind each network connection—a true gold mine of forensic artifacts. You can also include lists of ports for each service if you have services running on nonstandard ports, such as a web server on port 12345.

Once you've finished turning settings on or off, scroll to Step 2, then click the **Existing hosts** tab and select **Agent policy 1** so that the agent running on your first Elastic virtual machine will receive this new integration. Click **Save and continue**, then click **Save and deploy changes** at the confirmation pop-up. A banner should appear saying the new policy is deploying.

To view the events collected due to this integration, return to Kibana's Discover page. In the search bar, enter **event.category:"network"**. You should now see network logs from your host flowing in, meaning the integration applied successfully. If the events don't appear right away, wait a moment. The policy changes should take just under a minute to start working.

Iptables Firewall Logs

The Iptables integration reads Iptables firewall logs on Linux hosts. To add the integration to the policy, return to **Menu ▶ Fleet ▶ Agent policies ▶ Agent policy 1**, then click **Add integration**. Search for **Iptables**, then click the box that appears. Go to the **Settings** tab, install the assets as you did in the previous section, and then click **Add Iptables**.

This module can receive remote firewall logs, but in this example, you'll use it to read only local files. So, toggle the UDP and TCP network inputs **Off**, but leave the option for *journald* **On**. In the policy text field, ensure *Agent policy 1* will receive this new integration. Click **Save and continue**, then confirm the change in the pop-up.

Back in Discover, search for **event.category:"network" AND event .dataset:"iptables.log"** to verify that firewall events are streaming in. You can enable increased UFW logging by running the command sudo ufw logging medium, or use high to show many more events.

Integration Guidelines

For safety reasons, your policies should stick to using a small number of integrations. Each integration adds bytes to Elasticsearch, taking up storage space. In production environments, this storage can become expensive.

Not all of your agents need the same policies, however. If only a handful of agents pull data from network appliances or APIs, they can likely afford to run those integrations on top of your host collection policies. You can also define specific policies just for integrations. For example, you could update a hypothetical Elastic Defend policy (an integration focused on incident response and prevention) across your enterprise without impacting another cloud monitoring policy running on a smaller subset of hosts.

Incident response procedures can also benefit from the rapid application of new policies. Say an organization gets infected by malware, and analysts need to determine which internal hosts might spread the infection. Applying the Packet Capture integration to a particular office, division, or campus could provide a short-term enhancement to the data available for analysts. Once you've contained the incident, you can remove the Packet Capture integration.

It's also possible that you don't need an agent or its integrations at all. Several important integrations, such as those for reading host logs and tracing network events, perform activities already covered by Beats modules, including Filebeat and Packetbeat. As you saw in Chapter 4, deploying Filebeat is much simpler than deploying Elastic Agent, and plenty of compliance situations don't require much more than authorization and syslog events, provided by Filebeat's *system* module.

Once installed and configured, however, agent policies are much faster to update than even the fastest Beats changes, as you can perform these changes in the GUI rather than running command lines and altering Beats configuration files.

Stand-Alone Agents

What if you don't want to (or can't) connect a network segment directly to Elasticsearch and the fleet? For example, a network might isolate certain hosts via firewalls or *bastions*, hardened hosts through which network traffic is funneled. These isolated hosts likely can't directly connect to your Elasticsearch cluster and must route through a bastion first.

By creating a *stand-alone policy*, you can allow an agent to use integrations and collect data even when it isn't a member of the fleet. This stand-alone agent can send data to Logstash running on a bastion, or it could also send data to a local Kafka cluster so that tools in other network segments can connect to the isolated network and pull data from it. We'll cover Kafka in Chapter 10.

As you might expect, stand-alone policies don't include benefits like automatic policy updates or real-time integration pushes. Instead, each policy in Kibana allows you to view a raw YAML file, which you'll use shortly to configure the stand-alone agent.

The free Elastic Basic Subscription licensing doesn't allow you to define outputs for each policy; for example, you can't use Logstash with a custom policy only. Instead, you must use the default output for all policies. We'll manually configure a new Logstash output for when we copy the Agent policy 1 configuration from Kibana shortly.

Preparing the Virtual Machine

If you'd like to install the stand-alone agent on the same host as the existing, non–fleet server agent, you must first uninstall that agent by running `sudo /opt/Elastic/Agent/elastic-agent uninstall` on that host.

If you added the Elastic Defend integration on your own, the agent will have tamper protection enabled, which requires an additional policy token to be uninstalled. In Kibana, navigate to **Menu ▸ Fleet ▸ Agents**, then click the three dots next to the host running *Agent policy 1* and click **Uninstall agent**. Copy the command that appears in the pop-up, which includes an authorization token, then run the command to uninstall the agent.

If you instead set up a new virtual machine for this stand-alone agent, remember to update */etc/hosts*, a silly issue that has bitten me more than once. Follow the same steps as you did with the second Elastic Agent to create */opt/Elastic/Agent/certs/*, download the TLS files (including the password-protected private key), and change their permissions. Ensure you still have the Elastic Agent tarball and its extracted contents. Back up the original */opt/Elastic/Agent/elastic-agent.yml* file just to be safe:

```
$ sudo mv elastic-agent.yml elastic-agent.yml.backup
```

Next, you can connect the stand-alone agent to Logstash.

Receiving a Logstash API Key

With the virtual machine ready to go, we need an API key so that Logstash can send data to Elasticsearch with the access permissions needed to write Elastic Agent data and custom logs into the database. Using the hamburger menu in Kibana, scroll to the **Management** section, then click **Dev Tools**. Add the following API query to create a new API key for Logstash:

```
POST /_security/api_key
{
  "name": "standalone-logstash.local",
  "role_descriptors": {
    "logstash_writer": {
      "cluster": ["monitor"],
      "index": [
        {
          "names": [
            "logstash-*",
            "logs-*-*",
            "metrics-*-*",
            "traces-*-*",
            "synthetics-*-*",
            ".logs-endpoint.diagnostic.collection-*",
            ".logs-endpoint.action.responses-*",
            "profiling-*",
            ".profiling-*",
```

```
       "filebeat-*", "packetbeat-*", "metricbeat-*",
       "winlogbeat-*", "heartbeat-*", ".ds*"
     ],
     "privileges": ["auto_configure", "view_index_metadata", "create_doc"]
   }
  ]
 }
}
}
```

The bolded text, including the comma after .profiling-*, is a manual addition used to write data to Beats indexes. Be sure to experiment with these index permissions and eliminate what you don't need in production. The query should output a new API key, like the following:

```
{
  "id": "kwouKoOBFSso9JQdUCJj",
  "name": "standalone-logstash.local",
  "api_key": "ANI6NTBMQx2NNDj3UIAxkw",
  "encoded": "a3dvdUtvMEJGU3NvOUpRZFVDSmo6QU5JNk5UQk1ReDJOTkRqM1VJQXhrdw=="
}
```

Copy this output somewhere safe, because you won't be able to retrieve these values again. Note that Kibana has a GUI menu for adding API keys, but modifying access permissions still involves updating JSON values like the commands you just ran.

Configuring a Stand-Alone Agent Policy

To configure the stand-alone agent's policy, return to the fleet policy named *Agent policy 1*. Click **Actions**, then click **View policy**. Copy the massive block of text that appears into your editor of choice.

You should find the outputs and fleet sections of this configuration output at the top of the file, underneath a long id field and followed by a revision number. Replace all four of these sections with the following Logstash output configuration, as none of them matter for a stand-alone installation, and Elastic Agent will regenerate the ID dynamically after every service restart:

```
outputs:
  default:
    type: logstash
    ssl:
      certificate: /opt/Elastic/Agent/certs/wildcard.local.flex.cert.pem
      key: /opt/Elastic/Agent/certs/wildcard.local.flex.key.pem
      key_passphrase: abcd1234
      certificate_authorities:
        - /opt/Elastic/Agent/certs/ca-chain.cert.pem
    hosts:
      - logstash.local:5044
--snip--
```

The values for these settings should look familiar by now, even if the syntax is slightly different from those you saw when working with Filebeat and Winlogbeat. To use your previous *nopass* key without a password, omit the key_passphrase line and update the key filepath accordingly.

I recommend getting into the habit of using Kibana to copy and paste configurations into the stand-alone *elastic-agent.yml* file, reducing the likelihood of typos and human error. You can also create entire unused policies, with various integrations enabled and configured, to later copy into stand-alone agent configurations.

Save the modified configuration as *elastic-agent.yml* and copy it to the host that will run it into the directory extracted from the downloaded tarball, not inside of */opt/Elastic/Agent*. This is because the installation process copies the downloaded files into the */opt* directories and reads settings from the updated *elastic-agent.yml*.

Configuring Logstash

Now let's create a configuration for Logstash. You should have downloaded and extracted a Logstash tarball package and staged TLS files in its *certs* directory. Navigate to the location on the virtual machine at which you extracted Logstash. Next, create *elasticagent-mtls.conf* and add the following lines to it, substituting your filepaths for the placeholders:

```
input {
  elastic_agent {
    id => "elastic-agent-input"
❶ port => 5044
    ssl_enabled => true
    ssl_client_authentication => "required"
    ssl_certificate => "<path to TLS files>/wildcard.local.flex.cert.pem"
    ssl_key => "<path to TLS files>/wildcard.local.flex.key.pem"
    ssl_key_passphrase => "abcd1234"
    ssl_certificate_authorities =>
    [ "<path to TLS files>/ca-chain.cert.pem"]
  }
}
output {
  stdout { codec => rubydebug }
  elasticsearch {
    id => "elasticsearch-output"
    hosts => "https://elasticsearch01.local:9200"
    # id:api_key
❷ api_key => "kwouKoOBFSso9JQdUCJj:ANI6NTBMQx2NNDj3UIAxkw"
    data_stream => true
    ssl_enabled => true
    ssl_certificate => "<path to TLS files>/wildcard.local.flex.cert.pem"
    ssl_key => "<path to TLS files>/wildcard.local.flex.key.nopass.pem"
    ssl_certificate_authorities =>
    [ "<path to TLS files>/ca-chain.cert.pem" ]
  }
}
```

Note that some lines have wrapped due to space constraints; ensure that filepaths appear on the same lines as their respective settings.

Because Elastic Agent is built on top of the Beats family, the elastic _agent input allows individual Beats to connect on the same input and port ❶ so you can send Beats data to the input for your own testing. Consider *elasticagent-mtls.conf* to be an upgrade from the *beats-mtls.conf* file covered in Chapter 2, as it does everything that configuration does in addition to sending data to Elasticsearch.

The API key ❷ you generated previously uses the format id:api_key, wrapped in double quotes ("). The rest of the options define which Elasticsearch address to use and the TLS options. The data_stream option is the newer of two methods used to store data in Elasticsearch and is beyond the scope of this book. Also note that the elasticsearch output doesn't include the ssl_key_passphrase option, whereas the elastic_agent input does; this is a Logstash quirk.

Test the Logstash configuration and then start it by running the following commands from inside your Logstash directory:

```
$ bin/logstash -f conf.d/elasticagent-mtls.conf --config.test_and_exit
$ bin/logstash -f conf.d/elasticagent-mtls.conf --config.reload.automatic
```

With Logstash ready to receive data and send it to Elasticsearch, you can install the stand-alone Elastic Agent. Navigate to the Elastic Agent directory you extracted (or still had from the previous install), double-check that the new *elastic-agent.yml* file is present, and then run the following. Note that the client TLS arguments were defined in *elastic-agent.yml*, so you don't need them here:

```
$ sudo ./elastic-agent install --force
Installing service....... DONE
Starting service... DONE
Elastic Agent has been successfully installed.
```

Notice the output includes no message about enrolling the agent into the fleet, mentioning only that the agent successfully installed. Back in Kibana, on the Discover page, verify that events are flowing into Elasticsearch. The Logstash server you started manually should also show streaming output:

```
--snip--
"@version" => "1",
   "event" => {
  "module" => "system",
 "dataset" => "system.diskio",
"duration" => 2092543
--snip--
```

The data should parse into ECS in Logstash, but additional parsing may take place inside Elasticsearch because of the integration assets installed in the previous fleet-connected example.

Next, let's perform transformations inside of Elasticsearch.

Elasticsearch Ingest Pipelines

Beats modules and agent integrations use *ingest pipelines* to perform additional field transformations inside of Elasticsearch. These transformations might convert fields to the Elastic Common Schema, use regular expressions to parse dynamic message fields, or correct timestamps, to give a few examples. Ingest pipelines receive data from Beats, Elastic Agent, Logstash, or custom scripts and then process it before storing it in the database. These pipelines use *processors*, not to be confused with the processors used by Beats, to perform individual transformations.

Beats and Elastic Agent use pipelines slightly differently, even though the agent performs many of the same functions behind the scenes using Beats. For instance, Packetbeat uses a routing pipeline to identify what protocol a network event contains, such as DNS or HTTP; then, the routing pipeline passes the event to another dedicated ingest pipeline for that protocol before storing it in Elasticsearch. Elastic Agent still runs Packetbeat behind the scenes, but Elastic Agent sends events to service- or protocol-specific pipelines, then to custom pipelines for user-defined actions.

Don't think of ingest pipelines as necessarily operating in a sequential order. Rather, think of them as a hub-and-spoke model. You can use a pipeline processor inside one ingest pipeline (the *hub*) to route events through another, "dead end" ingest pipeline (the *spoke*), which doesn't route traffic back to the calling pipeline. Instead, the hub ingest pipeline treats the dead-end pipeline as an extra set of inline transformations to perform.

You shouldn't modify the ingest pipelines included with Beats and Agent directly. When you upgrade either tool to a new version, any custom changes you've made will essentially disappear, as the altered pipelines fall into disuse.

Instead, Elastic Agent pipelines all make calls to nonexistent *@custom* pipelines; these are the pipelines you're meant to create to hold your custom transformations and any calls to subsequent custom ingest pipelines. Custom pipelines won't be deleted or altered during an upgrade. You'll find references to custom pipelines inside each agent integration, and a global custom configuration.

Creating a Custom Ingest Pipeline

Let's consider an example of creating custom ingest pipelines, to modify data from DNS query logs as they're received by Elasticsearch. The Elastic Agent ingest pipeline for DNS events is named `logs-network_traffic.dns-X`
`.YY.Z` (where `X.YY.Z` is a pipeline-specific version number, not an Elastic

Agent version number). This DNS pipeline's raw JSON definition contains the following section, which refers to an @custom pipeline:

```
--snip--
{
  "pipeline": {
    "name": "logs-network_traffic.dns@custom",
    "ignore_missing_pipeline": true,
    "description": "[Fleet] Pipeline for the
    'network_traffic.dns' dataset"
  }
}
--snip--
```

The `logs-network_traffic.dns@custom` pipeline doesn't exist. Let's create it now.

Kibana includes a GUI menu system for creating pipelines, saving you from having to alter complex JSON structures via APIs. Let's create a simple pipeline that converts all DNS domain queries to uppercase.

In Kibana, navigate to **Stack Management** ▸ **Ingest Pipelines** in the hamburger menu. Click **Create pipeline**, then click **New pipeline**. Name the pipeline `logs-network_traffic.dns@custom`, the name of the nonexistent pipeline referenced previously. Toggle both "Add version number" and "Add metadata" radio buttons to **Enabled**.

In the "Add your first processor" section, click **Add a processor**. In the drop-down that appears, search for and then click **Uppercase**. In the Field text box, enter `dns.question.name`, and in the Target field box, enter `labels .my_uppercase_domain`. Recall that Beats, Agent, and Logstash events are formatted as JSON, and `dns.question.name` is an ECS field named for the nested series of values under `dns`, then `question`, then the domain `name`.

Toggle on both radio buttons for "Ignore missing" and "Ignore failures for this processor." Click **Add processor**, then scroll all the way to the bottom of the screen and click **Create pipeline**.

Testing the Pipeline

Let's generate some DNS data so we can confirm that the new pipeline works. From a host running *Agent policy 1*, use `curl` to access one of your favorite domains:

```
$ curl https://nostarch.com
--snip--
```

In Kibana, navigate to the **Discover** page, select the `logs-*` data view from the far-left drop-down menu next to the search bar (though the view should be on by default), then enter **network.protocol:dns** in the search bar. Pick one of the most recent events that appear, which should correspond to the domain you just accessed, then click the double-arrowhead line icon on the far-left side of the interface. In the menu for the event, look for the custom field `labels.my_uppercase_domain`. The field should show the value `NOSTARCH.COM`.

NOTE *Modify or delete the custom pipeline if you don't want to keep this custom field in the long term.*

Elasticsearch needs dedicated nodes running the *ingest* role in environments larger than a home lab or small test network. However, you can perform custom transformations using Logstash, a tool we'll cover in depth in Chapters 8 and 9. Using Logstash, you can transform data before it reaches Elasticsearch or another database. This is especially useful if Elasticsearch isn't the only destination for your data; for instance, you may want to back up data in the cloud, send select logs to an insider threat team, and parse other data that Beats and Elastic Agent don't support.

SAVING CONFIGURATIONS WITH GIT

Copy any commands and configurations you've saved for Elasticsearch and other tools in this chapter into a new directory named *elastic* in your local Git repository, and redact any important credentials. Track the files using `git add .` and then run `git status` to ensure your new files are tracked. Commit the changes by running `git commit -am "added elastic files"`. Finally, `git push` them to your remote repository.

Summary

Elastic Agent is a powerful tool that combines Beats and integration capabilities that you can tune to fit your environment's needs. In this chapter, you installed the Elasticsearch database, the Kibana frontend GUI, and an Elastic Agent running in three different ways: in the fleet server role, to manage other agents; as a fleet-connected agent collecting logs and receiving updates on demand; and as a stand-alone service operating independently of any other management. You also configured Logstash to receive data from Elastic Agent and then send it to Elasticsearch.

Next, let's explore Rsyslog, a tool for writing syslog messages to disk, relaying network events, standardizing messages, and much more.

7

WORKING WITH SYSLOG DATA

At the heart of Unix-like systems lies *syslog*, a message-logging format that has been a cornerstone of modern logging infrastructure since its introduction in the 1980s. Syslog messages contain important information about host actions, providing key insights for security analysts down the line. This chapter explores the format through Rsyslog, a high-performance, security-aware log collector used for working with syslog data.

We'll begin by examining syslog's logging priorities and consider how its severity levels and facilities work together to create a nuanced classification system for your log data. This information will be crucial for analysts down the line, as it will enable them to prioritize their security operations.

You'll then install Rsyslog and use it to read local logfiles, receive data sent over the network, write logs to disk, and forward data across the network. You'll use its components, such as templates and rulesets, to develop logging rules and create effective real-world configurations.

We'll conclude by walking through two real-world configuration examples: a log collection client able to transmit logs from hosts and a server relay capable of centralizing logs before forwarding them onward.

Logging Priorities

The syslog format classifies events using logging *priorities*, which are numeric values composed of two components: a *facility*, which describes the event source, and a *severity*, which describes its criticality. We reference facilities using the digits 0 through 23 and severities using the digits 0 through 7. To calculate a priority, multiply the facility by 8, then add the severity.

Log-reading systems typically convert facilities into human-readable keywords. These numerical codes and human-readable terms are described in the older, informational RFC 3164 and the newer RFC 5424 standard, which codify the syslog message formats that we'll use in this chapter. Note, however, that different operating systems may use facilities slightly differently:

kern (0) Kernel messages from the operating system's core

user (1) User-level messages

mail (2) Legacy mail system messages

daemon (3) Messages from system daemons, also called services

auth (4) Security and authorization messages

syslog (5) Messages generated internally by the syslog service

lpr (6) Legacy line printer subsystem messages

news (7) Legacy network news subsystem messages

uucp (8) Legacy Unix-to-Unix copy program messages

cron (9) Cron service messages

authpriv (10) Security and authorization messages that are more restrictive than auth

ftp (11) File Transfer Protocol service messages

ntp (12) Network Time Protocol service messages

log (13 and 14) Audit or alert messages, depending on the operating system

clock (15) Clock or cron service messages

local0 (16) through local7 (23) General-use facilities for custom application messages

It's worth noting that, in most cases, only the kernel can generate kern messages.

The logging severities become more critical as their numerical value decreases: debug (7), info (6), notice (5), warning (4), err (3), crit (2), alert (1), and emerg (0). RFC 5427 elaborates further on facilities and severities.

Lower priorities generally take precedence in alerts; for example, an emergency `kernel` event with priority 0 should receive more attention than an informational `clock` event with priority 126. Security analysts can use priority ranges to narrow down the number of events when looking for suspicious logins, network connections, and other process events.

Collecting Data with Rsyslog

Rsyslog is a freely available logging tool that conforms to the syslog standard. Like Filebeat and Winlogbeat, it can read, write, receive, and ship logs. For example, you could use Rsyslog to receive logs over the network and write their syslog-formatted data to a file, read files from the local host and send them to a remote database, or relay network logs without ever using the local disk.

Written in C, Rsyslog has over 20 different methods of receiving data and over 30 supported methods of sending data. The tool uses a modular approach to configuration, treating each feature as a setting you can turn on when needed. These modular configurations let you add or remove specific features in their own files, or you can add code blocks to existing files. For example, you could add a new logging destination, such as a Kafka cluster, by placing a new, short file into Rsyslog's main configuration directory.

Rsyslog supports conditional rules to route data to different destinations depending on your needs. It uses this conditional logic to apply *templates*, or standardized transformation definitions, before writing or sending data. We'll explore multiple ways to receive, process, and ship data shortly.

Installation

Begin by installing the base Rsyslog package, the documentation, and the OpenSSL and Kafka add-ons. If you're on Ubuntu or Debian, run the following command:

```
$ sudo apt install rsyslog rsyslog-doc rsyslog-openssl rsyslog-kafka
```

Using Rocky Linux, CentOS, and Red Hat Enterprise Linux, substitute dnf for **apt**.

On Windows, download the latest installer version available at *https://www.rsyslog.com/windows-agent/windows-agent-download/*, execute it, and follow the steps in the installation wizard.

Check the status of your new installation by running `systemctl status rsyslog.service`. If Rsyslog doesn't start automatically, start and enable it:

```
$ sudo systemctl start rsyslog
$ sudo systemctl enable rsyslog
```

Next, enable Transport Layer Security so you can encrypt Rsyslog's traffic.

Enabling TLS

Let's create a flex certificate for Rsyslog so it can both initiate and receive network connections. Using the same format as the previous OpenSSL configurations, create *~/tls/configs/openssl-flex-rsyslog.local.cnf*, then add the following lines, taking note of the bolded instances of rsyslog and relative filepaths:

```
################################################################
[ req ]
prompt             = no
default_bits       = 4096
default_md         = sha512
default_keyfile    = tls/keys/rsyslog.local.flex.key.pem
distinguished_name = flex_distinguished_name
req_extensions     = flex_cert
################################################################
[ flex_distinguished_name ]
countryName              = US
stateOrProvinceName      = MO
localityName             = St. Louis
organizationName         = Business, Inc.
organizationalUnitName   = Information Technology
commonName               = Rsyslog Flex
emailAddress             = none@localhost
################################################################
[ flex_cert ]
nsComment                = OpenSSL Certificate for Clients or Servers
subjectAltName           = @alternate_names
################################################################
[ alternate_names ]
DNS.1  = rsyslog
DNS.2  = rsyslog.local
```

Create a 4,096-bit key pair and certificate signing request:

```
$ openssl req -config ~/tls/configs/openssl-flex-rsyslog.local.cnf -new -out
tls/csr/rsyslog.local.flex.csr -outform PEM -passout pass:abcd1234
```

Sign the certificate signing request with the intermediate CA from Chapter 2, specifying the CA's flex_cert extensions:

```
$ openssl ca -batch -notext -config ~/tls/configs/openssl-intermediateca.cnf
-passin pass:abcd1234 -policy signing_policy -extensions flex_cert -out
~/tls/certs/rsyslog.local.flex.cert.pem -infiles
~/tls/csr/rsyslog.local.flex.csr
```

We now have the signed certificate, *rsyslog.local.flex.cert.pem*. Rsyslog's OpenSSL module regrettably can't decrypt private keys that use passphrases, so let's make a copy of the private key without it. Note that you can omit the -passin argument to be prompted for the passphrase on the command line:

```
$ openssl rsa -in ~/tls/keys/rsyslog.local.flex.key.pem -passin pass:abcd1234
-out ~/tls/keys/rsyslog.local.flex.key.nopass.pem
```

View the signed certificate to check that OpenSSL copied the extensions from the certificate signing request into the final certificate:

```
$ openssl x509 -in ~/tls/certs/rsyslog.local.flex.cert.pem -text -noout
--snip--
    X509v3 Extended Key Usage:
        TLS Web Client Authentication, TLS Web Server Authentication
    X509v3 Subject Alternative Name:
        DNS:rsyslog, DNS:rsyslog.local
--snip--
```

Finally, verify the certificate can be authenticated using our combined CA chain file:

```
$ openssl verify -CAfile ~/tls/certs/ca-chain.cert.pem ~/tls/certs/rsyslog.local.flex.cert.pem
~/tls/certs/rsyslog.local.flex.cert.pem: OK
```

Now that you have a working flex certificate, place the certificate and private key in */etc/ssl*, the system location for TLS files. Rsyslog runs as the *syslog* user, so we'll make root own the TLS files and *syslog* able to read them. First, make the *rsyslog* directory inside */etc/ssl*. Next, set its permissions to **750** so that the directory can be entered by the root and *syslog* users (execute) and so that files can be listed (read):

```
$ sudo mkdir /etc/ssl/rsyslog
$ sudo chmod 750 /etc/ssl/rsyslog
```

Linux system permissions are beyond the scope of this book, but you can learn more about them on Linux expert Vivek Gite's website, *https://www.cyberciti.biz/faq/how-to-use-chmod-and-chown-command/*.

Copy the CA chain file, signed certificate, and passphrase-less private key into */etc/ssl/rsyslog*:

```
$ sudo cp ~/tls/certs/ca-chain.cert.pem /etc/ssl/rsyslog/
$ sudo cp ~/tls/certs/rsyslog.local.flex.cert.pem /etc/ssl/rsyslog/
$ sudo cp ~/tls/keys/rsyslog.local.flex.key.nopass.pem /etc/ssl/rsyslog/
```

Set the root user and the *syslog* group as the file owners, and set the file permissions to **640** so that only root can read and write to them and the *syslog* group can only read them:

```
$ sudo chown -R root:syslog /etc/ssl/rsyslog/
$ sudo chmod 640 /etc/ssl/rsyslog/{ca-chain.cert.pem,rsyslog.local.flex.
cert.pem,rsyslog.local.flex.key.nopass.pem}
```

With TLS files in place, let's discuss Rsyslog configurations.

Custom Rsyslog Configurations

To determine where to read events from and where to send them, Rsyslog can use multiple configuration files. The main configuration, */etc/rsyslog .conf*, defines basic settings. For example, it loads Unix sockets to directly receive events from other programs, sets the default file permissions for new files, and defines the directory for modular configurations.

Modular configurations let you encapsulate related inputs and outputs into their own files, and they live in the */etc/rsyslog.d/* directory. This directory may include two modular configurations by default: *20-ufw.conf* and *50-default.conf*. Depending on the version of Ubuntu or RHEL you're using and if it's in the cloud, Rsyslog may also come with *21-cloudinit.conf*.

The UFW file contains log settings for Uncomplicated Firewall, installed by default on Ubuntu, which you configured in Chapter 2. The *50-default.conf* file contains an exceptional set of rules for system-level logging, and I recommend keeping it even when using other highly customized configurations because it defines entries for consuming core system logs. The *21-cloudinit .conf* file, if it exists on your system, contains settings for logging cloud-hosted systems.

By defining your own configurations, you can customize Rsyslog to fit your environment. To do so, you must understand the syslog format.

Basic vs. Advanced Formats

Rsyslog supports multiple configuration formats. Its *basic* format, commonly used by older systems, mirrors other logging programs and is popular because it uses a simple syntax for light tasks.

The basic format includes a selector comprising one or more combinations of logging facilities and priorities joined by a period, followed by a destination, such as a file or remote host:

```
kern.*    /var/adm/kernel
```

This example uses the kern facility to log kernel messages with any (*) severity to the logfile */var/adm/kernel*. In the first two uncommented lines of *50-default.conf*, you can see a slightly more complex example:

```
# 50-default.conf
--snip--
auth,authpriv.*              /var/log/auth.log
*.*;auth,authpriv.none       -/var/log/syslog
--snip--
```

The first line sends events from the auth and authpriv facilities with any severity to */var/log/auth.log*. The second line uses semicolons to list separate selectors for a single action; it sends events of any facility and severity, excluding auth and authpriv, to */var/log/syslog*. The severity none, a severity that doesn't exist, means do nothing. As a result, this line sends everything except the auth and authpriv logs to the *syslog* file.

The hyphen (-) indicates that the file isn't synchronized, or made consistent for all users, in real time. Because this file receives data at high speed, enabling file synchronization may cause messages to be dropped.

Also called RainerScript, after Rsyslog creator Rainer Gerhards, the *advanced* format is the recommended language for configuring Rsyslog, and the remainder of this chapter uses it. It can do everything the basic format can but also contains functions that perform logical checks and can edit logs and send them to multiple technologies, like Redis and Kafka. The format uses templates to apply standardized actions, which we'll cover shortly.

A third format, called *legacy rsyslog* or *obsolete legacy*, begins its lines with a dollar sign ($). The Rsyslog documentation warns, "Do not use obsolete legacy format. It will make your life miserable." We won't cover this format here.

Adding and Testing New Configurations

You'll add any new configurations you create to */etc/rsyslog.d/*. Then, you must test the configurations using the following command:

```
$ sudo rsyslogd -N 1
```

This command tests the validity of all configurations found in */etc/rsyslog.d/* that end with *.conf*, though you can also specify a single configuration with -f *filename*.

You'll need to restart Rsyslog every time you add a new configuration for the change to take effect. The following command does so:

```
$ sudo systemctl restart rsyslog
```

Next, let's discuss features of the advanced format.

Advanced Format Syntax

To start practicing using the advanced syntax, let's add a new configuration to Rsyslog. Make a new file called */etc/rsyslog.d/custom.conf* using your editor of choice for the configurations you create throughout this section.

Add the following configuration changes here, test them, then restart the Rsyslog service as you continue. This way, you'll have a central file you can store on Git for future use. You may comment lines with a hash mark (#) to disable any settings you don't want to use.

Global Properties

Global properties define settings that apply across the entire configuration file. Property names are case-insensitive throughout Rsyslog, meaning the term `defaultNetstreamDriverCAFile` is the same as `defaultnetstreamdrivercafile` (though the former is certainly easier to read).

For example, let's define global TLS settings in *custom.conf* using global properties, like the following snippet:

```
$ sudo nano /etc/rsyslog.d/custom.conf
global(
    defaultNetstreamDriverCAFile="/etc/ssl/rsyslog/ca-chain.cert.pem"
    defaultNetstreamDriverCertFile="/etc/ssl/rsyslog/rsyslog.local.flex.cert.pem"
    defaultNetstreamDriverKeyFile="/etc/ssl/rsyslog/rsyslog.local.flex.key.nopass.pem"
)
```

The first global option is the CA chain we placed in */etc/ssl/rsyslog/* earlier in the chapter, the second is the Rsyslog flex signed certificate, and the third is the private key without a passphrase.

Lower-level functions can override global properties if needed. Generally, however, most default global properties should suffice for complex projects and won't need tweaking.

While you could define global properties in any number of configurations, you can set individual options only once. For instance, if you include these TLS options in two different files, Rsyslog won't start, even if the values are identical between files.

Input Modules

Input modules provide Rsyslog with multiple ways to read or receive data. Rsyslog supports TCP, UDP, Kafka, Redis, HTTP, and many more input formats.

TCP and UDP

You must load, or import, a module before using it. For example, the following snippet loads the `imptcp`, or plaintext TCP, input module and configures port 5514 to receive non-TLS TCP input:

```
module(load="imptcp")
input(
    type="imptcp"
    port="5514"
)
```

Notice that the input statement references the `imptcp` input module using the `type` argument. Port numbers are unique to each protocol, so you could use the same port to receive plaintext UDP using the `imudp` module:

```
module(load="imudp")
input(type="imudp" port="5514")
```

You can use either spaces or line breaks to separate the module's arguments in parentheses. Feel free to use the style you prefer.

You defined paths to TLS files for Rsyslog in the previous global section. To load TCP using the TLS on port 51443, use the `imtcp` module (which differs from `imptcp`). We use port 51443 here because it combines 514, the conventional port used for syslog, and 443, conventionally used for TLS, but you can use any port above 1024 that you want.

Within the module, define the *stream driver*, which handles the OpenSSL encryption and additional settings:

```
module(load="imtcp"
    # OpenSSL
    streamdriver.name="ossl"
    # Mandatory TLS
    streamdriver.mode="1"
    # Certificate validation and subject name authentication
    streamdriver.authmode="x509/name"
    # Allowlist
    PermittedPeer=["logstash","logstash.local"]
)
input(type="imtcp" port="51443")
```

This code loads the `ossl` stream driver, which uses OpenSSL. (Alternatively, you could load the `gtls` module to implement GnuTLS, which supports passwords applied to private keys.) We set the stream driver mode to 1 to force TLS usage and set the stream driver authentication mode to x509/name to enforce certificate validation checks and subject-name authentication.

The permitted peers setting is optional but lets you add specific servers to an allow list for additional control. You can specify either IP addresses or resolvable domain names. After loading and configuring the module, use the `input` statement to initialize the port.

Kafka Clusters

Rsyslog can also read from a Kafka cluster by defining the Kafka broker addresses, a consumer group, and a topic in the configuration. We'll discuss Kafka further in Chapter 10, but a simple Kafka input for Rsyslog looks like the following:

```
module(load="imkafka")
input(
    type="imkafka"
    topic="syslog"
    broker=[
        "kafka01.local:9092",
        "kafka02.local:9092",
        "kafka03.local:9092"
    ]
    consumergroup="rsyslog"
    parsehostname="on"
)
```

Notice that we set the connection options in the `input` statement, not in the `module` statement. This is because the input statement is the portion that reaches out to Kafka, similarly to how the `imtcp` input initiates a listening port.

This code reads from a topic named `syslog` and connects to three brokers, starting with `kafka01`. The array in square brackets contains the multiple broker names, although you may also specify a single name in quotes like other strings. Kafka uses the `consumergroup` to track which messages have been sent to which recipients, per grouping. The `parsehostname` option allows Rsyslog to read the hostname from the received message for further processing, although this option is set to `off` by default.

Local Files

The `imfile` module reads from local files. By default, local files have the facility `local0` and the severity `notice`, but you can specify new settings on a per-file basis if needed, as we do in the following:

```
module(load="imfile")
input(
    type="imfile"
    file="/var/log/myapp.log"
    tag="myapp:"
    facility="local1"
    severity="info"
    freshStartTail="on"
)
```

This input overrides the defaults, specifying the `local1` facility and `info` severity. The option `freshStartTail` tells Rsyslog to begin monitoring only from the end of the file onward, discarding old logs. This may be useful when installing Rsyslog on existing or legacy systems with hundreds or thousands of logs stretching back years. The `tag` setting defines the syslog tag field included in the output message.

Rsyslog can use Unix sockets to receive data from other processes on the host system with the `imuxsock` module and can read local kernel messages with the `imklog` module. Both modules are enabled by default when you install Rsyslog inside its main configuration file, */etc/rsyslog.conf*. You can find a complete list of the more than 20 currently supported Rsyslog input modules at *https://www.rsyslog.com/doc/configuration/modules/idx_input.html*.

Output Modules

Outputs define locations to which to send data, whether writing it to a file or using a network protocol. Most of the input modules have output companions, but Rsyslog supports slightly more output varieties than it does inputs. Two of the most common outputs, `omfile` for writing to files and `omfwd` for sending data to another tool, don't need to be loaded.

By default, Rsyslog creates files with `0644` permissions for the user running Rsyslog, typically *root*. This access mode lets anyone read logs located in directories to which they have access. The easiest way to use this module is to give it a full filepath:

```
action(type="omfile" file="/var/log/myapp.log")
```

Outputs use *actions* to declare what should happen to the data. (Some people use the terms *output* and *action* interchangeably.) This single omfile output line would begin writing messages to */var/log/myapp.log* after a service restart.

The omfwd output contains many options that look like imtcp for configuring TLS connections, but take note that the stream driver parameters don't have periods in their names, as they do in imtcp:

```
action(
    type="omfwd"
    protocol="tcp"
    target="logstash.local"
    port="51443"
    # OpenSSL
    streamDriver="ossl"
    # Mandatory TLS
    streamDriverMode="1"
    # Certificate validation and subject name authentication
    streamDriverAuthMode="x509/name"
    # Allowlist
    streamDriverPermittedPeers="logstash,logstash.local"
    # Emit RFC 5424
    template="RSYSLOG_SyslogProtocol23Format"
)
```

This action specifies a TCP connection to the destination server *logstash .local* on port 51443 with the same TLS values used in the input examples. In this module, though, we specify the permitted peers as a comma-separated string, not as an array.

This action also uses a *template*, or predefined output format we'll discuss shortly, to send RFC 5424–compliant messages instead of the default RFC 3164. Let's discuss templates next.

Templates

Templates are Rsyslog's secret ingredient. Under the hood, every output uses templates to structure data for the variety of destinations Rsyslog supports. You can specify predefined templates, such as the previous RSYSLOG_SyslogProtocol23Format, or define your own, which can be helpful for tasks like reformatting odd legacy device logs and creating dynamic output filenames based on source hostnames. Define templates in the same configuration file as the rulesets that use them.

To access log data, templates reference message properties, which contain different components of a syslog message. For example, the property pri contains the calculated priority, the syslog tag has a process name and possibly its ID, and `msg` contains the message value. Consider the following RFC 3164 sample message:

```
<132>Dec 13 18:43:06 ubuntu04 mytool[4353]: hello world
```

When parsing it, Rsyslog would extract the following properties:

The priority (`pri`) `<132>`

The timestamp (`timestamp`) `Dec 13 18:43:06`

The hostname (`hostname`) `ubuntu04`

The syslog tag (`syslogtag`) `mytool[4353]`

The message contents (`msg`) `hello world`

Note that these are a small sampling of the available properties. Let's discuss how the string and list templates use these message properties.

String

String templates define strings of text containing variable placeholders. You can add constant text anywhere in the string, then set variables as placeholders for message properties in any order.

Suppose you want to prepend the string `PRIVESC`, for privilege escalation, along with the hostname to all events containing the `sudo` command as part of your alerting pipeline or internal audit workflow. This could help you detect attacks that abuse elevated privileges, although it would also capture legitimate administrator activity.

You could add such a tag by defining a simple string template like the following:

```
template(name="stringy" type="string"
string="PRIVESC::%hostname%::<%pri%>%timestamp% %hostname% %syslogtag% %msg%\n"
)

# Output
PRIVESC::ubuntu04::<86>Dec 13 23:54:10 ubuntu04 sudo:  pam_unix(sudo:session):
session closed for user root
```

We name the template `stringy` and set its type to string. Then we prepend the text `PRIVESC::` to the event, as well as the `hostname` property, wrapped in percent signs (`%`) to tell Rsyslog to add the property value parsed from the original message. A newline (`\n`) constant terminates the string. Like the global, input, and output settings previously discussed, templates support both newlines and spaces to separate arguments.

String templates can also use the *property replacer* engine to manipulate individual properties. The property replacer can extract specific characters using the `fromChar` and `toChar` fields and perform a multitude of transformations using the `options` field. The property replacer uses the following syntax:

```
%property:fromChar:toChar:options%
```

Note that we wrap the whole property replacement string in percent signs (%) and separate fields by colons (:).

Let's use the property replacer to make the `msg` field uppercase. Leave the `fromChar` and `toChar` fields blank, resulting in three colons in the middle of the replacement string, which also selects the whole string:

```
template(name="stringy" type="string"
string="PRIVESC::%hostname%::<%pri%>%timestamp% %hostname% %syslogtag%
%msg:::uppercase%\n"
)

# Output
PRIVESC::ubuntu04::<86>Dec 13 23:59:46 ubuntu04 sudo:  PAM_UNIX(SUDO:SESSION):
SESSION CLOSED FOR USER ROOT
```

We'll explore how to link templates to the rulesets and actions that use them shortly. Next, let's discuss list templates.

List

List templates provide a similar ability to modify messages with static and dynamic values, but they use a different syntax that some find easier to read.

Expanding on the string template example, let's say you want to prepend the string `FIREWALL`, along with the relevant hostname, to all firewall logs. A list template can achieve this using a mixture of constants and properties:

```
template(name="firewall" type="list") {
❶ constant(value="FIREWALL::")
❷ property(name="hostname")
  constant(value="::")
  constant(value="<")
  property(name="pri")
  constant(value=">")
  property(name="timestamp")
  constant(value=" ")
  property(name="hostname")
  constant(value=" ")
  property(name="syslogtag")
  constant(value=" ")
  property(name="msg" ❸ compressspace="on")
  constant(value="\n")
}
```

In a list template, we use `constant` and `property` keywords, followed by parameters, to define each portion of the message. This saves us from having to insert placeholders into a string, which might be difficult to read. Constants ❶ use a static value, such as the `FIREWALL::` prefix. Properties ❷ use the name of the Rsyslog property parsed from the message, such as `pri` and `timestamp`.

In addition, the `msg` field uses an option that compresses whitespace ❸. As a result, if a message has two or more consecutive spaces, Rsyslog will squash them into one.

Dynamic Filenames

Templates can create dynamic filenames based on property values like hostnames or IP addresses. The following shows a template that sends firewall messages received from the network to a custom file for each hostname:

```
template(name="hostnamefile" type="string"
string="/var/log/firewall-%hostname%.log")
```

This strategy might allow you to store logs based on retention and audit requirements or write logs to files that don't meet any other rule conditions as a catchall. We'll discuss rules and rulesets shortly.

JSON Output

For each message, Rsyslog creates a special JSON property called `jsonmesg` that contains all the message properties it has parsed. You can use it to conveniently send key-value messages downstream:

```
template(name="jsonify" type="list") {
  property(name="jsonmesg" compressspace="on")
  constant(value="\n")
}
```

Using this four-line template, a syslog message received by Logstash would appear with the following structure:

```
--snip--
        "protocol-version" => "0",
          "syslogfacility" => "16",
                   "rawmsg" => "<130>python-syslog-devlog.py: test critical",
          "syslogseverity" => "2",
                 "fromhost" => "ubuntu04",
                "syslogtag" => "python-syslog-devlog.py:",
                "inputname" => "imuxsock",
                 "app-name" => "python-syslog-devlog.py",
                 "hostname" => "ubuntu04",
              "fromhost-ip" => "192.168.8.152",
                      "pri" => "130",
                      "msg" => " test critical",
              "programname" => "python-syslog-devlog.py"
--snip--
```

Notice that `rawmsg` contains the priority in angle brackets, immediately before the syslog tag and message. This is often a "gotcha" when building your own templates, as new Rsyslog users may expect a typical syslog message that at least contains a timestamp, hostname, tag, and message.

This template relies on Rsyslog's specialty in understanding syslog, which reduces the configuration complexity needed downstream. We'll cover linking Rsyslog to Logstash later in this chapter.

Next, let's discuss the rulesets that govern actions within an Rsyslog configuration file.

Rulesets

In addition to the syntax covered so far, a configuration can use *rulesets* to determine how to process events. Rulesets apply if-else statements with various comparison operators, such as contains_i for case-insensitive string checks and re_match for regular expressions. They typically contain actions to direct traffic to various outputs, such as remote systems or the dynamically named files discussed in the previous section. Rulesets may be bound to an input or called from elsewhere in the configuration, including inside other rulesets.

Let's revisit the dynamic filename template to forward UFW logs to one file per hostname. The following ruleset pairs with this template:

```
❶ call myrules

❷ ruleset(name="myrules") {
    ❸ if $msg contains "[UFW " then {
        action(
            ❹ type="omfile"
            ❺ FileCreateMode="0640"
            ❻ dynaFile="hostnamefile"
        )
      ❼ stop
      }
}
```

First, we use a call statement ❶ to invoke the ruleset, named myrules ❷, as it's not bound to a specific input. If Rsyslog finds the string [UFW and a space in the message (msg) ❸, the action writes the message to a file ❹. The default omfile access mode is 0644, as defined in */etc/rsyslog.conf*; change it to 0640 so only *root* and *syslog* group members can read the file ❺. Invoke the dynamic filename template using the **dynaFile** option ❻.

All actions stop processing after the message has been sent ❼. Without the stop keyword, Rsyslog would continue to check additional rules, possibly leading to errant matches. Like most other settings in Rsyslog, we could write this action on a single line, with the options separated by spaces.

Rulesets and templates can work together to replace text. For example, the syslog tag in UFW firewall logs is the word kernel, indicating the source of the local event. Let's change it to the word popcorn to demonstrate how rulesets and templates interact. To start, we define a template with the details of the new tag:

```
template(name="popcorn" type="string"
    string="<%pri%>%timestamp% %hostname% %$!tag_fixed%%msg:::sp-if-no-1st-sp%%msg%\n"
)
```

This template sets up a standard RFC-compliant message with a few added Rsyslog features, shown in bold. The text $!tag_fixed is a variable that holds the new tag value you'll create in the ruleset accompanying this template.

Immediately after the tag, the template uses a property replacer to ensure that a single space separates the syslog tag and the message content; the sp-if-no-1st-sp modifier in the msg property does nothing if a space is present, but returns a single space if one isn't already there. Finally, just before the line terminator, we add another msg property, as the first either turned into a space or fizzled out as a result of the property replacer.

To apply this template and custom variable, we use the following rule:

```
call myrules
ruleset(name="myrules") {
  ❶ if re_match($fromhost-ip, "\127\\..*") and $msg contains_i "[UFW " then {
      ❷ set !tag_fixed = replace($syslogtag, "kernel", "popcorn");
      ❸ action(type="omfwd" template="popcorn" target=...
--snip--
```

First, we compare the $fromhost-ip property to a loose regular expression to ensure that a message emanates from the local host ❶. Then, we perform a case-insensitive check for the presence of UFW to confirm that the message comes from the firewall.

You can't override properties, but you can create new variables. In this case, we create a new variable called $!tag_fixed using the set command ❷ and make it the value of the existing syslog tag, with kernel replaced by popcorn. The dollar sign ($) indicates it's a variable, and the exclamation mark (!) means it's at the top level of a potentially nested data structure (as in the case of a plain string). Finally, omfwd sends the message downstream ❸.

When the action runs, it plugs the new tag_fixed into the template, and we see the following result downstream:

```
<4>Dec 14 23:24:05 ubuntu04 popcorn: [30250.776480] [UFW ALLOW] IN= OUT=ens33...
```

Replacing characters in messages is useful when you need to redact messages or standardize a property, such as making all hostnames lowercase. As a useful aside, you can also do case-insensitive regular expression comparisons using re_match_i or drop all trailing line terminators in the message field using %msg:::drop-last-1f%. Rsyslog rulesets simplify the process of directing logs where they need to go and allow for powerful editing capabilities.

Example Configurations

We've discussed Rsyslog components and how they interact. Now let's make two working configurations: a client that takes local host logs and sends them to Logstash and a central Rsyslog relay server that receives network logs, forwards them to Logstash, and simultaneously writes them to disk in files named after the host from which the logs originated. In both cases, we'll leave the default configurations *20-ufw.conf* and *50-default.conf* enabled.

Use these examples individually, not together. You can disable configurations by renaming them—for example, by changing custom.conf *to* custom.conf .disabled—*then restarting Rsyslog.*

To begin, let's make a simple Logstash configuration to use with the client and server Rsyslog configurations we create in this section. The following input receives TLS connections over TCP on port 51443 and then displays them on the screen and sends them to Elasticsearch using the outputs and TLS files from Chapter 6. We'll discuss these inputs and outputs in Chapter 8 and the filters used to parse data in Chapter 9:

```
input {
  ❶ tcp {
        port => 51443
     ❷ type => syslog
     ❸ mode => server
        ssl_enabled => true
     ❹ ssl_client_authentication => "required"
        ssl_certificate => "<path to TLS files>/wildcard.local.flex.cert.pem"
        ssl_key => "<path to TLS files>/wildcard.local.flex.key.pem"
        ssl_key_passphrase => "abcd1234"
        ssl_certificate_authorities =>
        [ "<path to TLS files>/ca-chain.cert.pem" ]
    }
}
output {
    stdout { codec => rubydebug }
    elasticsearch {
        id => "elasticsearch-output"
        hosts => "https://elasticsearch01.local:9200"
        # id:api_key
        api_key => "kwouKoOBFSso9JQdUCJj:ANI6NTBMQx2NNDj3UIAxkw"
        data_stream => true
        ssl_enabled => true
        ssl_certificate => "<path to TLS files>/wildcard.local.flex.cert.pem"
        ssl_key => "<path to TLS files>/wildcard.local.flex.key.nopass.pem"
        ssl_certificate_authorities =>
        [ "<path to TLS files>/ca-chain.cert.pem" ]
    }
}
```

Logstash has an unencrypted syslog input module available as a plug-in download, but its lack of TLS means we need to use a TCP listener ❶. We set the type ❷ to syslog, which adds a field we can use for filtering (but doesn't change any input settings). This TCP input runs in server mode ❸, which means it expects incoming connections and requires mutual client authentication (mTLS) ❹.

A Client

Let's create an Rsyslog client that forwards local host logs to Logstash. This client might be useful if you need a host to merely send logs to your data pipeline and not perform any parsing or storage. To configure an Rsyslog client, create a new file in */etc/rsyslog.d/* named *client.conf*:

```
global(
    defaultNetstreamDriverCAFile="/etc/ssl/rsyslog/ca-chain.cert.pem"
    defaultNetstreamDriverCertFile="/etc/ssl/rsyslog/rsyslog.local.flex.cert.pem"
    defaultNetstreamDriverKeyFile="/etc/ssl/rsyslog/rsyslog.local.flex.key.nopass.pem"
)
action(
    type="omfwd"
    protocol="tcp"
    target="logstash.local"
    port="51443"
    streamDriver="ossl"
    streamDriverMode="1"
    streamDriverAuthMode="x509/name"
    streamDriverPermittedPeers="logstash,logstash.local"
)
```

We add the global TLS configurations defined earlier in this chapter and use the omfwd output once again, specifying the local Logstash instance as the target. We don't need to load this output because Rsyslog loads it automatically. Put together, the configuration simply sends all data specified in the default configurations and any additional custom configurations to Logstash. If you want to keep the global settings in their own file, such as *global.conf*, you may do so and include only the action statement in *client.conf*.

Next, let's explore an Rsyslog server that receives network connections, relays them, and writes them to disk. Rename *clienf.conf* to *client.conf.disabled*, but don't restart Rsyslog yet.

A Server Relay

You may eventually set up a central log receiver for your organization to funnel traffic to your SIEM. Let's use Rsyslog to listen to the network for logs from various network appliances and hosts and then relay those logs to Logstash. Let's also conditionally write files to disk as a means of locally backing them up in case devices downstream go offline.

Make a copy of the client configuration, including the global section, from the previous section, naming it *server.conf*. We'll rearrange the configuration so that the omfwd action outputs data to the end of the file in a ruleset:

```
# Load TCP with TLS support (OpenSSL)
module(
    load="imtcp"
    streamdriver.name="ossl"
    streamdriver.mode="1"
    streamdriver.authmode="x509/name"
```

```
)
# Run module
input(type="imtcp" port="5443" ruleset="myrules")
```

We load the `imtcp` module, provide stream-driver options for TLS-wrapped TCP, and then configure the input statement with the port number 5443.

Make two more templates in *server.conf,* one that will write UFW events to their own firewall-specific logs and another for everything else. These templates define the filenames for events written to the local disk. Also make a ruleset named `myrules` to which the `imtcp` input is bound that sends all data to Logstash:

```
# Firewall events written to a file
template(
    name="firewallfile"
    type="string"
    string="/var/log/network/firewall-%hostname%.log"
)
# Non-firewall events written to a file
template(
    name="hostnamefile"
    type="string"
    string="/var/log/network/%hostname%.log"
)
# Ruleset used by imtcp
ruleset(name="myrules") {
  ❶ if $msg contains_i "[UFW " then {
        action(type="omfile" FileCreateMode="0640" dynaFile="firewallfile")
    }
    else {
        action(type="omfile" FileCreateMode="0640" dynaFile="hostnamefile")
    }
    # Action uses parentheses
  ❷ action(
        type="omfwd"
        protocol="tcp"
        target="logstash.local"
        port="51443"
        streamDriver="ossl"
        streamDriverMode="1"
        streamDriverAuthMode="x509/name"
        streamDriverPermittedPeers="logstash,logstash.local"
    )
}
```

First, we use `if` to check whether the event came from the firewall. The statement `contains_i` performs a case-insensitive match for [UFW (with a trailing space) ❶. If an event matches, Rsyslog writes it to a firewall log that includes the hostname in the filename. If the event didn't come from the firewall, the `else` branch writes the logs to a text file named for each hostname.

Notice that the ruleset doesn't place a stop statement after each action; we want messages to work their way through the if-else logic and eventually make it to the network output ❷ at the end of the ruleset. This ensures that, regardless of which file Rsyslog writes to, the data also gets sent to Logstash. In a more complex configuration, you'd probably place the omfwd action at the top of the logic, then add stop statements throughout the ruleset to immediately terminate remaining logic checks, which would speed up the configuration.

SAVING CONFIGURATIONS WITH GIT

Copy the commands and Rsyslog configurations from this chapter to a subdirectory called *rsyslog* in your local Git repository, and redact any passphrases you don't wish to share. Then push your code to your remote repository using the following Git commands:

```
$ git status
$ git add .
$ git commit -am "added rsyslog configurations and notes"
$ git push
```

The files should now be stored in your remote repository.

Summary

Rsyslog is a lightweight, fast, and extremely flexible tool for processing logs. In this chapter, you installed Rsyslog and learned its configuration layout. You explored global settings, inputs and outputs, templates, and rulesets. You also configured Logstash to receive messages from Rsyslog over TLS. Finally, you created two practical real-world configurations and stored them centrally using Git.

We've concluded our discussion of tools capable of reading logs directly from hosts. Next, we'll transition to working with network-based tools that transform and move data.

PART III

DATA TRANSFORMATION AND STANDARDIZATION

Once you've collected logs from devices across your environment, you might want to standardize them further by adding, removing, or renaming fields so they're easier for security analysts to find. If done properly, standardization could also enable you to feed your logs into automated response tools and machine learning solutions, allowing you to automate aspects of your security operations. Many tools exist to perform this kind of processing, but in this part of the book, we'll focus on an Elastic tool called Logstash. Chapter 8 introduces the input and output plug-ins you can use to craft your data transformation pipeline, and Chapter 9 discusses Logstash's transformation filters, which enable you to write custom logic to modify your data.

8

DATA MANIPULATION PIPELINES

Rsyslog and Filebeat can manipulate data to a certain extent, but if you intend to transform your data in extensive ways or standardize logs taken from different sources, it's worth creating dedicated transformation pipelines. *Transformation pipelines* can receive data from many technologies at once, transform it, and send it to multiple outputs simultaneously. This chapter covers Elastic Logstash, a versatile tool designed for this express purpose.

You'll install Logstash and then dive deep into its rich ecosystem of inputs and outputs, which can receive data via HTTP, interface with enterprise systems like Splunk and Elasticsearch, work with local files, and leverage distributed messaging systems like Kafka and Redis. We'll also discuss integrating with cloud storage solutions such as Amazon S3 and MinIO to receive data.

Logstash Pipeline Components

Logstash pipelines consist of three major components, referred to as plug-ins: inputs, filters, and outputs.

The more than 60 *input* plug-ins allow you to receive the data to transform. They support a wide variety of network protocols and files, much like the tools covered in previous chapters. We've already discussed the Beats, Elastic Agent, TCP, and Syslog inputs, but we'll explore more of them here, such as Redis, HTTP, and Kafka.

Filter plug-ins parse and transform data. Once an input receives data, filters use conditional logic to determine how to manipulate events. Chapter 9 covers filters extensively; here, we'll merely introduce them.

Logstash supports just over 60 *output* plug-ins, most of which are counterparts to input plug-ins. Unlike Filebeat and Elastic Agent, which support just one output at a time, Logstash lets you configure as many outputs as you need in your environment. Like filters, outputs support conditional logic and field comparisons, a capability that allows Logstash to route dozens or hundreds of data types to their respective destinations with relative ease.

Logstash Installation and Setup

You can run Logstash in two ways. To view the tool's standard output while testing, I recommend manually installing it from the tarball, as you did in Chapter 2. The tarball download will let you view results immediately, saving you from having to create and sift through a custom logfile or view partially processed results in Kibana. I'll assume you're using this download in this chapter.

To run the tool 24/7, however, you should instead use the apt or rpm packages. These help you consistently set up the tool across multiple nodes, automatically create service files, and perform upgrades for you.

Because you installed Elastic's GNU Privacy Guard key and the Elastic apt repository in Chapter 6, you can install Logstash with a single command on systems that use apt:

```
$ sudo apt update && sudo apt install logstash
```

On systems that use dnf, yum, and rpm, you must first install the GPG key:

```
$ sudo rpm --import https://artifacts.elastic.co/GPG-KEY-elasticsearch
```

Then, create the Elastic repository at */etc/yum.repos.d/elastic.repo*; be sure to substitute version numbers for *X.Y*:

```
[elastic-X.Y]
name=Elastic repository for X.Y packages
baseurl=https://artifacts.elastic.co/packages/X.Y/yum
gpgcheck=1
gpgkey=https://artifacts.elastic.co/GPG-KEY-elasticsearch
enabled=1
autorefresh=1
type=rpm-md
```

Finally, with the GPG key and repository in place, use **yum** or **dnf** to install Logstash:

```
$ sudo dnf install logstash
```

If you're downloading Logstash for the first time, change into the extracted directory and create a dedicated configuration directory. You should already have a directory named *config* containing Logstash settings, so make *conf.d* to hold the configurations you'll create in this chapter:

```
$ mkdir conf.d
```

You'll use the following commands throughout the chapter to test individual configurations. They should look familiar to you, as we've run them in almost every chapter so far. You'll execute these commands from inside the Logstash directory extracted from the tarball:

```
$ bin/logstash -f conf.d/your-config.conf --config.test_and_exit
$ bin/logstash -f conf.d/your-config.conf --config.reload.automatic
```

In "Logstash to Logstash" on page 167, you'll begin running multiple configurations at once using the *pipelines.yml* file, in which case you can shorten the command by dropping the filename argument:

```
$ bin/logstash --config.test_and_exit
$ bin/logstash --config.reload.automatic
```

Use CTRL-C to stop Logstash from inside of the terminal in which you started it.

Enabling TLS

In Chapter 2, you created a flex certificate for Logstash. That certificate has the necessary clientAuth and serverAuth extensions so Logstash can connect to Kafka and Redis while also accepting incoming connections. Alternatively, you may convert to using the wildcard certificate from Chapter 6.

Using the existing flex certificate is perfectly acceptable. Converting to the wildcard certificate may make managing certificates easier in your lab setup. Ultimately, we want an encrypted connection; either method will work throughout the rest of the book.

Configuring Java Virtual Machine Options

Logstash uses a Java implementation of Ruby called JRuby, which runs in the Java Virtual Machine. The JVM interprets Java code and provides memory and thread management. Logstash stores its JVM settings in *jvm.options*, including the minimum (-Xms*<value>*) and maximum (-Xmx*<value>*) RAM utilization sizes. Set both values to 1GB, which is sufficient for running the code in this book.

You might want to increase allocated RAM if you add more CPU workers to process queued items, or if you increase the processing batch sizes to push more items through your pipeline. Elastic recommends capping these values at 8GB (the default value) and keeping both minimum and maximum values equal. If you exceed 8GB, ensure that the values don't exceed 50 to 75 percent of installed physical RAM. The following snippet from *jvm.options* shows these options; note the use of g in place of GB:

```
-Xms8g
-Xmx8g
--snip--
```

Elastic recommends against tweaking the remainder of *jvm.options* unless you're a Java expert and absolutely need to alter settings that directly affect memory management, internal Java logging, or array-nesting limits. You can find calculations for more advanced use cases in the official Elastic documentation at *https://www.elastic.co/guide/en/logstash/current/jvm-settings.html*.

Installing Codecs

Codecs are transforming functions that can convert data between formats. Most codecs work in both input and output statements to support easier filtering. We'll cover four codecs in the following sections: json_lines, line, plain, and nmap.

The json_lines codec recognizes newline-delimited JSON and parses its key-value structure so Logstash filters can use the data immediately. The line codec handles individual lines of data, whether it be from syslog, a file, or something else. The plain codec is useful for prestructured data, such as messages from Kafka or Redis. It removes line breaks, so don't use it to read a text file and then write the same data to a new file. These three codecs come preinstalled with Logstash.

The nmap codec converts XML output from the Nmap network-scanning tool into JSON for Logstash. Combined with the HTTP input we'll cover shortly, this enables you to automate the detection of and response to open ports on your network. This codec doesn't rename the JSON fields to align with the Elastic Common Schema, and it doesn't come bundled with Logstash, so let's acquire it now. Run the following command from the Logstash directory:

```
$ bin/logstash-plugin install logstash-codec-nmap
```

With the plug-in installed, let's move on to inputs and outputs.

Inputs and Outputs

In this section, we explore new inputs and outputs for working with HTTP data, transmitting data to other tools in API requests, reading from and writing to files, and performing Logstash-to-Logstash communications. We'll also read data from other common components of a data engineering pipeline, including Kafka, Redis, and Amazon Simple Storage Service (S3).

Note that Logstash is flexible when it comes to whitespace. You may use spaces, tabs, newlines, or any combination of the three to organize your code. Logstash uses curly brackets ({ and }) and square brackets ([and]) to detect blocks of related code. In the following sections, we'll use two or four spaces of indentation, adjusting for readability and printing limitations, but snippets of code on GitHub use tabs.

HTTP POST Requests

Logstash can receive HTTP POST requests containing data in the body of the request or retrieve data from HTTP-based API services. Behind the scenes, the HTTP input also loads the JSON codec so Logstash can immediately use what it receives.

Receiving Data from Nmap

To practice working with HTTP inputs, let's create a Logstash configuration that ingests data from the widely known Nmap network scanning tool. Centralizing this scan data can be useful in the case of an audit, for retroactive analysis, or to validate and verify any authorized activities during incident response.

Save the following configuration as *nmap-http.conf* in your Logstash *conf.d* directory:

```
input {
    http { ❶
        id => "nmap-http-input" ❷
        host => "0.0.0.0"
        port => 8443
        ecs_compatibility => v8
        codec => nmap { ❸
            # Don't nest hosts in a single document.
            emit_hosts => false ❹
        }
        ssl_enabled => true
        ssl_certificate => "/home/j/tls/certs/wildcard.local.flex.cert.pem"
        ssl_key => "/home/j/tls/keys/wildcard.local.flex.key.pem"
        ssl_key_passphrase => "abcd1234"
        ssl_certificate_authorities => [ "/home/j/tls/certs/ca-chain.cert.pem" ]
        ssl_client_authentication => "optional"
    }
}
```

```
filter { ❺
    if [@metadata][input][http][request][headers][x_nmap_target] {
        mutate {
            copy => {
            "[@metadata][input][http][request][headers][x_nmap_target]" => ❻
            "[labels][nmap_target]" }
        }
    } else {
        mutate {
            add_field => { "[labels][nmap_target]" => "not_provided" } ❼
        }
    }
}

output {
    stdout {
        codec => rubydebug { metadata => true } ❽
    }
    elasticsearch {
        id => "nmap-elasticsearch-output"
        hosts => "https://elasticsearch.local:9200"
        api_key => "kwouKoOBFSso9JQdUCJj:ANI6NTBMQx2NNDj3UIAxkw"
        data_stream => true
        ssl => true
        ssl_certificate_authorities => "/home/j/tls/certs/ca-chain.cert.pem"
    }
}
```

This configuration runs an HTTP input ❶ on all available interfaces on TCP port 8443. We add an optional ID to it ❷ to make identifying performance issues easier. Logstash creates IDs internally for each input, filter, and output plug-in when it starts, but these IDs change with each service start unless we specify them in the configuration. Setting ID values becomes useful when we have two or more of the same plug-ins, are using Kibana monitoring features (not covered in this book), or are using the Logstash monitoring APIs. Next, the Nmap codec ❸ specifies that each open port on a host will be its own document ❹, which is preferable for running database queries with Elasticsearch.

We'll cover filters extensively in Chapter 9, but the filter used here ❺ copies a hidden metadata field ❻ containing a custom HTTP header we'll set shortly into the field labels.nmap_target. This allows you to keep track of when a specific scan occurred and what the target was. If the custom HTTP header wasn't sent, the filter adds a fallback value ❼. Finally, we add a further option to the standard output ❽ to display the otherwise invisible metadata fields. If you just want to view the events on the standard output, you may comment out the Elasticsearch output.

Test and then run the Logstash configuration:

```
$ bin/logstash -f conf.d/nmap-http.conf --config.test_and_exit
$ bin/logstash -f conf.d/nmap-http.conf --config.reload.automatic
```

Next, let's generate some data for Logstash to ingest. Run a scan of your home or lab network using Nmap and send the output to XML. The following command uses the 192.168.1.0/24 network; substitute your own as needed:

```
$ nmap -n --reason --open -sT -T4 -F 192.168.1.0/24 -oX nmap_results.xml
```

This TCP connect scan (-sT) command doesn't resolve DNS names (-n); it merely shows open ports and the reason they're considered so, checking for the top 100 most common ports (-F). It uses a speed (-T4) one step faster than default: level 3. Nmap writes the scan results to an XML file (-oX), *nmap_results.xml*.

Use curl to POST the *nmap_results.xml* file to Logstash, substituting your own directory paths:

```
$ curl --cacert "/home/j/tls/certs/ca-chain.cert.pem" -H
"X-Nmap-Target: 192.168.8.0/24" https://logstash.local:8443
--data-binary @/home/j/nmap_results.xml
```

The -H option adds a custom header to the HTTP request containing the scan target, an idea proposed by Elastic developer Andrew Cholakian in 2016. This header makes it easier to keep records of all of your scans.

Logstash should show the parsed file upload on standard output and ship the results to Elasticsearch. The following snippet includes the header value we set using curl in the labels.nmap_target field, the state of the port, and other values from the Nmap XML file:

```
--snip--
    "type" => "nmap_port",
    "ipv4" => "192.168.1.103",
    "ipv6" => nil,
      "ip" => "192.168.1.103",
  "labels" => {
      "nmap_target" => "192.168.1.0/24"
  },
    "port" => {
  "number" => 80,
   "state" => "open"
  "reason" => "syn-ack",
"protocol" => "tcp",
--snip--
```

Inside Kibana, you can find your results using the type:nmap* query. Because you added the option metadata => true in the Ruby debug output, you'll see the metadata fields on standard out, but they won't appear in Kibana.

Outputting Data to Splunk

Logstash's HTTP output allows you to send data to APIs or connect to third parties in cases when HTTP is the only common language between them and Logstash. For example, *Splunk* is a popular database and SIEM tool that uses its own proprietary protocols for sending data. It also supports receiving data over HTTPS, so if you're migrating data from other tools to Splunk, you may need to use Logstash as an intermediary.

Because many organizations use Splunk and Elasticsearch simultaneously, it's worth gaining a passing familiarity with sending data between them, so we'll cover this topic here. If you don't wish to use Splunk, try instead configuring an output to create an HTTP-to-HTTP pipeline.

To configure Splunk to receive Logstash data over HTTP, follow my guide at *https://github.com/bonifield/logstash-to-splunk*. Once you've received your authorization token, use the following output block to send data to Splunk via the POST method:

```
output {
    http {
        id => "http-output-splunk"
        content_type => "application/json" ❶
        http_method => "post" ❷
        url => "https://your-splunk-server:8443/services/collector/raw"
        headers => ["Authorization", "Splunk c6012558-7817-45e0-a3a5-7dfc876e1bf3"] ❸
        ssl_certificate => "/home/j/tls/certs/wildcard.local.flex.flex.pem"
        ssl_key => "/home/j/tls/keys/wildcard.local.flex.key.pem"
        ssl_key_passphrase => "abcd1234"
        ssl_certificate_authorities => [ "/home/j/tls/certs/ca-chain.cert.pem" ]
    }
}
```

We set the Content-Type header ❶ to application/json, indicating that the recipient should expect JSON. We use the POST request method ❷ because this request contains data in its body. We also specify a custom header containing an authorization token ❸.

API Requests

Logstash's *HTTP Poller* reaches out to web APIs to retrieve data. This is especially useful for connecting to public or enterprise services that can't send data in other ways, such as to retrieve information from weather APIs, pulling updates from threat intelligence websites, or even interacting with cloud-native logging tools.

To demonstrate its use, we'll create simulated APIs that return data using a Python web server, then request them using http_poller. (Don't worry; this isn't a Python programming chapter, and you don't need to know Python to use the following commands.)

We'll use a *virtual environment*, a container for a project's dependencies, which keeps a project resistant to version changes elsewhere on your system. On your Linux host, install the Python package *virtualenv*:

```
$ sudo apt install python3-virtualenv
```

Virtual environments contain a *symbolic link*, or shortcut, to your system's Python binaries, allowing the project to run "in a bubble" and act as a stand-alone environment. First, create a new directory using *virtualenv* to contain the packages you'll need. Then, use the virtual environment's Python package installer, pip, to install the web server *Flask* and the OpenSSL wrapper *pyopenssl*:

```
$ virtualenv myapp
$ myapp/bin/pip install flask pyopenssl
```

Next, create *app.py* at the same parent directory as your *myapp* directory. Add the following code, which establishes two endpoints, one that returns plain strings and another for JSON:

```
❶ #!myapp/bin/python

❷ import json
  from flask import Flask

  app = Flask(__name__)

❸ @app.route('/')
  def homepage():
      message = "Hello, world! This is a plain string."
      return message

❹ @app.route('/json/')
  def jsonpage():
      message = {"message":"Hello, world!", "message_type":"This is a JSON
      structure."}
    ❺ return json.dumps(message)

❻ if __name__ == "__main__":
    ❼ app.run(debug=True, ssl_context="adhoc")
```

This short script uses the Python binary symbolic link in the virtual environment ❶. We import the JSON ❷ and Flask modules so we can access bits of code needed to start the web server. Using Flask's *decorators*, which enhance certain object functions in Python, we create HTTP URL endpoints, or paths, for / ❸ and */json/* ❹ and define the contents they return in their functions. The JSON endpoint dumps a Python key-value dictionary into a JSON string ❺. When we invoke the script from the command line ❻, the web server will start with an ad hoc TLS certificate ❼.

Make the script executable and launch it. You should be able to reach the endpoints on localhost port 5000 using HTTPS:

```
$ chmod +x app.py
$ ./app.py
Running on https://127.0.0.1:5000
Press CTRL+C to quit
--snip--
```

Test the APIs with curl, using the -k option to ignore TLS verification:

```
$ curl -k https://localhost:5000/
Hello, world! This is a plain string.
$ curl -k https://localhost:5000/json/
{"message":"Hello, world!", "message_type":"This is a JSON structure."}
```

Now you have two APIs to practice connecting to. To send data to them, create *http-poller.conf* in your Logstash *conf.d* directory:

```
input {
    http_poller {
        id => "httppoller-api-input"
    ❶ urls => {
        ❷ mytextapi => {
            method => get
        ❸ url => "https://127.0.0.1:5000/"
        ❹ headers => { Accept => "text/plain" }
        }
        ❺ myjsonapi => {
            method => get
            url => "https://127.0.0.1:5000/json/"
        ❻ headers => { Accept => "application/json" }
        }
    }
    ❼ #schedule => { cron => "* * * * * UTC"}
    ❽ schedule => { every => "5s"}
        type => "myapi"
    ❾ metadata_target => "http_poller_metadata"
        ssl_verification_mode => "none"
    }
}

output {
    stdout { codec => rubydebug }
}
```

Within the http_poller input type, the urls ❶ statement allows us to nest multiple API queries. These APIs can have any names you want, so choose descriptive ones, such as mytextapi ❷ and myjsonapi ❺. Each API configuration block contains the HTTP request method, the URL including the desired endpoint in the URL path ❸, and custom headers ❹ ❻. The mytextapi block connects to the plain-string endpoint we configured, and myjsonapi connects to the */json/* endpoint. The schedule statement supports making connections based on cron intervals ❼ and every syntax ❽, in addition to others. The every syntax in this configuration runs every five seconds, although you may use 5m for five minutes, 1h for every hour, or some other value. This input tracks requests sent and received, so we nest them in their own dedicated parent field, http_poller_metadata ❾, to avoid any parsing conflicts later.

Logstash should begin to query the custom APIs every five seconds. The plaintext base path API should produce the following:

```
--snip--
      "type" => "myapi",
   "message" => "Hello, world! This is a plain string.",
      "tags" => [
   [0] "_jsonparsefailure"
--snip--
```

Notice that your string message is in the message field, but a new _json parsefailure tag has appeared. The HTTP Poller uses the JSON codec by default, but as the codec couldn't parse the plain string, it applied the tag to let us know that something went wrong. You may choose to remove the tag by using a filter because the input successfully retrieved the data we wanted or make a separate http_poller input with the plain codec.

The JSON API should produce the key-value pairs we're expecting:

```
--snip--
        "message" => "Hello, world!",
   "message_type" => "This is a JSON structure.",
           "type" => "myapi",
--snip--
```

In this output, we see that the parsed JSON matches the dictionary we defined in the API script.

Reading and Writing Files

Logstash can read local logfiles on disk, much like Filebeat, before processing them in its pipelines and sending them elsewhere. It can also output log data to files.

Reading Local Logs

It's typically better to use Filebeat or Elastic Agent rather than Logstash for reading files from servers because they use fewer system resources. However, if you need to send files to a server already running Logstash in your data pipeline, you can easily read the logs and ingest them into your SIEM.

The file input has two main modes: tail and read. *Tail mode* monitors the latest entries in an active file; Logstash can optionally start from the beginning of the file rather than the end. *Read mode* processes closed or finalized files. It's worth noting that although the documentation says read mode will delete a file once consumed, it in fact leaves the files intact, which may be a welcome bug. Both modes use a *since database* to track the last position in the file from which Logstash has read.

To practice using read mode, add the following to a configuration file named *file-io.conf*:

```
input {
    file {
        id => "file-input-varlog"
    ❶ mode => "read"
    ❷ path => "/var/log/custom.log"
    ❸ sincedb_path => "/tmp/sincedb"
    ❹ ignore_older => "10 weeks"
        #mode => "tail"
        #start_position => "beginning"
    }
}
```

Within the file input, we specify read mode ❶ and a path to a custom logfile ❷ we want to consume. The path option also supports wildcards and can recurse through a directory structure. The sincedb_path file ❸ keeps track of the files Logstash has consumed. We also tell Logstash not to read any files older than 10 weeks ❹. The commented lines provide example syntax for using tail mode.

Writing Data to Disk

The file output writes data to disk. By default, it uses the json_lines codec and adds more JSON fields to the output event. If you want to write unstructured files, such as relayed syslog output or some other text data, change the codec to line and specify that you want only the message field. If you don't change the codec, Logstash will add the event.original field and additional session metadata, outputting a JSON message potentially more than triple the size of the original input.

Add the following to the *file-io.conf* file created previously:

```
output {
    file {
        id => "file-output-tmp"
        path => "/tmp/output.log"
    ❶ codec => line {
        ❷ format => "%{[message]}"
        }
    }
}
```

In this output block, we specify the full filepath to write to and the line codec ❶. By default, this codec prepends the time at which Logstash processes the event and the hostname of the Logstash server to the original message. Using the format option ❷, we specify that we want only the message field, which contains just the original message. The `format` option uses C-style *printf*, or print formatted, strings to specify exactly what to include in the output. You may also add static values or the content of other fields here, resembling the Rsyslog templates you used in Chapter 7.

Kafka

Logstash connects to Kafka *topics*, or data streams, as a member of a *consumer group*, which is a group of subscribers treated as a single entity for load balancing. If five Logstash servers belonging to a single consumer group subscribed to the same topics, Kafka would distribute the events between each of them, increasing overall throughput. By contrast, if all the Logstash servers were in different consumer groups connected to the same topics, they would all receive copies of the same data. We'll discuss Kafka in depth in Chapter 10.

Configuring Kafka Inputs

Logstash initiates the connection to Kafka; then Kafka pushes the requested data to Logstash. Here is the Kafka input, which subscribes to Kafka topics to receive data:

```
input {
    kafka {
        id => "kafka-input"
      ❶ bootstrap_servers => "kafka01.local:9093,kafka02.local:9093"
      ❷ group_id => "logstash"
        security_protocol => "SSL"
        ssl_endpoint_identification_algorithm => "https"
      ❸ ssl_keystore_location => "wildcard.local.flex.pkcs12"
        ssl_keystore_password => "abcd1234"
      ❹ ssl_keystore_type => "PKCS12"
      ❺ ssl_key_password => "abcd1234"
      ❻ ssl_truststore_location => "truststore.jks"
        ssl_truststore_password => "abcd1234"
        ssl_truststore_type => "jks"
      ❼ topics => ["filebeat", "metricbeat", "packetbeat", "winlogbeat"]
    }
}
```

In this input block, we specify the bootstrap servers ❶ Logstash should use to connect to Kafka for the first time using a comma-separated string of values. Once Logstash connects to Kafka, Kafka decides which of its nodes, or servers, would best serve the new connection. Kafka may then redirect Logstash to the other nodes for data transfer. We specify the consumer group using a group ID ❷ and then specify TLS settings, providing the PKCS12 keystore ❸ and its password, the keystore type ❹, and the passphrase for the private key ❺ inside of the keystore. We also need to set the truststore location ❻, which contains the CA chain file, its type, and a password if you set one. We subscribe to multiple topics at once ❼ using an array of string values.

Publishing Data to a Cluster

The Kafka output acts as a *publisher*, connecting to a Kafka cluster and then sending data to it:

```
output {
    kafka {
        id => "kafka-output"
    ❶ bootstrap_servers => "kafka01.local:9093,kafka02.local:9093"
    ❷ client_id => "logstash"
        security_protocol => "SSL"
        ssl_keystore_location => "wildcard.local.flex.pkcs12"
        ssl_keystore_password => "abcd1234"
        ssl_keystore_type => "PKCS12"
        ssl_key_password => "abcd1234"
        ssl_truststore_location => "truststore.jks"
        ssl_truststore_password => "abcd1234"
        ssl_truststore_type => "jks"
    ❸ topic_id => "%{[@metadata][beat]}"
    }
}
```

We use the same bootstrap servers ❶ to make the initial connection to Kafka. Instead of specifying a consumer group, we set a client ID ❷, used to identify a publisher during debugging. We specify the same TLS settings for the keystore and truststore. Logstash uses topic_id ❸ to specify the topic to send data to. The topic name in this example uses a printf-style variable that references a metadata field containing the name of the Beats data being processed. In this way, Logstash can route data to the appropriate topic based on the event being processed.

Redis

We briefly mentioned Redis in Chapter 4 as a supported Filebeat output. Redis is a tool that holds data in RAM, making it useful for caching and ephemeral database lookups. In this section, we'll use it as a *queued log relay*, which adds events to a queue so other programs may retrieve them. In Chapter 13, we'll use it to distribute threat intelligence indicators, such as IPs and domains, to our Logstash hosts.

Connecting to Channels and Lists

Logstash supports three Redis modes: list, channel, and multiple channels. *List mode* operates much like a Kafka topic: Data enters a queue, where it stays in RAM until it's consumed or expires. *Channels* operate much like a radio broadcast: Data is published to a channel and immediately distributed to the world, regardless of whether anyone is listening. Lastly, you can match patterns using the wildcard character (*) to subscribe to multiple channels, such as using *beat to subscribe to anything Beats related. We'll cover Redis in greater detail in Chapter 13.

As of this writing, Logstash's support for enabling TLS with Redis has a bug. To work around it, you may use encrypted tunneling tools like Stunnel or SSH to securely link Logstash servers to Redis. Redis listens on localhost TCP port 6379 by default, and we'll need an SSH tunnel to connect to the remote, localhost-only service. Run the following command on the host running Logstash:

```
$ ssh -N -L 6379:127.0.0.1:6379 -l j 192.168.8.138
```

This command doesn't send commands (-N) and forwards only local ports to the remote server (-L), allowing us to initiate connections. The first 6379 is the port on the Logstash side of the tunnel, which Logstash will use to connect to Redis. The localhost IP address 127.0.0.1 indicates that the SSH tunnel will be able to access only localhost services on the distant end of the tunnel. The second 6379 is the port on the remote side of the tunnel we want to connect to. We use -l (lowercase L, not the number 1) to specify the login name, j, and then the IP address of the Redis server.

Put together, this command drills a hole to the server running Redis so we can connect to its localhost-only port. Another option would be to configure a persistent *systemd* service to automatically connect to the service on boot and handle reconnecting after disconnections.

The following input statements connect to both a Redis channel for "broadcasts" and a list from which to pull queued items:

```
input {
    redis {
        id => "redis-channel-input"
        host => "localhost"
        port => 6379
      ❶ password => "<long-Redis-password>"
      ❷ data_type => "channel"
      ❸ key => "mychannel"
    }
    redis {
        id => "redis-list-input"
        host => "localhost"
        port => 6379
        password => "<long-Redis-password>"
      ❹ data_type => "list"
        key => "mylist"
    }
}
```

Input IDs are particularly useful in this example, as without ID values, any errors would simply list "Redis" as the issue, even though we have two Redis inputs. Naming these inputs will help us address problems in the future or analyze network performance for each input.

Both inputs connect to localhost on port 6379, which uses the SSH tunnel to transparently link them to the Redis server on the distant end. Redis uses a strong random password to authorize connections, and both inputs specify that password ❶. The channel input ❷ connects to the channel *key*, or name, mychannel ❸. The list input ❹ specifies its key, mylist, to pull queued data.

Outputting Data to Channels and Lists

Redis outputs support the same list and channel options, except that sending data to a list allows us to use batch settings. Note also that Redis holds all data in RAM, which can be memory intensive, and if you're transmitting large amounts of data, you may not necessarily need to include all fields. Depending on your use case, you could use filters to prune data to take up less space in memory or send only unparsed messages and then perform parsing later in your pipeline. We'll cover using filters to prune or keep data in Chapter 9.

The following output sends data to a Redis list named mylist2:

```
output {
    redis {
        id => "redis-list-output"
        host => "localhost"
        port => 6379
        password => "<long Redis password>"
    ❶ data_type => "list"
        key => "mylist2"
        # Batches only work with lists.
    ❷ batch => true
    ❸ batch_events => 50
    ❹ batch_timeout => 5
    }
}
```

The output plug-in options share several connection settings with the corresponding input plug-in. In this case, since we're sending data to a list ❶, we can enable sending data in batches ❷ rather than making one RPUSH Redis command per event. We send data in batches of 50 events ❸ but specify a timeout ❹ in seconds, which will occur even when there aren't 50 events ready to send.

Amazon S3 and MinIO

Amazon S3 is an object storage solution that is part of the Amazon Web Services (AWS) cloud. Logstash can connect to S3 *buckets*, which are conceptually like directories, to store files or read ones placed there by other programs.

S3 isn't free; it's priced based on the amount of data you store and the amount of data transferred to and from your buckets. *MinIO*, a free object storage software alternative to S3, uses the same APIs for compatibility but lacks some of S3's more niche features. Logstash can also use most of the same S3 input and output plug-ins to connect to MinIO. (We'll look at certain capability gaps shortly.) Configuring S3 and MinIO is well beyond the scope of this book, but you can find extensive documentation and video tutorials on the internet.

The Logstash S3 input downloads files in a bucket to temporary files. You can download all files or just those specified with a prefix, such as *2040*. It then reads those temporary files to push their data through filters before sending them to the output plug-ins. This allows you to control which logs Logstash consumes and which it ignores.

The term *prefix* has additional meaning in AWS terminology that you can read about at *https://repost.aws/knowledge-center/s3-prefix-nested-folders -difference*, but for the purposes of this section, it relates to the first characters in a filename when used in the S3 input or to a subdirectory when used in the S3 output.

Ingesting Bucket Files

The S3 input scans the files in a bucket at intervals specified in the configuration. Logstash will reread the same files at every interval unless you specify options to move and delete files after they're consumed, which you'll see in the following snippet.

WARNING *As of this writing, the ability to back up and delete files using Logstash works only on S3 and not on MinIO, so beware of this limitation lest you duplicate your data.*

In this example, we use Logstash to download the files in an Amazon S3 bucket and display the results in the terminal. Save this file as *s3-input .conf*, substituting your own endpoint and access key values:

```
input {
    s3 {
        id => "s3-input"
        type => "s3-input"
      ❶ bucket => "mylogs"
      ❷ endpoint => "<s3-or-minio-endpoint-url>"
      ❸ access_key_id => "Vfzt54o4w6lmEHMbEqVj"
        secret_access_key => "bir2etGNAjTsMFBXxIRXEaa3fOxOLYAqF7e5X3t1"
      ❹ prefix => "202"
        interval => 120
      ❺ region => "us-east-1"
        sincedb_path => "/home/j/Downloads/logstash/sincedb_s3"
        temporary_directory => "/tmp/logstash"
      ❻ backup_add_prefix => "processed-"
        backup_to_bucket => "archive"
        delete => true
      ❼ additional_settings => {
          ❽ "force_path_style" => true
          ❾ "follow_redirects" => true
            "ssl_verify_peer" => true
            "ssl_ca_bundle" => "/home/j/tls/certs/aws.cert.pem"
        }
    }
}
output { stdout { codec => rubydebug }}
```

We specify the bucket `mylogs` ❶ located at the bucket endpoint address ❷ (which is notably one of the only globally unique address schemes in the AWS cloud environment). The access key ❸ is functionally like a username, and the secret access key is its password. The prefix ❹ in this case is 202, which would return filenames starting with 2020, 2021, and so forth. This configuration runs with an interval of 120 seconds, or two minutes.

The region must match your bucket's location, although it will always remain the default of `us-east-1` ❺ if you're using MinIO. We also set a *since* database to keep track of what's been read so far and a temporary directory to store downloaded files.

After Logstash has consumed a file, it creates a copy of the file, gives it the `processed-` prefix ❻, moves it to the archive bucket, and then deletes the original. These backup functions work only on AWS, not MinIO. We specify additional settings ❼, including forcing the path style to which Logstash writes. Forcing the path style to be `true` ❽ means the bucket name will be appended to the endpoint URL as a path; otherwise, the bucket would be prepended as a subdomain.

We also make Logstash follow redirects ❾, which typically occur only during the first 24 hours after creating a bucket in AWS, using 307 Temporary Redirect response codes to find the proper address. Lastly, we force Logstash to verify the S3 certificates against an Amazon CA. If you're using MinIO and a custom CA like the one we created in Chapter 2, your custom CA would go here.

Pushing Files to Buckets

The Logstash S3 output provides an easy method of sending your data to an external system if you need to store logs in the long term for compliance or legal reasons. Like the S3 input, it creates temporary local files and then pushes finalized files into the object storage bucket, using prefixes to organize the data. Its options work in both Amazon S3 and MinIO.

The following snippet uses a file input to monitor logs and then store them in S3 or MinIO. Save this configuration as *s3-output.conf.*

```
input {
    file {
        id => "file-input-examplelogs"
        path => ["/home/j/example-logs/*.log"]
        sincedb_path => "/home/j/Downloads/logstash/sincedb"
        start_position => "beginning"
    }
}
output {
    s3 {
        id => "s3-output"
        bucket => "mylogs"
        endpoint => "<s3-or-minio-endpoint-url>"
        access_key_id => "so1h8PaQPjQGjzIUlJcP"
        secret_access_key => "QxVKAWGmWxDU6NszhZcxLITgSLYkHcFV1CEcErb6"
      ❶ prefix => "%{+YYYY-MM-dd}"
```

```
❷ validate_credentials_on_root_bucket => false
  # Send to S3 after 256 MB or .25 minutes (15 seconds)
❸ size_file => 256000000
❹ time_file => 0.25
❺ codec => line { format => "%{message}" }
  additional_settings => {
      "force_path_style" => true
      "follow_redirects" => true
      "ssl_verify_peer" => true
      "ssl_ca_bundle" => "/home/j/tls/certs/aws.cert.pem"
  }
❻ canned_acl => "private"
  }
}
```

This configuration reads from the mylogs bucket at the specified end-point, making use of an access key ID and secret access key. The prefix ❶ uses the *printf* variable format to store data according to the year, month, and day. By default, Logstash attempts to verify that it can write to the bucket and, in doing so, stores small text files indicating success. We disable this validation ❷ so we don't accumulate unwanted junk files.

The temporary files that store data from the input module finalize and then upload to S3 either after reaching 256MB ❸ or after 15 seconds (0.25 minutes) ❹. We use the line codec ❺ to preserve input data as is, using a format option to keep just the original text; the codec adds a trailing newline. We specify the same TLS settings as we did for the input. The canned ACL ❻ uses permissions predefined by AWS; in this case, private (the default option) grants the owner full control over the object, and nobody else has any access rights.

The following command can append data endlessly to test logs:

```
$ while true; do date +'%Y-%m-%d %H:%M:%S.%N' >> ~/example-logs/timestamp.log && sleep 1; done
```

Doing so is useful when sending test data with changing timestamps to S3 or MinIO using the previous configuration.

Logstash to Logstash

Logstash formerly relied on the *Lumberjack* protocol to move data between different Logstash servers. Elastic eventually built this protocol into the Beats input, enabling one server to send data using the Lumberjack output and another to receive it using the newer Beats input. Now Logstash has matching logstash input and output plug-ins to provide the same features as the Beats plug-ins, such as backpressure support and proper load balancing.

In the following example, we'll make use of pipelines to run multiple configurations that can send data to each other. Let's generate some test data, then create two configurations: one running the logstash output and another running the logstash input. If we define these configurations in the *pipelines.yml* file that Logstash uses to manage multiple inputs and outputs, the configurations can run simultaneously.

Create *logstash-input.conf*, which will receive data and then display it in the terminal:

```
input {
    logstash { ❶
        id => "logstash-input"
        port => 9800 ❷
        ssl_enabled => true
        ssl_client_authentication => "required"
        ssl_certificate => "/home/j/tls/certs/wildcard.local.flex.cert.pem"
        ssl_key => "/home/j/tls/keys/wildcard.local.flex.key.pem"
        ssl_key_passphrase => "abcd1234"
        ssl_certificate_authorities => [ "/home/j/tls/certs/ca-chain.cert.pem" ]
    }
}

output {
    stdout { codec => rubydebug }
}
```

We define the logstash input ❶ and TCP port 9800 ❷, which is the default for this plug-in. The rest of the options should look familiar by now, as they establish a mutually authenticated TLS connection.

Next, create *logstash-output.conf*, which will generate the data for the test pipeline:

```
input {
    generator { ❶
        id => "generator-input"
        count => 1 ❷
        lines => [ "Uno", "Dos", "Tres" ] ❸
    }
}

filter {
    sleep { time => 2 } ❹
}

output {
    logstash {
        id => "logstash-output"
        hosts => [ "logstash.local:9800" ]
        ssl_enabled => "true"
        ssl_verification_mode => "full"
        ssl_keystore_path => "/home/j/tls/certs/wildcard.local.flex.pkcs12" ❺
        ssl_keystore_password => "abcd1234" ❻
        ssl_certificate_authorities => [ "/home/j/tls/certs/ca-chain.cert.pem" ]
    }
}
```

First, we use the generator input ❶ to create a single test event ❷ for each of the terms in the lines array ❸. If we didn't specify the number of events to generate, Logstash would iterate over these lines repeatedly as fast as it could until we canceled it. Generator inputs can be useful for testing filter parsing when working with new data sources.

We use a sleep filter ❹, which forces the test pipeline to slow down so both pipelines have time to start. Don't use a sleep filter in production unless your use case requires slowing down your system. Because we'll create three lines and apply a two-second sleep filter, this configuration will take around six seconds ($3 \times 2 = 6$) to show results in your terminal.

Although the Logstash input supports PKCS8 certificates and encrypted keys, the Logstash output doesn't. Instead, the output supports only PKCS12 keystores, which contain both the certificate and encrypted key ❺, or an unencrypted PKCS8 key (not displayed) and its separate certificate, like the input module. We also set the keystore password ❻.

Now we must define the pipeline. Within the *configs* (not *conf.d*) subdirectory in your Logstash directory, open *pipelines.yml* in an editor and add the following lines:

```
- pipeline.id: logstash-input
  path.config: "/home/j/Downloads/logstash/conf.d/logstash-input.conf"
  pipeline.workers: 1
  pipeline.ordered: true

- pipeline.id: logstash-output
  path.config: "/home/j/Downloads/logstash/conf.d/logstash-output.conf"
  pipeline.workers: 1
  pipeline.ordered: true
```

We specify an ID for each configuration. We add the paths to the relevant configuration files and then specify one worker thread each. The pipelines are ordered because we want the Logstash input to start first so it's ready to receive the generator output (even though we slowed the output pipeline using sleep). Note that you can't use ordered pipelines when a configuration has more than one worker thread.

Let's start the pipeline. Since we specified the configuration filepaths in *pipelines.yml*, we can eliminate the -f argument, simplifying the command to just two arguments:

```
$ bin/logstash --config.reload.automatic
```

After about six seconds, the following output should appear:

```
--snip--
      "message" => "Uno",
--snip--
      "message" => "Dos",
--snip--
      "message" => "Tres",
--snip--
```

In most cases, we specify the pipeline ID defined in *pipelines.yml* within the configuration files. This is because the ID acts as a *virtual address* for Logstash to route traffic between pipelines on the same node. In this example, though, we simulated remote Logstash instances communicating by way of hostname and port number. We'll use pipeline IDs later in this chapter.

Null Output

The null output exists only to help test input and filter plug-in performance. When an event reaches the null output, it disappears forever. If you want to test performance metrics using a monitoring cluster or other means of watching Logstash, use the following output:

```
output { null {}}
```

If you must drop a subset of real events, it's better to use the drop filter, which we'll cover in Chapter 9. This filter immediately drops events to prevent the processing of data you'll eventually discard.

Virtual Addressing in Pipelines

As you learned in the previous section, pipelines encapsulate the processes that transform data inputs into data outputs. This is a fancy way of saying that they make individual configurations work together to process data. Pipelines can prepare data for either storage in a database or sending elsewhere for further processing, including to other pipelines.

Pipeline IDs assigned in *pipelines.yml* act as virtual addresses within a single Logstash node. Configuration files may use these virtual addresses in both input and output statements. For example, a single pipeline might receive all Beats data, which then uses multiple output statements to route data to a dedicated Filebeat pipeline, a Winlogbeat pipeline, and so on.

Previously, we used the Logstash input and output configurations inside *pipelines.yml* to communicate via hostname and port number. Let's make new configurations and use the pipeline input and output plug-ins to demonstrate virtual addressing. Create the following *generator-to-pipeline.conf* configuration:

```
input {
    generator {
        id => "generator-input"
        lines => [ "Uno", "Dos", "Tres" ]
    }
}
```

```
output {
  ❶ pipeline {
        id => "pipeline-output-from-generator"
      ❷ send_to => "display-stdout"
    }
}
```

This configuration uses the pipeline output ❶ to send data to a named ID ❷ we'll create in *pipelines.yml* shortly. We need a pipeline to receive the generator data. Create another configuration titled *display-stdout.conf*:

```
input {
    pipeline {
        id => "pipeline-input-from-generator"
      ❶ address => "display-stdout"
    }
}

output {
    stdout { codec => rubydebug }
}
```

This configuration uses the pipeline input, specifying the address ❶, or pipeline ID. Finally, modify *pipelines.yml* to include only the following lines:

```
- pipeline.id: generator
  path.config: "/home/j/Downloads/logstash/conf.d/generator-to-pipeline.conf"
  pipeline.workers: 1
  pipeline.batch.size: 25
  pipeline.batch.delay: 50
  queue.type: persisted

- pipeline.id: display-stdout
  path.config: "/home/j/Downloads/logstash/conf.d/display-stdout.conf"
  queue.type: persisted
```

In this file, we still define one pipeline worker thread, but we also specify a batch size of 25 with a delay of 50 milliseconds. With these options, Logstash will send batches of events to the output when either 25 events have entered its queue or the time delay has elapsed. The persisted queue means certain inputs can support the acknowledgment of data received, such as HTTP, and can have their queued data written to disk instead of held in memory while in flight.

Pipelines don't have to interact with one another. If you need multiple inputs and unrelated outputs, just add them to *pipelines.yml*. Logstash pipelines provide the ability to strategically map what data flows where, while avoiding the technical details contained in the individual configuration files.

Summary

Logstash is a versatile tool that supports receiving a variety of data sources, transforming them as needed, and sending them to many kinds of outputs. In this chapter, you configured several inputs and outputs to explore using Logstash to receive and send data. You also managed multiple pipelines at once to simulate data flowing between disconnected systems and sending data between pipelines on the same system using virtual addressing.

This chapter focused on Logstash inputs, outputs, and pipelines. In the next chapter, we'll examine Logstash filters in depth. Filters are Logstash's transformational workhorse and the primary source of its value in data engineering and standardization.

9

TRANSFORMATION FILTERS

In the previous chapter, you began configuring data transformation pipelines by defining Logstash inputs and outputs. This chapter covers Logstash filters, which allow you to parse, manipulate, enrich, add, and delete data passing through a system.

You'll use two essential approaches to parsing logs: the versatile grok filter for complex pattern matching and the lightweight dissect filter for simpler, performance-critical operations. Then, you'll learn how to handle event timestamps, a critical aspect of security analysis, to ensure that your logs maintain accurate information. You'll also learn how to remove irrelevant data from logs, split fields, apply control flow logic to compare values, and create inline Ruby scripts.

For simplicity, all examples in this chapter will use generator inputs to avoid relying on dynamic data provided by other sources, such as Filebeat or Rsyslog. We'll also use the standard output plug-in to show the filter results in the terminal window as we start, stop, and reload Logstash.

NOTE   *You configured Logstash in Chapter 8. Ensure that your Logstash directory contains a* conf.d *directory in which to save the configurations you create in this chapter.*

Logstash Filters for Data Transformation

Logstash filter plug-ins transform input data before sending it to output plug-ins. These transformations can extract, manipulate, add, remove, and enrich data in streaming events. For example, consider the following sample useragent filter, which parses a web browser's user agent string into new fields:

```
input {...}

filter {
  useragent {
    source => "my_browser_useragent_field"
  }
}

output {...}
```

Many Logstash filters use the syntax *key => value*. The key is commonly a field or setting, and the value is generally some data you wish to add to or update in an event. In this instance, Logstash would parse the field my_browser_useragent_field into additional JSON fields:

```
--snip--
"user_agent" => {
    "version" => "129.0.0.0",
    "name" => "Chrome",
--snip--
```

Logstash has close to 50 filters for transforming events. Many, including mutate, contain options for renaming or copying field values. Other filters, such as urldecode or extractnumbers, parse or extract more specific types of information. The cidr and translate filters let you enrich data, and the ruby filter, expectedly, lets you execute Ruby code.

A configuration can include more than one filter. When Logstash runs, it compiles all inputs, filters, and outputs into a single input-filter-output feed. It's a good idea to use multiple filters, as they enable you to encapsulate logic for specific use cases, making it easier for other users of your pipelines to understand what you're doing. We'll explore several types of filters in the following sections and discuss behaviors common to all filters.

Remember that Logstash is flexible about whitespace, and you can use newlines, spaces, or tabs in your configurations. Using a single line to specify a new filter can be helpful for emphasizing its logic, keeping it from turning into a tangle of newlines and curly brackets.

Extracting Data from Messy Inputs

Filters can be useful for working with *unstructured* data, or data that isn't organized into rows and columns or into key-value pairs like JSON or YAML. Let's make a configuration to simulate a common occurrence: receiving syslog events in multiple formats. For example, consider the following input:

```
input {
  generator {
    count => 1
    lines => [
      "<191>Jan 19 17:22:43 ServerThree MyApp[45788]: DNS 192.168.8.138 36728 -> 8.8.8.8 53", ❶
      "Jan 19 17:22:43 ServerThree MyApp[45788]: DNS 192.168.8.138 36728 -> 8.8.8.8 53", ❷
      "Jan 19 17:22:43 ServerThree MyApp: DNS 192.168.8.138 36728 -> 8.8.8.8 53" ❸
    ]
  }
}
```

This generator input simulates three syslog messages with slightly different structures. The first is an RFC 3164–compliant syslog message containing a priority, timestamp, hostname, program name, process ID, and message ❶. The second line is similar, except it omits the syslog priority ❷. The third line omits both the priority and the process ID ❸.

All three lines contain a space after the colon that follows the program name. You may recall from Chapter 7 that a space in this location can cause parsing issues, but it shouldn't affect the following Logstash filters.

Let's transform these text events into JSON fields that databases or analysts can use. Once you've standardized the data, you can use analysis techniques to correlate and aggregate fields. By contrast, if you kept the original log strings, you'd need to run separate command line tools or wildcard database queries for each log format, which would be computationally expensive and slow.

To structure the data, we'll use *grok*, a popular regular expression–based language built into Logstash. We'll also use the dissect filter to parse fields using a position-based syntax.

Let's start parsing the simulated syslog messages. Before you begin, create the file *grok-dissect-date.conf* in your Logstash *conf.d* directory and add the previously shown generator input to it. Below the input, add this filter:

```
filter {
❶ mutate {
  ❷ remove_field => [ "[event][sequence]", "[message]", "[host]", "@version" ]
  }
}
```

We include a mutate filter, instead of a prune filter, to demonstrate alternative ways to trim down the output fields the generator creates ❶. In this case, we're removing everything except the field event.original, which contains the lines from the generator ❷.

Extracting Unstructured Data with grok

The grok filter uses regular expression patterns to extract unstructured or semistructured data into usable fields. It follows the pattern %{*syntax: semantic*}, where *syntax* is the name of a predefined format, such as NUMBER or WORD, and *semantic* is a reference used by Logstash to create fields.

For example, the grok statement %{DATA:[host][name]} would extract a sequence of nonspace characters (DATA) and save those characters as the field host.name. The square brackets represent nested JSON fields, meaning name is hierarchically underneath host. The dotted name format, host.name, is an industry-standard syntax for describing nested data used by Beats and Elastic Agent in configurations. We'll cover JSON field references throughout this chapter.

Add the following filter to *grok-dissect-date.conf*; note that the long string after [event][original] in the match setting should be a single line:

```
filter {
  grok {
❶ id => "grok_syslog"
    match => {
❷ "[event][original]" => [
"(<%{POSINT:[log][syslog][priority]}>)?%{SYSLOGTIMESTAMP:syslog_timestamp}
%{DATA:[host][name]} %{DATA:[process][name]}(\[%{POSINT:[process][pid]}\])?
:%{GREEDYDATA:message}"
      ]
    }
  }
}
--snip--
```

Always use an ID to label grok filters ❶. Regular expressions can cause performance hits if poorly written, and you can identify these issues by looking for the filter ID in the message string of error messages.

This filter matches the event.original field ❷ against a regular expression string. We place this string in an array. Although we check only one pattern here, you may add as many as you need, separated by commas. Please note that this string is a single line, broken here for space reasons, with a space between the syslog_timestamp expression and host.name.

Let's walk through the regular expression piece by piece. First comes the snippet that checks for the syslog priority:

```
(<%{POSINT:[log][syslog][priority]}>)?
```

The positive integer (POSINT) syntax declares the type of semantic at that location in the string and assigns it the name log.syslog.priority. If there were something other than a positive integer in this position, such as a hostname or IP address, the grok match would fail.

In regular expressions, a question mark (?) instructs the code to look for zero or one occurrences of the preceding *token*, or group of characters treated as a single item. It also attempts to match the shortest number of characters possible. We wrap the expression in parentheses to make it a single token, allowing the question mark quantifier to take effect.

Put together, this grok checks for the presence of a positive whole number between angle brackets at the beginning of an event, which would correspond to the format of the syslog priority.

The grok then looks for the syslog timestamp immediately following the previous capture group:

```
%{SYSLOGTIMESTAMP:syslog_timestamp}
```

This regular expression uses the prebuilt SYSLOGTIMESTAMP pattern to detect various timestamp formats and saves the field in syslog_timestamp. There's a space following this expression because there is typically a hostname or process name following the timestamp, separated by a space, in syslog messages.

The next chunk looks for the hostname:

```
%{DATA:[host][name]}
```

The DATA syntax is a useful catchall when you know you're looking for a contiguous set of characters that terminates at whitespace. Following a space, %{DATA:[process][name]} checks for the process that created the event.

Next is the pattern for the process ID, if it exists:

```
(\[%{POSINT:[process][pid]}\])?
```

The process ID should always be a positive whole number, so we use the POSINT syntax and create the semantic process.pid. However, syslog events may wrap the process ID in square brackets ([and]), which are reserved special characters in regular expressions. We use backslashes (\) to *escape* the square brackets, telling the regular expressions to treat them as literal characters.

Here is the final part of this pattern:

```
%{GREEDYDATA:message}
```

The syntax GREEDYDATA essentially means "from here until the next pattern or until the end of the event." In this instance, we capture everything from after the colon until the end of the syslog message in a single field, message. With these fields extracted, we can continue processing the event.

The extracted message field captured every character after the colon of the previous expression. This means it begins with a space if the event is RFC compliant. We don't want whitespace at the beginning of the message, so let's remove it with a mutate filter:

```
filter {
  mutate {
    strip => [ "[message]" ]
  }
}
```

We've placed the mutate keyword in its own filter for readability, but you could encapsulate the logic in a single filter by placing it immediately following the grok statement's closing bracket.

The strip function within the mutate filter removes leading and trailing whitespace, cleaning up the field for the next step in parsing: dissecting the message field.

Extracting Reliably Ordered Data with dissect

The dissect filter is grok's counterpart for unstructured but reliably ordered data. While faster, it lacks the robust abilities of a full regular expression engine.

Notice that our input's generator lines all have the same output syntax in the syslog message field:

```
DNS 192.168.8.138 36728 -> 8.8.8.8 53
```

Because these messages all have the same positional syntax, we can use dissect to easily parse them by position into usable fields. The following dissect filter tokenizes the syslog message into ECS-aligned fields. Place it immediately following the previous mutate filter:

```
filter {
  dissect {
    id => "dissect_networkinfo"
❶ mapping => {
❷ "[message]" => "%{[network][protocol]} %{[source][ip]} %{[source][port]}
    -> %{[destination][ip]} %{[destination][port]}"
    }
  }
}
```

Note that the message field should appear on one line, with a space after the -> characters; we've added a line break here due to space constraints. The filter's mapping keyword ❶ extracts key-value pairs from the message field ❷. The dissections use the same %{field} format as grok, but noticeably lack grok's required syntax patterns and regex expressions. This static mapping extracts network, IP, and port information from our event.

Handling Inaccurate Syslog Timestamps

Next, we need to tell Logstash how to handle the syslog timestamp extracted by grok. If Logstash doesn't receive a @timestamp field in an incoming event, it adds the current timestamp. While the receipt time may be close enough to the event's timestamp for actively streaming data in the same time zone, it poses a problem when reading old files, receiving delayed or queued events, and receiving data from other time zones.

Our generator produced the syslog timestamp Jan 19 17:22:43. Under the dissect block and within the filter block, add the following date filter:

```
filter {
❶ if [syslog_timestamp] {
    date {
    ❷ timezone => "Europe/Madrid"
    ❸ match => [
        "[syslog_timestamp]", "yyyy-MM-dd HH:mm:ss.SSS Z",
        "MMM dd yyyy HH:mm:ss", "MMM  d yyyy HH:mm:ss",
        "MMM dd HH:mm:ss", "MMM  d HH:mm:ss", "ISO8601"
        ]
    }
  } # Ends the "if" statement
} # Ends the filter block
```

Let's say we know this server is in Madrid, Spain, and this application sends events using local time, not Greenwich Mean Time, also known as Coordinated Universal Time (UTC). First, we check if the syslog_timestamp field exists ❶, and if it does, we continue. Logstash can use if statements to control the execution of filters. These statements let you check for a condition and then run some filter only if the condition is met. Note that the timestamp formats listed after [syslog][timestamp] can be listed on one continuous line or separated with newlines and indentation, as shown here.

If the condition isn't met, optional else if statements can check for other conditions, and an optional else statement can provide a default option to run if all others fail. We'll show more control flow examples, including else if and else statements, in the following sections.

We specify the time zone ❷ using a string from the Java time library; Elastic uses this specific format. We then provide a list of formats against which to match the field ❸. We close the dissect filter, the if statement, and finally the filter block.

Add the trusty standard output plug-in to view the output in your terminal:

```
--snip--
output {
  stdout { codec => rubydebug }
}
```

Before running any Logstash commands, check your indentation. We broke the configuration sections up to discuss them, so let's make sure your file is structured properly. The filters should be indented for readability, as in the following skeleton:

```
input {
  generator {}
}
filter {
  mutate {}
}
filter {
  grok {}
}
```

```
filter {
  mutate {}
}
filter {
  dissect {}
}
filter {
  date {}
}
output {
  stdout {}
}
```

If your formatting looks good, run the following commands to test the configuration and then launch Logstash:

```
$ bin/logstash -f conf.d/grok-dissect-date.conf --config.test_and_exit
$ bin/logstash -f conf.d/grok-dissect-date.conf --config.reload.automatic
```

Your final output should look like the following:

```
{
                "host" => {
        "name" => "ServerThree"
    },
             "network" => {
         "protocol" => "DNS",
        "transport" => "UDP"
    },
               "event" => {
        "original" => "<191>Jan 19 17:22:43 ServerThree MyApp[45788]: UDP DNS
192.168.8.138 36728 -> 8.8.8.8 53"
    },
              "source" => {
          "ip" => "192.168.8.138",
        "port" => "36728"
    },
         "destination" => {
          "ip" => "8.8.8.8",
        "port" => "53"
    },
                 "log" => {
        "syslog" => {
            "priority" => "191"
        }
    },
    "syslog_timestamp" => "Jan 19 17:22:43",
             "message" => "UDP DNS 192.168.8.138 36728 -> 8.8.8.8 53",
          "@timestamp" => 2040-01-19T16:22:43.000Z,
             "process" => {
         "pid" => "45788",
        "name" => "MyApp"
    }
}
--snip--
```

The grok and dissect filters successfully parsed the three different syslog messages into usable JSON fields.

While modules from Filebeat and Elastic Agent do a great job of parsing common data formats, the grok, dissect, and date filters give you control over how data is extracted from messy inputs.

Enriching Data

Enriching data is the process of adding context to otherwise uninteresting individual pieces of data. As examples, let's enrich data using the CIDR and translate filters. The CIDR filter checks IP addresses against an array or file of network addresses; if it finds a match, it applies custom tags or fields, such as a label for a specific office building or network appliance. The translate filter similarly looks up fields from an event in an array or file and adds new tags or fields.

Create a file called *cidr-translate.conf* in your Logstash *conf.d* directory. Add the following input and prep filters:

```
input {
  generator {
    count => 1
    add_field => {
      "[source][ip]" => "192.168.8.133"
      "[destination][ip]" => "192.168.8.138"
    }
  }
}

filter {
  mutate {
    remove_field => [ "[event]", "[message]", "[host]", "@version" ]
  }
}
```

This simple generator adds the source.ip and destination.ip fields, and the mutate filter removes fields we don't need for this example.

Network Identification with the CIDR Filter

The CIDR filter can be useful for identifying network logs using more than just an IP address. For example, it can allow you to organize logs by geographic region or campus location. Enriching data in flight also allows us to send copies of "interesting" logs to network operations for troubleshooting or to auditing teams to verify connections to external networks.

In this example, we'll use the filter to tag *homenet* information, meaning we'll distinguish our internal network's traffic from the rest of the world's. These tags will help us determine whether network logs show inbound, outbound, or internal traffic. Tagging traffic direction enables analysts to quickly assess incoming scans, outbound file transfers, and other potential threats to the network.

Add the following to your configuration:

```
filter {
❶ cidr {
    id => "cidr_tag_sourcehomenet"
❷  address => [ "%{[source][ip]}" ]
❸  network => [ "10.0.0.0/8", "172.16.0.0/12", "192.168.0.0/16" ]
❹  add_field => {
      "[source][geo][name]" => "Office Building 1234"
      "[source][geo][city_name]" => "St. Louis"
      "[source][geo][region_name]" => "Missouri"
      "[source][geo][country_name]" => "United States"
    }
❺  add_tag => "source_homenet"
  }
  cidr {
    id => "cidr_tag_destinationhomenet"
    address => [ "%{[destination][ip]}" ]
❻  network_path => "/home/j/lookups/networks-stlouis.list"
❼  refresh_interval => 30
    add_field => {
      "[destination][geo][name]" => "Office Building 1234"
      "[destination][geo][city_name]" => "St. Louis"
      "[destination][geo][region_name]" => "Missouri"
      "[destination][geo][country_name]" => "United States"
    }
    add_tag => "destination_homenet"
  }
}
```

The first CIDR filter ❶ compares the source.ip field ❷ in the current
event with an array of IP addresses ❸. If it finds a match, it adds geographi-
cal fields ❹ describing the name and location of the IP address. The filter
also adds the tag source_homenet ❺, indicating that this traffic is emanating
from your network.

The second CIDR filter checks the destination.ip field and adds more
directional data to the event and the destination_homenet tag, meaning the
network traffic is destined for your network. Instead of using an array of values, which is hard to update in a running configuration, it uses network_path
to specify a file of addresses to check ❻. By default, the file should contain
one IP address per line. The refresh interval ❼ specifies how often the filter should check the file for updates—in this case, every 30 seconds. (The
default is 10 minutes.)

Key-Value Lookups with translate

The translate filter works like the CIDR filter, except it checks for key-value
pairs instead of a list of network ranges. It uses either an inline dictionary
or a dictionary file containing YAML key-value pairs, comma-separated values, or JSON.

Let's use several translate filters to enrich data in multiple ways. Many servers require static IP addresses to remain accessible to services, so we can use the IP address fields in the event to add hostnames to the data. Once we have these hostnames, we can add other information about the hosts, such as the names of the system owners, the operating systems they're running, or their business criticality:

```
filter {
❶ if "source_homenet" in [tags] {
    # Using a YML file with key-value pairs
    translate {
      id => "translate_sourceip_to_hostname"
❷    source => "[source][ip]"
❸    target => "[host][name]"
❹    fallback => "no_match_sourceip"
❺    dictionary_path => "/home/j/lookups/ip-to-hostname.yml"
      refresh_interval => 5
❻    refresh_behaviour => "merge"
❼    #override => true
    }
    # Using an inline hash/dictionary
    translate {
      id => "translate_hostname_to_userfullname"
      source => "[host][name]"
      target => "[user][full_name]"
      fallback => "no_match_hostname"
❽    dictionary => {
        "logstash.local" => "Alice Allison"
        "elasticsearch.local" => "Bob Robertson"
      }
    }
    mutate {
❾    copy => { "[user][full_name]" => "[source][user][full_name]" }
    }
  }
}
```

If the value source_homenet appears in the tags field ❶, a translate filter uses the source field ❷ to specify the key to check for in the dictionary and then populates the target field ❸ with the matching value. If the filter can't find the key in the dictionary, the fallback option ❹ populates no_match, which may be useful for troubleshooting gaps in your asset inventory. The dictionary_path option ❺ points to the file containing the lookup data and uses a refresh_interval, as we did with the CIDR filter.

The refresh_behaviour ❻ (note the "u") is set to merge (the default setting), which means Logstash will add new or updated values found during the file refresh to its in-memory dictionary alongside existing values.

The commented-out override option ❼ means that if the target field already exists, Logstash will write over the target field's value with the dictionary match. By default, the translate filter won't replace information present in the target field if it already exists, and unless you specify a target field to hold any dictionary matches, the filter will replace the source field's value with the value from the dictionary match. Thus, specifying override here ensures that matches always write to the target field and that the filter never alters the source field you're comparing. Fallback strings will write over any existing values if you set override to true, so be careful with its use. We'll leave it commented out for this example. Alternatively, you can remove it.

In the second translate filter, we use an inline dictionary ❽ instead of pointing to a file and don't specify a refresh interval. In the mutate filter ❾, we copy the user.name value into part of the source field to enable further directional analysis and user attribution. Be careful adding host-level data like usernames to network data; a different user than you expect may be at the keyboard, or the user may have taken their laptop to a different campus on another network segment, so let proper analysis be your guide to ground truth.

In the previous filter, we used a dictionary file containing one YAML key-value pair per line to define how to translate the data. The following is the contents of this *ip-to-hostname.yml* file. Note that the space after the colon is mandatory in YAML formatting:

```
"192.168.8.133": "logstash.local"
"192.168.8.138": "elasticsearch.local"
```

Let's add a second set of translations to traffic bound for our network, indicated by the presence of the destination_homenet tag:

```
filter {
  if "destination_homenet" in [tags] {
    translate {
      id => "translate_destinationip_to_destinationdomain"
❶    source => "[destination][ip]"
❷    target => "[destination][domain]"
      fallback => "no_match_destinationip"
      dictionary_path => "/home/j/lookups/ip-to-hostname.yml"
      refresh_interval => 5
      refresh_behaviour => "merge"
    }
    translate {
      id => "translate_destinationdomain_to_destinationuserfullname"
      source => "[destination][domain]"
❸    target => "[destination][user][full_name]"
      fallback => "no_match_destinationdomain"
      dictionary_path => "/home/j/lookups/system-owners.yml"
      refresh_interval => 5
      refresh_behaviour => "merge"
    }
  }
}
```

In these filters, we check the `destination.ip` field ❶ and populate the `destination.domain` field with the corresponding hostname ❷. We then take the domain field ❸ and use it to map the destination system owner's name if a match is found in the dictionary.

The following shows the contents of *system-owners.yml*. Again, take note of the single space after each colon:

```
"logstash.local": "Alice Allison"
"elasticsearch.local": "Bob Robertson"
```

Data enrichment suits many business and security use cases, but it comes with a cost: storage. Every field and tag added to an event also adds bytes. For small-scale operations, these extra fields may have little impact, but if your organization processes millions or billions of events per day, those fields may account for multiple hard drives' worth of storage.

Carefully consider where to add enrichment fields. Do they provide value to your analytics? Once enriched, can you drop other fields to compensate for increased event size? Will your analysts even use the added fields? It's important to strike a balance between "nice to haves" and storage limitations.

Let's discuss logical control flow statements in filters in more detail, in this case to determine if a network event is entering into, leaving from, or on the inside of our network.

Adding Directional Tags

In the previous section, we tagged network events to indicate whether they were inbound or outbound by using `if-else` statements to control code processing. Let's take the configuration one step further by adding a new field to hold this direction information. It's often worth creating such a field because otherwise, your Kibana query to find outbound traffic might look like this:

```
tags:source_homenet AND NOT tags:destination_homenet
```

While effective, this query is clunky for analysts, who must know the names of the specific tags in order to search for events. By creating a new field derived from the tags, you could enable analysts to write outbound traffic queries like the following:

```
network.direction:outbound
```

This `network.direction` field creates a more intuitive search experience for your analysts and makes scripted API queries simpler to design. The following filter checks each event's tags to create the new field:

```
filter {
  if [source][ip] and [destination][ip] { ❶
    if "source_homenet" in [tags] and "destination_homenet" in [tags] { ❷
      mutate { add_field => { "[network][direction]" => "internal" } }
    }
    else if "source_homenet" in [tags] and "destination_homenet" not in [tags] { ❸
      mutate { add_field => { "[network][direction]" => "outbound" } }
    }
    else if "source_homenet" not in [tags] and "destination_homenet" in [tags] {
      mutate { add_field => { "[network][direction]" => "inbound" } }
    }
    else { ❹
      mutate { add_field => { "[network][direction]" => "unknown" } }
    }
  }
}
```

First, we check for the presence of both source and destination IP address fields ❶. If neither is present, we'll save some CPU cycles by skipping all subsequent checks. Otherwise, we use another nested `if` statement ❷ to check the traffic direction.

If an event has both the source and destination tags, a `mutate` filter sets `network.direction` to `internal`. If it has just one of these tags, we use `else if` to apply the `outbound` or `inbound` values to the new field ❸. If the event has neither tag, `else` sets the traffic to `unknown` ❹, which should trigger alerts that something may be wrong with network devices or a CIDR file is incomplete. We close the curly brackets belonging to the top-level `if` statement and the `filter` block.

With the `network.direction` field added to the event, let's see the result. Add the standard output plug-in below all of the filters and save the file:

```
output {
  stdout { codec => rubydebug }
}
```

Once again, check that your filters are properly nested in curly brackets, that quoted strings are closed, and that options are separated from their values using =>. I've been stung by these mistakes many times over the years! Then run Logstash:

```
$ bin/logstash -f conf.d/cidr-translate.conf --config.test_and_exit
$ bin/logstash -f conf.d/cidr-translate.conf --config.reload.automatic
```

Your final output should look like the following:

```
{
      "@timestamp" => 2040-01-12T04:22:17.184746833Z,
            "host" => {
```

```
                "name" => "logstash.local"
        },
        "destination" => {
                "geo" => {
                        "city_name" => "St. Louis",
                             "name" => "Office Building 1234",
                     "country_name" => "United States",
                      "region_name" => "Missouri"
                },
                "domain" => "elasticsearch.local",
                    "ip" => "192.168.8.138",
                  "user" => {
                     "full_name" => "Bob Robertson"
                }
        },
            "source" => {
                "geo" => {
                        "city_name" => "St. Louis",
                             "name" => "Office Building 1234",
                     "country_name" => "United States",
                      "region_name" => "Missouri"
                },
                  "ip" => "192.168.8.133",
                "user" => {
                   "full_name" => "Alice Allison"
                }
        },
            "user" => {
                "full_name" => "Alice Allison"
        },
            "network" => {
          "direction" => "internal"
        },
                "tags" => [
          [0] "source_homenet",
          [1] "destination_homenet"
        ]
}
```

Interesting possibilities for data enrichment arise when using the CIDR and translate filters to combine business inventories with cybersecurity data. For example, scripts could query Active Directory for host information and post it to an internal Git instance, which Ansible can then distribute for Logstash to pull from. Similarly, well-structured data that Logstash has enriched can be pulled from the SIEM to automate blocks or generate alerts based on traffic patterns.

Field Comparison

Logstash supports many methods of comparing fields to values, values to fields, and fields to other fields, as well as determining regular expression matches and array membership. Field comparisons are the backbone of

Logstash control flow, as they enable us to perform specific kinds of parsing under certain conditions. This section explores these comparisons. You could insert each of the comparisons we'll cover into an if statement, replacing the snippet in bold:

```
if [some][field] == "some_value" {
--snip--
```

Let's start by checking a field's equality and inequality to another value.

Equality and Inequality

The most basic way to compare fields is with an equality (==) or inequality (!=) check. You can also join multiple comparisons with and or use and not to exclude the results of a comparison. Parentheses can encapsulate your logic for readability and ensure the logic works as intended.

You should wrap strings in quotation marks, but not integers or floats. Reference fields using their square bracket notation, without quotation marks, and place each nested field in its own subsequent bracket:

```
[event][code] == 11
[event][code] == 11.0
[event][code] != "eleven"
[http][request][method] == "POST" and [http][response][status_code] == 200
[user][name] == "bob" and not ([event][code] == 11 and [host][name] == "bobpc")
```

These examples use == to check if [event][code] is 11, 11.0, or eleven. Next, we join two conditions that check HTTP fields using and, meaning both conditions must match to be true. Lastly, we check if [user][name] equals bob and that the conditions in parentheses don't match using and not.

If you're referencing a field with a literal dot in the name, you can use the format [example.dotfield], but it's best practice to rename the field to a nested JSON object to align with Elastic Common Schema.

Field Existence

You can check for a field's existence by referring to it after an if statement or use an exclamation mark to check for nonexistence. For example, if you want to check that winlog.event_data.SourceIp exists but source.ip doesn't before you attempt to rename the former to the latter, use the following snippet:

```
if [winlog][event_data][SourceIp] and ![source][ip] {
--snip--
```

Checking for existence is a great way to ensure you're not about to overwrite a value you may want to keep or copy elsewhere.

Membership

The in operator allows you to check an item's membership, or presence, in an array of terms, a string, or another field. This operator is easier to use than equality checks for multiple values because its syntax is more concise and readable.

Array of Terms

Check if a field's value is present in an array using the in or not in operators:

```
[host][name] in [ "MyHostname", "MyOtherHostname", "YetAnotherHostname" ]
[host][name] not in [ "NotMyServer", "AlsoNotMyServer" ]
```

Arrays must have two or more members, even if they're the same. For instance, you can't compare a field to an array with a single item:

```
# Doesn't work
[host][name] in [ "MyHostname" ]
```

If you absolutely insist on using an array to check a single value, you could add your single term to the array twice, though it's better to just use a string or regular expression match in this case.

You also can't compare an array field to an array. Assuming the host.ip field has the value ["192.168.99.99", "fe80::1234:5678:1a:2bcd"], the following snippet won't work even though the field and the array contain the exact same values:

```
# Doesn't work
[host][ip] in [ "192.168.99.99", "fe80::1234:5678:1a:2bcd" ]
```

We'll use a Ruby filter to compare array fields in "Writing Filters with Ruby Scripting" on page 195.

Strings in Fields, Fields in Strings, and Fields in Fields

You can check for either a whole or partial string in a field or an exact term or number in an array field using in:

```
# Checking whether a string is part of field
"JamesB" in [user][name]
# Checking whether a string is in an array field
"logstash-is-great" in [tags]
```

Conversely, you can check if a field's value is part of a string, in another field, or in an array field:

```
# Checking whether a field is part of string
[user][name] in "JamesBonifield"
# Checking whether a field is part of another field
[user][name] in [source][user][name]
# Simulating some array field
[user][name] in [ "JamesBonifield", "SomeOtherUser" ]
```

These comparisons are features unique to strings; numbers, including integers and floats, can't be checked in this way. In the case of numbers, you may use the equality (==), inequality (!=), less than (<), greater than (>), less than or equal to (<=), and greater than or equal to (>=) operators.

Regular Expressions

Logstash supports regular expression-based field comparisons, but use them cautiously, as complex or poorly written regular expressions may add significant processing overhead to your logic. You must also escape special regular-expression characters like slashes, dots, parentheses, opening brackets, and other symbols, as they have functional meanings if not escaped.

Note that these comparisons are distinct from the regular expressions you previously used with grok; whereas grok parses one field into many others, the regular expressions described in this section perform comparisons that trigger (or don't trigger) your control flow logic.

The regular expression comparison uses the equals-tilde (=~) comparison operator and places regular expression terms inside a set of forward slashes (/). You may include multiple terms inside the forward slashes, delimited with a pipe character (|).

An example of regular expression matching, checking if a field matches anything containing either auth.log or ufw.log, looks like the following:

```
[log][file][path] =~ /auth\.log|ufw\.log/
```

Earlier in the chapter, you parsed a username and domain from a Windows field. The following regular expression checks the field for one or more characters (the first .), a backslash (the escaped \), and one or more characters (the second .) after the backslash:

```
[winlog][event_data][UserName] =~ /.\\./
```

When you're performing regular expression matches, the case-insensitive mode modifier (?i) often comes in handy. Everything to the right of the modifier gets matched as case-insensitive, and everything to the left remains case-sensitive:

```
# Only "WORLD" will be case-insensitive.
[message] =~ /HeLlO|(?i)WORLD/
# Both words will be case-insensitive.
[message] =~ /(?i)HeLlO|WORLD/
```

Now that we've thoroughly covered how to compare fields, let's discuss parsing key-value data.

Parsing Key-Value Pairs from Structured Syslog Data

The previous examples worked with unstructured data, but suppose the message conformed to a standard format, such as syslog, defined in RFC 5424. The kv filter can parse key-value pairs from consistently formatted strings into their own fields. As an example, create *kv.conf* and add the following to it:

```
input {
  generator {
    count => 1
    add_field => { "[sd]" => "[sip=192.168.8.133|dip=8.8.8.8]" }
  }
}

filter {
❶ prune { whitelist_names => [ "sd" ] }
}

filter {
❷ mutate { gsub => [ "[sd]", "[\[\]]", "") }
❸ kv {
    source => "[sd]"
    target => "[parsed]"
  ❹ field_split => "\|"
  }
}

output { stdout { codec => rubydebug }}
```

We use prune instead of mutate to allow whitelist_names to preserve the field we want to keep and drop all others ❶. We then remove the leading and trailing square brackets with gsub ❷ because their only significance in this example is marking the start and end of the structured data. In the kv filter ❸, we specify the source field sd, the destination top-level field parsed, and the escaped pipe delimiter using field_split ❹. This should parse the fields into parsed.sip and parsed.dip, which we can rename later to ECS. Test and then run the configuration:

```
$ bin/logstash -f conf.d/kv.conf --config.test_and_exit
$ bin/logstash -f conf.d/kv.conf --config.reload.automatic
```

You should see something like the following output:

```
{
    "parsed" => {
        "sip" => "192.168.8.133",
        "dip" => "8.8.8.8"
    },
        "sd" => "sip=192.168.8.133|dip=8.8.8.8"
}
```

The kv filter saves time whenever we need to parse data whose keys and values have consistent separators.

Splitting Fields and Avoiding Backslashes

Inevitably, you'll encounter backslashes (\) in fields you want to parse, notably from Windows systems, but likely from web applications and Linux systems as well. Backslashes are commonly used to escape certain nonprintable characters, like newlines (\n) and tabs (\t), and as a result, they themselves must be escaped if you're trying to use them to search many SIEMs, databases, and command line tools. Windows uses them in everything from system paths to usernames, which adds an unwanted layer of complexity when querying data.

For example, a query term in Kibana for a Windows path might look like C:\\Windows\\System32. Failing to properly escape the backslashes by using two of them would result in the single backslashes escaping the characters immediately following them, causing the database to look for the string C:indowsystem32.

In this section, we'll take a standard Windows username that includes a domain and split it into two valuable fields: user.domain and user.name. This filter will also demonstrate replacing all backslashes with forward slashes (/), adding another layer of standardization to your data, as Kibana requires us to escape backslashes but not forward slashes. Create a new configuration named *split-username.conf* inside your Logstash *conf.d* directory and then follow along.

Input

The following input simulates a field parsed from Windows event log XML data. Note that the add_field operation doesn't require the username's backslash to be escaped because Logstash treats the new field as a literal:

```
input {
  generator {
    count => 1
    add_field => { "[winlog][event_data][UserName]" => "StLouisOffice\James" }
  }
}

filter {
  prune {
    whitelist_names => [ "winlog" ]
  }
}
```

For the sake of example, we're using the prune filter again to preserve all fields starting with winlog. This filter comes in handy in the real world when sending data to external teams, auditors, or even third parties; it enables you to keep only the fields they need and automatically drop the rest.

Mutate

The following filter checks for backslashes, makes a temp field so as to not alter the original, replaces backslashes with forward slashes, and assigns field values and cleanup:

```
filter {
❶ if [winlog][event_data][UserName] =~ /.\\./ {
    mutate {
❷   copy => { "[winlog][event_data][UserName]" => "[utemp]" }
    }
    mutate {
❸   gsub => [ "[utemp]", "[\\]", "/" ]
❹   split => [ "[utemp]", "/" ]
      add_field => {
❺     "[user][domain]" => "%{[utemp][0]}"
        "[user][name]" => "%{[utemp][1]}"
      }
❻   remove_field => [ "[utemp]" ]
    }
❼ } else {
    mutate {
      copy => { "[winlog][event_data][UserName]" => "[user][name]" }
    }
  }
  mutate {
❽   lowercase => [ "[user][domain]", "[user][name]" ]
  }
}
```

When using the `mutate` filter with many functions, note that it follows an order of operations that can catch you off guard if you aren't familiar with it. While Logstash processes configurations top to bottom, individual mutate filters may behave differently. I recommend reading the "Processing Order" section of Elastic's online documentation for the `mutate` filter to better understand its behavior.

First, the filter checks for backslashes ❶ using the `=~` operator and a regular expression pattern. We'll discuss this specific field comparison and more later in this chapter. We copy ❷ the original field into a new temporary field, utemp. Because copy is last in the `mutate` filter's processing order, it needs its own mutate block above the rest of the operations.

Next, we use gsub ❸ on the utemp field to replace all characters listed in a regular expression character class (the escaped backslash inside the square brackets) with a forward slash. We then split the utemp field ❹ on the new slash, creating an array that contains two objects we can interact with. We add the `user.domain` ❺ and `user.name` fields by accessing the index positions of the array. As with most programming languages, index positions start at zero, not one.

Once the fields have been assigned, we remove the temporary field ❻, since it's just a copy of the XML field we've processed into an array and we no longer need it. After that logic block has been closed, we reach the `else` statement for the topmost logic; if there wasn't a backslash in the original field ❼, we copy it into the user.name field. Finally, we use the lowercase function ❽ of the mutate filter to further standardize the data. Note that the original field is still there because we used copy; if you want to directly modify the original field instead of creating a duplicate, use rename in place of copy.

Next, let's view the output from these filters on the terminal.

Output

Add the standard output to the end of the configuration:

```
output {
  stdout { codec => rubydebug }
}
```

As with the previous sections, ensure your curly brackets and quotation marks are properly closed. Check the configuration and then launch Logstash:

```
$ bin/logstash -f conf.d/split-username.conf --config.test_and_exit
$ bin/logstash -f conf.d/split-username.conf --config.reload.automatic
```

You should see the following output appear on your screen:

```
{
    "winlog" => {
        "event_data" => {
            "UserName" => "StLouisOffice\\James"
        }
    },
      "user" => {
        "domain" => "stlouisoffice",
          "name" => "james"
    }
}
```

This processing might seem like a lot of work for just two fields, but keep in mind that you can easily expand the steps to alter any number of fields. The copy, gsub, split, add_field, remove_field, and lowercase all support manipulating multiple fields at a time, as do most filter plug-ins.

The gsub filter is somewhat different from the other filters, which use key-value pairs with the => operator. To perform multiple fields and character replacements, gsub uses sets of three arguments for each operation, and it looks like the following:

```
filter {
  gsub => [
    "[field_one]", "[\\]", "/",
    "[field_two]", "\|", "; "
  ]
}
```

With this configuration complete, let's discuss using Ruby code directly in Logstash.

Writing Filters with Ruby Scripting

Ruby is an object-oriented programming language that uses methods, control flow, variables, and other common features. You can write your own Ruby filters, either inline or in a separate script file, to further control the processing of your data, which is useful in cases when no other Logstash filter can efficiently do what you need.

NOTE   *Because complex scripts may add overhead to your filters, always use a filter ID to enable troubleshooting and performance analysis.*

Logstash's internal event API controls how filters, including Ruby ones, access or create field values in streaming events. To get a field's value for use in a Ruby filter, use event.get("[*field*]"). To set a field's value, use event .set("[*field*]","*value*"). To remove a field, use event.remove("[*field*]").

Let's use both the get and set APIs in an example. Create a new configuration named *ruby-simple.conf* and add the following generator input:

```
input {
  generator {
    count => 1
    add_field => {
      "[host][ip]" => [ "192.168.99.99", "fe80::1234:5678:1a:2bcd" ]
      "[test][ip]" => [ "192.168.99.99", "fe80::1234:5678:1a:2bcd" ]
    }
  }
}
```

The host.ip and test.ip fields are arrays with the exact same values. We'll use them to demonstrate how to compare arrays, a filtering capability gap we identified earlier in this chapter.

Init and Code

The Ruby filter supports two options for including inline code: init and code. The init option runs once at startup, making it ideal for storing static values, calculations that run once, and methods or functions. The code block executes for every event and can access the event's API variables.

Let's create a filter that adds the field agent.forwarder, which holds the hostname of the current Logstash server, to an event. This field can help you track an event's path across your logging infrastructure. It also enables you to monitor feed health; if one server stops sending data or drops its logging volume, you'll know where to begin investigating. Add the following lines to your configuration:

```
filter {
  ruby {
    id => "ruby_add_agentforwarder"
    init => '
    ❶ require "socket"
    ❷ @@hostname = Socket.gethostname
    '
    code => '
    ❸ event.set("[agent][forwarder]", @@hostname)
    '
  }
}
```

Within the init section, we use require ❶ to load the socket class, which can access certain underlying system details. Next, we create a class variable, denoted by the double at signs (@@) ❷. This variable is available to other Ruby filters within the same pipeline but, importantly, is only instantiated once at startup.

Within the code section, we use the variable to add the agent.forwarder field ❸ to each event using the event API format. Note that the init and code sections begin and end with single quotes and everything inside of those sections uses double quotes.

Array Comparisons

Earlier in the chapter, you learned that we can't compare array fields to other arrays using Logstash syntax. Let's accomplish this task with Ruby. We'll iterate over both array fields in the input (although you may use other means of comparing arrays such as intersections, includes, subsets, and supersets) and use a nested Ruby do loop to check for matches:

```
filter {
  ruby {
    id => "ruby_array_comparison"
    code => '
    ❶ arr1 = event.get("[host][ip]")
      arr2 = event.get("[test][ip]")
      if arr1 && arr2
      ❷ arr1.each do |item1|
        ❸ arr2.each do |item2|
            if item1 == item2
            ❹ if event.get("[tags]")
              ❺ event.set("[tags]", event.get("[tags]") << "match_"+item1)
                else
              ❻ event.set("[tags]", ["match_"+item1])
                end
            end
          end
        end
      end
```

```
❼ if event.get("[tags]")
    event.set("[tags]", event.get("[tags]").uniq)
  end
  '
  }
}
```

First, we create new variables arr1 and arr2 to hold the contents of each IP address field we're comparing and use the event API to get the fields ❶. Note that, instead of creating arr1 and arr2, you could use event.get().each, but that code is less readable.

If arr1 and arr2 both exist and aren't nil (nonexistent), we then call the .each method ❷ to begin a do loop for each array. Like a for loop in other languages, a do loop iterates over every item. In this case, we iterate over every item in the first array and then every item in the second. Everything between do and end is called a *block* and encapsulates processing logic. The object passed into the block is indicated between the pipes; in this case, item1 ❷ and item2 ❸ in the next line.

After checking whether the two items are equal (which leads to more sets of blocks), we check if the field tags exists ❹. If it does, we append a custom string match_itemX ❺ to the tags array using the << operator. If tags doesn't exist (represented by nil), we create the tags array field ❻ using the same custom string. We have to check the tags field because if it doesn't exist but we try to append values to it anyway, the operation will fail. We then close out each loop with end. Finally, outside of all loops, we check for tags again and set it to a new version of itself ❼ that only holds unique values using the uniq method.

Last, add the standard output:

```
output {
  stdout { codec => rubydebug }
}
```

Test and then run the configuration:

```
$ bin/logstash -f conf.d/ruby-simple.conf --config.test_and_exit
$ bin/logstash -f conf.d/ruby-simple.conf --config.reload.automatic
```

You should see something like the following output:

```
{
    "agent" => {
        "forwarder" => "ubuntu01"
    },
     "test" => {
        "ip" => [
            [0] "192.168.99.99",
            [1] "fe80::1234:5678:1a:2bcd"
        ]
    },
     "host" => {
```

```
        "ip" => [
            [0] "192.168.99.99",
            [1] "fe80::1234:5678:1a:2bcd"
        ]
    },
     "tags" => [
            [0] "match_192.168.99.99",
            [1] "match_fe80::1234:5678:1a:2bcd"
    ]
--snip--
```

This example covered some useful Ruby syntax elements you can use in your own scripts. Note that Ruby is flexible about whitespace and indentation; for example, the four consecutive end keywords from the previous example could all go on one line. You might also find it helpful to use elsif, Ruby's equivalent of the else if statement.

Other helpful methods include upcase to convert a string to all capital letters, downcase to convert a string to all lowercase characters, and capitalize to capitalize only the first character of a word. The join method creates a string from an array of terms, and split conversely splits a string into an array. The methods to_s and to_s(16) convert data to strings or hex strings, respectively. You can also validate whether a variable is in fact a string:

```
if mystring.is_a?(String)
--snip--
if !mystring.is_a?(String)
--snip--
```

With some Ruby skills in your arsenal, let's cover how to drop events we don't want to spend processing cycles on.

Dropping Data to Save CPU

In Chapter 8, we used the null output to make events disappear instead of sending them downstream. We've also used filters like prune to remove or allow a subset of the data. The drop filter gives you more flexibility to control eliminating data, and it removes the data at the filter level, keeping you from spending CPU cycles on the event further down the pipeline.

Suppose you have a new network appliance that is flooding your SIEM with event codes you've determined provide little to no value. The following filter would drop those logs:

```
filter
  if [event][code] == 123456789 {
    drop{}
  }
}
```

The filter's only option is percentage, which allows you to drop a certain percentage of whatever events meet the filter's conditions. If you only need to sample data such as router network flow logs and sampling isn't enabled or supported upstream on the appliances, use the drop filter to meet your collection requirements. If you wanted to keep just 5 percent of the problematic event codes by dropping 95 percent of all events from your new appliance, use the following:

```
filter
  if [event][code] == 123456789 {
    drop { percentage => 95 }
  }
}
```

It's best to place drop filters as high as logically possible in your configurations, though it's even better to eliminate them at or closer to the source.

SAVING CONFIGURATIONS WITH GIT

In your local Git repository, create a new directory for your filters if you didn't already, then copy your configurations and additional notes there, and redact any credentials. Track the new files with **git add** **.** and then commit them by running **git -a -m** *<message>*. Finally, run **git push** to add them to your remote repository.

Summary

Logstash filters provide immense capabilities for extracting, transforming, and enriching data. You can use Logstash to parse and manipulate data, add or remove fields, map network addresses to hostnames and users, use event fields to add terms from dictionary files, run Ruby scripts, and more.

In this chapter, you used generator inputs and preparation filters to stage data for the examples. Then, you used a number of filters to read and use timestamps, process names and IDs, and substitute characters. You also enriched data, made fields from key-value pairs, and performed many types of field comparisons. You explored regular expression matching, control flow, and Ruby's capabilities using inline filters.

Next, we'll cover Apache Kafka, a distributed event-streaming tool that serves as the backbone of many enterprise data pipelines and ties in seamlessly with Beats and Logstash.

PART IV

DATA CENTRALIZATION, AUTOMATION, AND ENRICHMENT

This final part of the book discusses strategies for further improving your cybersecurity data pipeline by centralizing security logs and automating configurations. Chapter 10 covers Kafka, a data broker that allows other parties in your organization to request access to specific pieces of security information as needed. In Chapters 11 and 12, we discuss how to automate the configuration and management of the tools covered in previous chapters, improving efficiency. Chapter 13 explains how to rapidly check incoming logs for suspicious fields gleaned from threat intelligence by using the caching tools Redis and Memcached.

10

CENTRALIZING SECURITY DATA

Once organizations have collected logs from across their environment, they may want to allow multiple tools to access these logs as needed. For example, security teams may want to review sensor alerts, whereas auditors may need to see access logs. In this chapter, we'll cover centralizing logs with Apache Kafka, which stores inputs in one platform and then allows consumers to access only the data they need via standard application programming interfaces.

We'll begin by examining Kafka's fundamental components: its producers and consumers, the role of brokers and controllers, and its topics and partitions. Next, you'll learn how to configure brokers, manage topics, and implement proper data replication strategies that ensure the data remains available when needed.

Over the course of the chapter, you'll configure two Kafka servers and then connect them to tools covered previously, including Rsyslog, Filebeat, and Logstash. Finally, you'll push and pull data from Kafka.

Kafka Fundamentals

Kafka forms the core of many organizations' data pipelines by providing centralized access to streaming data while separating the data publishers from the data consumers. As long as both applications can connect to Kafka, they don't need any further ability to interact with one another.

The tool can run as a stand-alone server or in a *cluster* of two or more nodes working together. It replicates the data it receives to other nodes running in the same cluster, making it highly reliable, as it can suffer multiple server outages before data is degraded or destroyed. It can also redistribute its data, so a server taken out of the cluster for maintenance will offload its data to other nodes before shutting down.

Kafka itself doesn't initiate network connections, other than between its own cluster nodes. Both the nodes sending data to Kafka and those requesting data from it must first connect to it, removing requirements for consumers to continuously listen for data. Those that want to send data can do so, and those that want to receive data can just ask for it.

Kafka used to rely on a separate tool called Zookeeper to manage metadata for its server nodes and data. Newer versions of Kafka use an internal metadata-management protocol called Kafka Raft, or KRaft, which we'll use in this chapter. KRaft allows users to manage settings for only one tool, rather than those for both Kafka and Zookeeper.

Understanding Kafka's terminology will help you grasp its complex functionality. Let's explore its key concepts and their usefulness in data engineering.

Producers, Consumers, and Consumer Groups

Producers are the entities sending, or *publishing*, data to an event stream, and *consumers* are the entities receiving, or *subscribing*, to that stream. Producers and consumers are typically applications, such as Filebeat or Logstash. They may also describe an actual person using tools included with Kafka to manually send test data or read messages.

Consumer groups assign each individual consumer in a group its own small segment of a data stream to receive, allowing applications to receive the data more quickly. Consider students taking turns reading a book aloud in school; each student would read a section of the book before passing the text to the next person to read. Now imagine instead that every student read their assigned pages simultaneously (and that the students somehow retained everything they heard), allowing them to complete an entire book in one class period. This is how a consumer group works. The concurrent processing of small data segments dramatically increases the potential throughput for consumer applications.

Brokers and Controllers

Kafka nodes filling the *broker* role manage the sending of data between producers and consumers. Producers and consumers primarily interact with brokers. Kafka *controllers* handle management functions within the cluster, such as determining which nodes are responsible for each event stream, which node is the leader for a given dataset, and when it can store certain metadata as a snapshot before deleting it from live streams.

In this chapter, our nodes will fulfill both the broker and controller roles. In production environments, you may configure separate brokers and controllers in cases when your clusters have dozens or hundreds of nodes. You may also assign a handful of nodes to both roles to avoid the cost of using dedicated hardware or cloud computing instances.

Topics

Kafka manages events using *topics*, individual collections of append-only event logs. *Messages* are the events stored in a topic. Topics are the main unit of data sent between producers and consumers; Kafka appends published messages to a topic, and consumers subscribe to the topic to receive new messages. Topics are logical groupings and may span multiple physical or virtual servers.

Topics allow you to organize your events. For example, you might create topics dedicated to separate tools like Filebeat, Winlogbeat, or Rsyslog. You may also have topics for alerts from sensors, suspicious user logins, or certain database transactions. In the shopping world, you'll find purchasing topics used by both fulfillment software and real-time shipping notifications.

As a best practice, Kafka topics should align to a dataset or support a single business purpose: In other words, they should provide one kind of data to meet a specific demand.

Partitions

Topics may contain more data than one server can hold. To accommodate this fact, Kafka breaks topics down into *partitions*, which are smaller units of key-value pairs.

Whereas topics are logical *collections* of data, partitions are the data *structures* used to store and move data in Kafka. Topics can logically span multiple servers, but individual partitions must fit on a single host. We'll use commands later in this chapter to create topics for our tools with a specific number of partitions.

Within a partition, keys are offset positions, and values are individual streaming messages. Kafka uses the offsets to determine which messages within a topic a subscriber application has received. Kafka's internal `__consumer_offsets` topic tracks this data (and may use gigabytes of storage per server if the cluster has many consumer groups).

When a topic has two partitions, Kafka splits any received data between them. You may have more partitions than brokers; if a cluster has two broker nodes and four partitions, each node might have two writeable partitions available. This *over-provisioning* increases write throughput, although you should use replication (covered in the next section) to create read-only copies of your data for consumers.

You can only ever increase the number of partitions in a topic because Kafka has no means of consolidating writeable partitions, meaning the data in deleted partitions would disappear. There are ways to bypass this restriction, such as by using a consumer to read events from a topic and then immediately publishing them into a new topic with a smaller number of partitions, effectively "draining" a topic of messages before deprecating it.

Importantly, a single partition's write speed is approximately 10MB per second, though it may be higher depending on the drive speed or CPU. At 10MB per second, a single partition could potentially process 864GB of data per day. Generally, you should use 3 to 10 partitions for a single topic.

Data Replication

Replication, or data copying, specifies additional copies of a partition to make. A *replication factor* of three means Kafka keeps three read-only copies of a partition, and the data would remain available even if two servers failed. Replication is a built-in feature of Kafka; partitions with no replication technically have a replication factor of zero.

Recall that a single broker may have multiple partitions, but each partition represents a writeable segment of a topic's data. When a partition is replicated, Kafka assigns a broker as the *leader* for that partition, meaning it receives all writes for that partition. Kafka then assigns *follower* brokers, which subscribe internally to the partition leader, thus creating *read-only replicas*, available for consumer use alongside the leader. If the leader broker suddenly crashes, an internal election process occurs, a new partition leader is elected, a read-only copy of the data becomes writeable, and a new read-only replica is created elsewhere.

The replication factor can't be larger than the number of brokers in a cluster, as you can have only one leader partition (the writeable copy) per broker. You can, however, use one broker as the leader for multiple different partitions, which represent different data in the topic. Generally, Kafka developers recommend a replication factor of three for most use cases, which, at a minimum, requires three brokers.

In a nutshell, the replication factor directly affects how fast consumers receive data. If you had a topic with five writeable partitions and a replication factor of three, your cluster would generate and maintain 15 readable partitions that your consumers could access.

Replication requires storage space, so plan accordingly if you need to balance write and read speeds in large clusters. Interestingly, increasing the replication factor too much may actually *decrease* throughput, due to the latency that occurs while copying data between brokers to read-only partitions, opening file handles on your hard drives, and coordinating metadata.

Listeners and Metadata

When clients, whether publishers or subscribers, connect to Kafka, they don't immediately start sending data to or receiving data from the node they connect to. Instead, clients receive metadata from Kafka containing connection information for the broker, including the partitions the client will use to consume messages. It's somewhat common for dedicated *bootstrap* hosts, with more resources than other servers in a cluster, to handle incoming network connections before routing the client to the appropriate node.

Listeners are simply sockets created by Kafka to accept incoming connections from clients and other nodes. Listeners are often assigned hostnames or IP addresses that are only resolvable from an interface on the internal network; by default, though, they use 0.0.0.0, which represents all available interfaces. If certain clients can't access internally resolvable names, you'll need an external *advertised listener* to which clients can connect.

When Kafka sends metadata back to clients, the included connection information may contain an advertised listener if configured, which should contain a hostname or IP address and a port reachable by your potential clients. Listeners are mandatory, but advertised listeners aren't, because if advertised listeners are left undefined in Kafka's configurations, Kafka just uses the listener values for all network communications. In this chapter, we'll use both settings.

Streams and Connectors

You can interact directly with Kafka messages within a topic using *streams*. Streams allow you to write Java or Scala programs that run their own algorithms on the data in transit.

Because Kafka isn't a database, its data is constantly moving, so processing it is like counting fish in a stream. (Apache's own example of using streams involves counting unique words within messages as Kafka receives them.) In a cybersecurity context, streams may allow you to perform real-time alerting on business-critical assets before data even appears in a SIEM. We won't write any streams code in this chapter, but you should know that it's possible to do so.

Connectors are pieces of software created for systems and services that don't natively support Kafka to send or retrieve data. In this chapter, you'll use tools from previous chapters, like Rsyslog and Logstash, to act as connectors.

Creating a Kafka Cluster

In this section, we'll use two Ubuntu virtual machines as a miniature Kafka cluster. Although Kafka developers and gurus recommend using an odd number of servers to facilitate voting on leaders and other tasks, we'll stick to two for demonstration purposes. To set up multiple Kafka nodes with identical configurations in one fell swoop, you can learn Ansible, which we'll cover in Chapters 11 and 12.

Create a new virtual machine with 4GB RAM, two processors, and 50GB storage. Then, create a full, nonlinked clone of the new virtual machine, and update */etc/hostname* and */etc/hosts* on each host with the hostnames *kafka01* and *kafka02*, respectively. Finally, update and reboot the machines. I recommend taking a snapshot of this fresh state in case you have to roll back any upcoming changes.

Setting Up the Network

We'll use two virtual network interfaces for each virtual machine: one in the 10.0.0.0/8 network and one in the 192.168.0.0/24 network. This design simulates the use of different networks for interbroker and client-to-broker communications. If you don't want to add new virtual network interface cards (NICs), it's perfectly fine to use the same network for both purposes while practicing.

Kafka's underlying TLS infrastructure requires resolvable hostnames to connect to each node, as the signed certificates don't use IP addresses in the Subject Alternative Name section. If you have a DNS server, add the following entries to it, or update the */etc/hosts* file on each node to reflect a numbered naming convention, such as *kafka01.local*, *kafka02.local*, and so forth. This allows each host to know where to find every other node in the cluster. If you're using two networks, set the domains in the 10.0.0.0/8 network to **internal** instead of local using your editor of choice. The following shows a snippet from */etc/hosts*:

```
--snip--
10.0.0.211          kafka01
10.0.0.211          kafka01.internal
192.168.8.138       kafka01.local
10.0.0.212          kafka02
10.0.0.212          kafka02.internal
192.168.8.136       kafka02.local
--snip--
```

After updating your DNS server or */etc/hosts*, add firewall rules to allow TCP ports 22, 9093, and 9094. Your Kafka nodes will use port 9093/TCP for interbroker communications and 9094/TCP for incoming client connections. Port 22/TCP is for Secure Shell. Run the following command on systems that use UFW:

```
$ sudo ufw allow 22,9093,9094/tcp
```

On systems that use Firewalld, run this command instead:

```
$ sudo firewall-cmd --zone=public --add-port={22,9092,9093}/tcp --permanent
$ sudo firewall-cmd --reload
```

With network preparation done, let's move onto creating a new user, staging files, and installing prerequisites.

Creating Users and Directories

Let's create a dedicated user to run Kafka, appropriately named *kafka*. On each virtual machine, add the *kafka* user and set their password to *abcd1234*; on RHEL, substitute wheel for sudo:

```
$ sudo useradd -s /bin/bash -d /home/kafka -m -G sudo kafka
$ sudo passwd kafka
```

We need to create directories for files we'll copy shortly. The following commands create the directories */data/kafka* and */opt/kafka/certs* and set the appropriate access permissions; feel free to also make and use */etc/ssl/kafka/* or another directory that meets your certificate policy:

```
$ sudo mkdir -p {/data/kafka,/opt/kafka/certs}
$ sudo chmod 700 {/data/kafka,/opt/kafka/}
$ sudo chown -R kafka:kafka {/data/kafka,/opt/kafka/}
```

Kafka persists all data to disk, and the */data/kafka* directory will hold that live data, including partitions and replications. In production environments, it should use high-speed, durable solid state or nonvolatile memory express (NVMe) drives. The */opt/kafka/certs* directory holds TLS files only and doesn't need any special drives of its own.

Installing Kafka and a Java Development Kit

Kafka is Java based, so you'll need to install the Java Development Kit, Open-JDK, on your Kafka nodes. Run the following command on Ubuntu:

```
$ sudo apt install openjdk-11-jdk -y
```

If you're running RHEL, CentOS, or similar builds instead of Ubuntu, use the following command on your Kafka nodes; note that the OpenJDK name is slightly different from the Ubuntu version:

```
$ sudo dnf install java-11-openjdk -y
```

You'll also need OpenJDK on your main workstation, where you generate TLS files, so you can make Java-specific certificate containers in the next section. Logstash and Elasticsearch also support these Java certificate containers, and you'll get extra mileage from installing it on your main workstation if you want to try using the containers with those tools.

Back on the Kafka virtual machines, switch to the new *kafka* user, entering the password *abcd1234* when prompted, to begin staging files:

```
$ sudo su - kafka
$ cd ~
```

Download the binary tarball from the Apache website with the highest Scala version, available at *https://kafka.apache.org/downloads*. You can right-click the tarball hyperlink, copy the address, and then use wget to download the files on each broker virtual machine. After the file has been downloaded, extract it into */opt/kafka* (substitute version numbers as necessary):

```
$ wget https://downloads.apache.org/kafka/VERSION/kafka_VERSION.tgz
$ tar -xzf kafka_X.XX-Y.Y.Y.tgz --strip 1 -C /opt/kafka/
```

With your Kafka files staged, it's time to make TLS certificates.

Enabling TLS

Kafka receives client connections and initiates them between brokers, so create flex certificates and keys for each Kafka node. We covered flex certificates in Chapter 2 and created a wildcard certificate in Chapter 6.

If you want to send certain Kafka management metadata over a separate network (10.0.0.0/8), which we covered in "Setting Up the Network" on page 208, add another Subject Alternative Name to each host's certificate that includes the *.internal* domain. Without the domain in your SANs, you'll likely encounter troublesome TLS errors.

Kafka uses *Java KeyStores (JKS)* to store signed certificates, keys, and CA files. To make a JKS file, you'll need *keytool*, which is part of Java Development Kit packages such as OpenJDK. You should have installed OpenJDK in the previous section on your main workstation and on your Kafka nodes.

JKS files are simply file containers, so they can't import private keys, but they can import PKCS#12 (P12 or PFX) files that contain both a private key and signed certificate. Create P12 files for each node; the following example uses the hostname *kafka01.local*, so be sure to substitute your own hostnames:

```
$ openssl pkcs12 -export -inkey tls/keys/kafka01.local.flex.key.pem -in
tls/certs/kafka01.local.flex.cert.pem -out
tls/certs/kafka01.local.flex.pkcs12
```

You'll be prompted to enter a password for the private key you're importing into the P12 file, as well as a password for creating the new P12 file. If you're scripting this process and you accept the risk of entering passwords on the command line, you may add the following arguments:

```
-passin pass:<privatekey password> -passout pass:<P12 password>
```

Keytool considers P12 files to be stores. The following command imports the P12 store into a new password-protected JKS file:

```
$ keytool -importkeystore -srckeystore tls/certs/kafka01.local.flex.pkcs12
-srcstoretype pkcs12 -destkeystore tls/certs/kafka01.local.keystore.jks
```

You should be prompted for the new JKS file's password, then the P12 file's password. Again, if you wish to skip prompts in favor of scripting future deployments, you may add these arguments:

```
-srcstorepass <P12 password> -storepass <new JKS password> -keypass
<private key password> -noprompt
```

You should now have *kafka01.local.keystore.jks*. Repeat this process for both brokers, substituting *kafka01* for *kafka02* as needed.

Let's make one more file, a keystore technically called a *truststore*, for holding the CA chain. You need only one of these, which you'll copy to all your Kafka nodes:

```
$ keytool -keystore tls/certs/truststore.jks -alias CAChain -import -file
tls/certs/ca-chain.cert.pem
```

Using a Python web server or your transfer tool of choice, copy the keystores and truststore to each respective node. Run the following on the workstation containing your TLS files in the TLS directory:

```
$ python3 -m http.server 8000
```

Next, run these commands on each broker node:

```
$ wget 192.168.8.133:8000/certs/kafka01.local.keystore.jks -P /opt/kafka/certs/
$ wget 192.168.8.133:8000/certs/truststore.jks -P /opt/kafka/certs/
```

Now let's configure Kafka's settings.

Configurations

Because you've already set up the Kafka package and TLS files, all you need to do to configure the tool is update two existing configuration files. When running in both broker and controller roles, Kafka's primary configuration is */opt/kafka/config/server.properties*. Kafka also has specific *broker.properties* and *controller.properties* files you can use when running a cluster whose nodes each have distinct modes. I recommend using these files instead of *server .properties* for large production deployments, as their names are clearer and they compartmentalize your configurations. These files contain almost all the same settings and showcase the ones you most likely should use for each role.

The */opt/kafka/config/client-ssl.properties* file is a legacy configuration for local clients and command line tools included in the Kafka package. While production environments should use *consumer.properties* or *producer.properties* instead, you may want to use *client-ssl.properties* for one-off connections and testing.

Previous versions of Kafka that used Zookeeper, notably between versions 2.8 and 3.9, stored KRaft configurations in */opt/kafka/config/kraft/*, while Zookeeper configurations were stored one directory level below them in *config*. As of Kafka version 4.0, Kafka dropped the *kraft/* portion of the filepath, storing KRaft configurations into the main *config* directory.

As always, back up the original configuration before you proceed. Because you'll create a new configuration from scratch over the course of this chapter, use mv (move) instead of cp (copy):

```
$ cd /opt/kafka/config/
$ mv server.properties server.properties.original
```

With the original configuration backed up, let's create the new one with our cluster and TLS information.

Configuring Server Properties

We'll create Kafka's configuration in sections. Using your editor of choice, add the lines from this section to a new */opt/kafka/config/server.properties* file. Start with the following lines:

```
node.id=211
process.roles=broker,controller
bootstrap.servers=SSL://kafka01:9094,SSL://kafka02:9094
log.dirs=/data/kafka
```

The first option sets the node's ID to the last octet of its internal IP address, 10.0.0.**211**. This is a lab value; in large or production deployments, use a dedicated numbering system. Update **node.id** on your other nodes, as the number must be unique for each server. This node fills both broker and controller roles.

The bootstrap servers list has a listener conveniently named SSL, which we'll discuss shortly, and node addresses used for the initial cluster connection. These don't need to be a complete or even extensive list of brokers because once a new node successfully connects to a cluster and exchanges metadata, it won't reference this setting anymore. We also save Kafka's operational, live-streaming files to */data/kafka*, which we created earlier in this chapter.

The following lines describe Kafka's listeners, which map out which sockets should fill each role. For listeners and advertised listeners, the option's format is *LISTENER_NAME://hostname:port*. The listener's name lets us reference this socket elsewhere in the configuration. Recall that we're using port 9093 for controller communications and 9094 for client interactions. Add the following lines:

```
listeners=CONTROLLER://kafka01.internal:9093,SSL://kafka01.local:9094
advertised.listeners=SSL://kafka01.local:9094
inter.broker.listener.name=SSL
listener.security.protocol.map=CONTROLLER:SSL,SSL:SSL
```

The listener setting creates the CONTROLLER and SSL listeners. Both clients (via advertised.listeners) and brokers will use the SSL listener. The security protocol map uses the listener name on the left side of the colon and a communication protocol on the right. In this case, both CONTROLLER and SSL listeners will use TLS (referenced as SSL).

If you're not using two network interfaces or didn't add .internal to your certificate SANs, just remove .internal (bolded in the previous code listing) from the controller hostnames and use the kafka01 or kafka02 hostnames with or without .local, which should already be in each broker's */etc/hosts* files. If you've been following along with this book, you should have *hostname* and *hostname*.local entries in all of your certificates, and your */etc/hosts* or DNS entries should route *kafka01* and *kafka02* to the appropriate 10.*x* IP addresses. As you update each node in your cluster, be sure to change the hostnames in both listeners.

The controller list is comma separated and uses the format BROKER_ID@ hostname:port; note you may need to change 211 and 212 if you used different IDs for the brokers:

```
controller.quorum.voters=211@kafka01:9093,212@kafka02:9093
controller.listener.names=CONTROLLER
```

The list of voters should be a complete list of controllers in the cluster. Because we specified inter.broker.listener.name in a previous snippet, we need to specify the listener for controllers too. Now let's add our TLS files:

```
ssl.keystore.location=/opt/kafka/certs/kafka01.local.keystore.jks
ssl.keystore.password=abcd1234
ssl.key.password=abcd1234
ssl.truststore.location=/opt/kafka/certs/truststore.jks
ssl.truststore.password=abcd1234
ssl.client.auth=required
ssl.endpoint.identification.algorithm=https
```

These settings should look familiar by now, even if you're reading these specific settings for the first time. The keystore contains the signed certificate and private key for this node. Following these are the passwords for the keystore and the private key. Update the keystore name on each node's configuration.

Next are the truststore path and password, followed by ssl.client.auth and ssl.endpoint.identification.algorithm, which create the mutual TLS (mTLS) requirement.

Now we can specify behaviors for our topics:

```
log.message.timestamp.type=LogAppendTime
delete.topic.enable=true
auto.create.topics.enable=false
```

By setting LogAppendTime, we tell Kafka to calculate message retention based on how long it has held an individual message, regardless of the timestamp included in the event's metadata. Otherwise, if Kafka were set to retain only seven days' worth of data but you sent it data from logfiles that were months or years old, Kafka would immediately drop them once received! We also allow topics to be deleted and disallow dynamic topic creation.

The remaining values are defaults from the original *server.properties,* shown here for the sake of completeness:

```
num.partitions=1
log.retention.hours=168
log.segment.bytes=1073741824
log.retention.check.interval.ms=300000
offsets.topic.replication.factor=1
transaction.state.log.replication.factor=1
transaction.state.log.min.isr=1
num.network.threads=3
num.io.threads=8
socket.send.buffer.bytes=102400
socket.receive.buffer.bytes=102400
socket.request.max.bytes=104857600
num.recovery.threads.per.data.dir=1
```

These options specify that new topics should have only a single partition unless otherwise specified and retain messages for 168 hours, or one week. The remaining default settings cover log sizes, metadata retention rates, network input and output, and worker threads used when Kafka starts and shuts down, dumping or reading files from disk. If you find your disk space filling up unexpectedly and need to trim your data retention, these are some of the key settings to tune.

Defining the Connection Settings

The configuration */opt/kafka/config/client-ssl.properties* contains minimally required connection information and SSL/TLS settings. We'll use it for the purposes of this example. After backing up the original file, if present, update the configuration or create a new one with the following lines, substituting your servers and keystores as needed:

```
bootstrap.servers=SSL://kafka01.local:9094,SSL://kafka02.local:9094
security.protocol=SSL
ssl.keystore.location=/opt/kafka/certs/kafka01.local.keystore.jks
ssl.keystore.password=abcd1234
ssl.key.password=abcd1234
ssl.truststore.location=/opt/kafka/certs/truststore.jks
ssl.truststore.password=abcd1234
```

We'll use this file shortly with Kafka's included command line tools to create our topics.

Creating Cluster IDs

Kafka clusters use an internal identifier to track their members. Use the following command *once* to generate a random 22-character string, then save it so you can copy it onto the other node. Please note this command uses backticks (`` ` ``) and no single quotes:

```
$ echo `</dev/urandom tr -dc A-Za-z0-9 | head -c 22`
BSjh5WvShpH3pERXbMIJPr
```

Next, apply the ID to *both nodes* using the following command:

```
$ /opt/kafka/bin/kafka-storage.sh format -t BSjh5WvShpH3pERXbMIJPr
-c /opt/kafka/config/server.properties
metaPropertiesEnsemble=MetaPropertiesEnsemble(metadataLogDir=Optional.empty,
dirs={/data/kafka: EMPTY})
Formatting /data/kafka with metadata.version 3.7-IV4.
```

With the ID in place, we can add the service file before starting the Kafka cluster.

Using Systemd for Automatic Startup

Because we extracted Kafka's files from a tarball and never installed a package, we need a Systemd service file to handle automatic startup. Kafka comes with tools to gracefully manage startup and shutdown functions on each broker, so we'll use those to start, stop, and restart Kafka as needed.

With superuser privileges, create */etc/systemd/system/kafka.service* using your editor of choice and add the following lines:

```
[Unit]
Requires=network.target remote-fs.target
After=network.target remote-fs.target

[Service]
Type=simple
#SyslogIdentifier=kafka
User=kafka
ExecStart=/bin/sh -c '/opt/kafka/bin/kafka-server-start.sh
/opt/kafka/config/server.properties > /data/kafka/kafka.log 2>&1'
ExecStop=/opt/kafka/bin/kafka-server-stop.sh
Restart=on-abnormal

[Install]
WantedBy=multi-user.target
```

The ExecStart line uses */bin/sh* to launch the *kafka-server-start.sh* helper tool. It will use the *server.properties* file you just made and redirect terminal output to */data/kafka/kafka.log*. The ExecStop line gracefully terminates the Kafka processes. Also note the commented SyslogIdentifier line, which lets you set a specific program name in syslog messages for this process. After adding the service file, run the following command so systemd identifies the new service file:

```
$ sudo systemctl daemon-reload
```

Ensure that you've configured both nodes before continuing. Substitute *kafka01* for *kafka02* as necessary and ensure that the TLS files are in the right spots and referenced accordingly in the configurations. Also check that network connectivity works between the hosts and that they have the expected IP addresses. Next, let's start Kafka to begin processing data.

Running Kafka

So far, we've made a new user, created keystores containing TLS files, updated configurations, and generated a service file ready to launch Kafka. Let's start the Kafka brokers.

Starting Brokers

To start both brokers at the same time, run the **systemctl** command on both Ubuntu virtual machines:

```
$ sudo systemctl start kafka
```

After a second or two, run the **status** command:

```
$ systemctl status kafka
```

You should see the status in green (shown here in bold):

```
kafka.service
    Loaded: loaded (/etc/systemd/system/kafka.service; disabled;
            vendor preset: enabled)
    Active: active (running) since Wed 03-27 19:24:32 UTC; 20h ago
  Main PID: 60321 (sh)
     Tasks: 99 (limit: 4515)
    Memory: 619.6M
       CPU: 8min 52.178s
--snip--
```

To check for errors, run **tail -f** on the *kafka.log* file to view logs on your terminal as Kafka creates them. Errors should be hard to miss, as they fill the screen before causing a shutdown message to appear:

```
$ tail -f /data/kafka/kafka.log
```

If neither cluster says it's shutting down, congratulations! Your first multi-node Kafka cluster using custom TLS infrastructure is up and running. If you receive TLS errors, you may need to remove .internal references from your *server.properties* configuration, check that your certificates are correct, or verify that DNS entries are accurate. Also ensure you created the truststore, which contains the CA chain.

Creating Topics

We'll create a topic, test its data on *kafka01*, and then use *kafka02* to read the data, ensuring both systems are working as intended. On *kafka01*, use the appropriately named *kafka-topics.sh* to create a simple test topic, encryptedtesttopic:

```
$ /opt/kafka/bin/kafka-topics.sh --create --bootstrap-server kafka01.local:9094
--command-config /opt/kafka/config/client-ssl.properties --replication-factor 1
--partitions 1 --topic encryptedtesttopic
```

The test topic specifies the *client-ssl.properties* configuration because it emulates other client connections and uses only a single partition and replication factor. You should see the following output in your terminal:

```
Created topic encryptedtesttopic.
```

If you're still tailing *kafka.log* on either server, you should see one of the servers display the following text indicating success:

```
[2040-12-28 16:05:26,013] INFO Created log for partition testtopic-0 in
/data/kafka/encryptedtesttopic-0 with properties {} (kafka.log.LogManager)
```

The message appears on one server only because we used a replication factor of one and a single partition.

Next, use the same *kafka-topics.sh* tool on *kafka01* to list all topics in the cluster, which should show the single test topic you just created:

```
$ /opt/kafka/bin/kafka-topics.sh --bootstrap-server kafka01.local:9094
--command-config /opt/kafka/config/client-ssl.properties --list
```

You should see the following output:

```
Encryptedtesttopic
```

You may also see the __consumer_offsets topic, which includes the internal topic for tracking cluster metadata if you already sent data to your cluster.

Publishing Messages

Now that you've verified the topic's presence, publish a test message from *kafka01*:

```
$ echo Hello, World sent from kafka01 | /opt/kafka/bin/kafka-console-producer.sh
--bootstrap-server kafka01.local:9094 --producer.config
/opt/kafka/config/client-ssl.properties --topic encryptedtesttopic > /dev/null
```

We pipe echo into *kafka-console-producer.sh*, which also uses the *client-ssl .properties* configuration. Note the use of the --producer-config option, rather than the previously used `--command-config`. The command should exit without errors once complete.

Subscribing to Topics

Switch to *kafka02*, then use *kafka-console-consumer.sh* to simulate a consumer subscribing to a topic:

```
$ /opt/kafka/bin/kafka-console-consumer.sh --bootstrap-server kafka01.local:9094
--consumer.config /opt/kafka/config/client-ssl.properties --topic
encryptedtesttopic --from-beginning --max-messages 1
```

Note the `--from-beginning` switch. You can omit this to receive only the latest data between tests; otherwise, you'll receive all data retained by Kafka in that topic. This command uses `--consumer-config` to reference *client-ssl.properties*.

You should see your message appear in the terminal:

```
Hello, World sent from kafka01
Processed a total of 1 messages
```

Because you included the argument `--max-message 1`, the tool should show only one event and then exit.

Creating Tool-Specific Topics

Now that you've verified that the cluster can create topics, store and deliver messages, and facilitate interactions between brokers, let's create tool-specific topics.

You'll use *kafka-topics.sh* once again, except you'll specify a replication factor of two to store data on both nodes and create three partitions. These settings should provide approximately 30MB per second of write throughput (though your settings may be higher depending on your hardware).

We'll start with the `filebeat` topic:

```
$ /opt/kafka/bin/kafka-topics.sh --create --bootstrap-server kafka01.local:9094
--command-config /opt/kafka/config/client-ssl.properties --replication-factor 2
--partitions 3 --topic filebeat
```

You should see the following output, like your test topic:

```
Created topic filebeat.
```

Repeat this command to create topics named `winlogbeat`, `elasticagent`, `rsyslog`, and so forth.

Now that the cluster is running and ready to receive data, try different ways of organizing your data to see what fits your needs. For example, create additional technology-based topics like the ones you just made, such as for the pfSense firewall and Suricata (a network intrusion detection system). Or create generic, category-based topics, such as firewall and sensor.

Connecting to External Tools

In this section, you'll use tools you're already familiar with to connect to Kafka. Rsyslog, Filebeat, and Logstash make great connectors, as they are purpose-built for the logs and events you'll encounter in cybersecurity analysis.

Rsyslog

Rsyslog, covered in Chapter 7, makes its modules available as stand-alone packages, so let's install its Kafka plug-ins. You can do so on your main workstation, either of the Kafka virtual machines, or some other virtual machine, so long as it has Rsyslog and can communicate with your Kafka hosts via hostname. If you installed Rsyslog on a Debian or Ubuntu host and didn't install the plug-in in Chapter 7, run the following command:

```
$ sudo apt install rsyslog-kafka
```

On RHEL, CentOS, and Rocky Linux, use dnf instead of apt.

Publishing

The following configuration sends logs collected by other Rsyslog configuration files to Kafka. Using your editor of choice, create */etc/rsyslog.d/rsyslog -omkafka.conf*:

```
module(load="omkafka") ❶
action(
    type="omkafka" ❷
    broker=["kafka01.local:9094","kafka02.local:9094"] ❸
    topic="rsyslog"
    confParam=[ ❹
        "compression.codec=snappy", ❺
        "security.protocol=ssl",
        "ssl.key.location=/etc/ssl/rsyslog/rsyslog.local.flex.key.pem",
        "ssl.key.password=abcd1234",
        "ssl.certificate.location=/etc/ssl/rsyslog/rsyslog.local.flex.cert.pem",
        "ssl.ca.location=/etc/ssl/rsyslog/ca-chain.cert.pem"
    ]
)
```

First, load the omkafka module ❶ before using it inside an action ❷. Specify the brokers as a single comma-separated string inside an array ❸, using the format *hostname:port* for each entry. The omkafka module uses the *librdkafka* C/C++ library from Confluent, and we specify its connection-specific options in the confParam array ❹. We also specify the Snappy compression codec ❺, which saves CPU at the expense of slightly lower compression rates. The remaining settings reference your TLS files, which you should have saved previously to */etc/ssl/rsyslog*.

On one of your Kafka nodes, run *kafka-console-consumer.sh* without a maximum limit to view the syslog event stream in real time:

```
$ /opt/kafka/bin/kafka-console-consumer.sh --bootstrap-server kafka01.local:9094
--consumer.config /opt/kafka/config/client-ssl.properties --topic rsyslog
```

After a few moments, you should see syslog messages streaming in your terminal. Next, let's subscribe to Kafka to pull events.

Subscribing

The following configuration pulls Kafka events and writes them to a file. This might be useful if you need to archive logs in a certain topic for compliance or policy reasons. You'd typically compress these logs once they reach a certain size, then send them to *cold* (low cost and slow) storage for the long term.

Create */etc/rsyslog.d/rsyslog-imkafka.conf* and add the following lines to it:

```
❶ module(load="imkafka")

❷ input(
    type="imkafka"
    broker=["kafka01.local:9094","kafka02.local:9094"]
❸ consumergroup="rsyslog"
❹ topic="filebeat"
    confParam=[
      "compression.codec=snappy",
      "security.protocol=ssl",
      "ssl.key.location=/etc/ssl/rsyslog/rsyslog.local.flex.key.pem",
      "ssl.key.password=abcd1234",
      "ssl.certificate.location=/etc/ssl/rsyslog/rsyslog.local.flex.cert.pem",
      "ssl.ca.location=/etc/ssl/rsyslog/ca-chain.cert.pem"
    ]
)

❺ call archiveFilebeat

❻ ruleset(name="archiveFilebeat") {
    if $msg contains_i "filebeat" then {
❼ action(type="omfile" FileCreateMode="0640" File="/tmp/archive.filebeat")
    }
}
```

First, load the imkafka module ❶, then use the input plug-in ❷ and specify the imkafka type. After specifying the broker array, set the consumer group ❸ to rsyslog and topic to filebeat ❹ so we can consume its events. The remaining input options, including confParam, are the same as *rsyslog-omkafka.conf*, as both modules use librdkafka. We call ❺ the ruleset ❻, and after rudimentary checks, we write the output ❼ to */tmp/archive.filebeat*.

You might wonder why we're writing to *tmp* instead of */var/log*. Well, if you're following along with this chapter, you're about to use Filebeat to send */var/log* contents to Kafka via the Filebeat topic. However, we're already consuming the Filebeat topic with Rsyslog, creating a feedback loop. By writing to *tmp* for this demonstration, you'll avoid a comical mess of recursively nesting the same JSON message until your hard drives fill up. Avoid feedback loops in your home lab, your production networks, and certainly when playing music on stage in small venues.

Filebeat

We briefly touched on sending data to Kafka using Filebeat in Chapter 4. Let's revisit those examples in the context of your new cluster.

Publishing

Recall that Filebeat supports only one output at a time, so you must set enabled: false for any other outputs you may have configured in *filebeat .yml* in previous chapters before proceeding. Next, from your downloaded Filebeat directory, enable Filebeat's system input module so it can read system and authorization logs:

```
$ ./filebeat modules enable system
```

In your Filebeat directory, within *modules.d/system.yml*, ensure both system and authorization enabled settings are set to true:

```
--snip--
- module: system
  syslog:
    enabled: true
  auth:
    enabled: true
--snip--
```

Inside *filebeat.yml*, define the following Kafka output, then restart Filebeat so it can take effect:

```
filebeat.config.modules:
  path: ${path.config}/modules.d/*.yml
  reload.enabled: true
  reload.period: 3s

output.kafka:
  enabled: true
❶ hosts: [ "kafka01:9094", "kafka02:9094" ]
❷ topic: "filebeat"
❸ client_id: "my-awesome-server-running-filebeat"
  ssl.enabled: true
❹ ssl.verification_mode: full
  ssl.certificate: "/etc/ssl/elastic/filebeat.local.flex.cert.pem"
```

```
ssl.key: "/etc/ssl/elastic/filebeat.local.flex.key.pem"
ssl.key_passphrase: "abcd1234"
ssl.certificate_authorities:
  - /etc/ssl/elastic/ca-chain.cert.pem
```

Note that I've included the `filebeat.config.modules` options to allow you to enable or disable modules without restarting Filebeat in the future for testing purposes. List the bootstrap servers ❶ in an array, the topic to which to publish events ❷, and the unique identifier ❸ of the server running Filebeat. Also require mTLS ❹ and define the relevant filepaths, as in other Filebeat configurations.

You can start Filebeat either using *systemctl*, if installed as a service, or manually from inside your download path with the following command:

```
$ ./filebeat -e
```

This command shows Filebeat's internal activity logs on the terminal instead of writing them to a file. This allows for much easier troubleshooting if connection errors occur.

Subscribing

Let's also expand on our discussion of subscribing to Kafka using the examples in Chapter 4. Add the following input to *filebeat.yml*:

```
filebeat.inputs:
- type: kafka
  enabled: true
  id: kafka-input
❶ hosts:
    - kafka01:9094
    - kafka02:9094
❷ topics: [ "rsyslog" ]
❸ group_id: "filebeat"
❹ tags: [ "from-kafka-via-filebeat" ]
  ssl.enabled: true
  ssl.verification_mode: full
  ssl.certificate: "/etc/ssl/elastic/filebeat.local.flex.cert.pem"
  ssl.key: "/etc/ssl/elastic/filebeat.local.flex.key.pem"
  ssl.key_passphrase: "abcd1234"
  ssl.certificate_authorities:
    - /etc/ssl/elastic/ca-chain.cert.pem
```

The `hosts` array ❶ contains the same options as the Kafka output, just in list form. We're consuming from the `rsyslog` topic ❷ as a member of the `filebeat` consumer group ❸, potentially sending data through processing modules before reaching the output module. We also set a custom tag ❹ to track events through the pipeline. The remaining TLS options are the same as in previous Filebeat configurations.

In Chapter 4, we included the `ndjson` parser in the input because we knew the topic would only ever contain JSON. But as the `rsyslog` topic likely won't exclusively contain JSON unless you've configured this setting across your entire business, you should drop the parser or add conditional logic.

Logstash

Logstash is a great out-of-the-box Kafka client due to its easy setup and ability to use multiple inputs and outputs simultaneously. Logstash best operates as the "first mile" between programs that can't connect to Kafka, as the "last mile" between Kafka and Elasticsearch, or between Kafka topics as an enrichment worker that reads one topic and writes to another.

Publishing

Let's use the Logstash output from Chapter 8 to show a full, usable configuration. The following configuration accepts Elastic Agent and Beats data over mTLS and, based on the Beat type, forwards it to the corresponding Kafka topic.

The following configuration makes it easy to begin using Kafka in your enterprise if it's already using Beats or Elastic Agent and Logstash. The settings allow you to test and build your Kafka cluster, begin forking data to it, and then eventually connect producers to Kafka directly:

```
input {
  elastic_agent {
    port => 5044
    ssl_enabled => true
    ssl_client_authentication => "required"
    ssl_certificate => "/etc/ssl/elastic/wildcard.local.flex.cert.pem"
    ssl_key => "/etc/ssl/elastic/wildcard.local.flex.key.pem"
    ssl_key_passphrase => "abcd1234"
    ssl_certificate_authorities => [ "/etc/ssl/elastic/ca-chain.cert.pem" ]
  }
}

filter {
  mutate {
    add_tag => [ " logstash-to-kafka" ]
  }
}

output {
  stdout { codec => rubydebug { metadata => true }}
❶ if [agent][type] =~ /(?i)beat/ {
    kafka {
      id => "kafka-output"
      bootstrap_servers => "kafka01.local:9094,kafka02.local:9094"
❷     client_id => "logstash"
      security_protocol => "SSL"
❸     ssl_keystore_location => "/etc/ssl/elastic/wildcard.local.flex.pkcs12"
      ssl_keystore_password => "abcd1234"
❹     ssl_keystore_type => "PKCS12"
      ssl_key_password => "abcd1234"
```

```
    ❺ ssl_truststore_location => "/etc/ssl/elastic/truststore.jks"
       ssl_truststore_password => "abcd1234"
    ❻ ssl_truststore_type => "jks"
    ❼ topic_id => "%{[@metadata][beat]}"
      }
    }
}
```

All Beats and the Elastic Agent add the `agent.type` field to events, so we check whether the field contains the case-insensitive string beat ❶. We set the client ID to `logstash` ❷ (though ideally this value should be a unique identifier, like a hostname). The Kafka output requires either PKCS#12 containers ❸ or JKS keystores ❺. You must specify the container formats ❹ ❻. Finally, we publish data into the Kafka cluster dynamically based on the value in `@metadata.beat` ❼.

Subscribing

Let's use the Kafka input for Logstash also covered in Chapter 8. When Logstash consumes events from Kafka, Logstash places all received event data in the `event.original` field. Because Beats data was originally JSON, the structured data appears as a single large, escaped string. We need a JSON parser to expand the string into its original key-value format.

The following configuration subscribes to Kafka topics and parses JSON data if the event came from a Beats topic:

```
input {
    kafka {
        id => "kafka-input"
        bootstrap_servers => "kafka01.local:9094,kafka02.local:9094"
    ❶ group_id => "logstash"
        security_protocol => "SSL"
    ❷ ssl_endpoint_identification_algorithm => "https"
        ssl_keystore_location => "/etc/ssl/elastic/wildcard.local.flex.pkcs12"
        ssl_keystore_password => "abcd1234"
        ssl_keystore_type => "PKCS12"
        ssl_key_password => "abcd1234"
        ssl_truststore_location => "/etc/ssl/elastic/truststore.jks"
        ssl_truststore_password => "abcd1234"
        ssl_truststore_type => "jks"
    ❸ topics => ["filebeat", "winlogbeat", "rsyslog"]
    ❹ decorate_events => "extended"
    }
}

filter {
  ❺ if [@metadata][kafka][topic] =~ /(?i)beat$/ {
        json {
            id => "json_parse_kafka_eo"
            source => "[event][original]"
        }
    }
```

```
❻ if [event][original] == [message] {
      mutate {
          remove_field => [ "[event][original]" ]
      }
   }
}

output {
    stdout { codec => rubydebug { metadata => true } }
}
```

First, we add this Logstash application to the logstash consumer group ❶.
We define HTTPS as the protocol to use to identify endpoints ❷, which
means Logstash verifies the Kafka hostnames in the server's certificates.

After the TLS settings, we list topics in an array ❸. The decorate_events
option ❹ adds Kafka metadata fields to the event, including the field
@metadata.kafka.topic that we'll use in the first filter. We check that field
using regular expressions, and if it loosely matches a Beats program, the
JSON parser ❺ runs, which should expand the original Beats fields into
the event. We also check that event.original matches the message field ❻,
which is the behavior expected of Beats and Logstash, due to various parser
needs; if they match, we remove event.original to save bytes later in storage.

Kafka Pipeline Design Considerations

In a data pipeline involving Kafka, your enrichment processes are flexible
during the design stage but become somewhat more rigid once your cluster
becomes operational. Let's discuss the pros and cons of various Logstash
placements to support a Kafka deployment.

Placing Logstash *before* Kafka allows you to parse, clean, and enrich
data before it enters Kafka. It also ensures that consumer messages entering Kafka are JSON and allows your Kafka nodes' firewall rules to accept
publisher connections from the Logstash hosts only. The variety of input
modules available to Logstash might be easier for an organization to use
instead of other Kafka connectors or installing client-side modules. This
design may place a heavy burden on Logstash to receive all enterprise data,
however, and likely necessitates running a load balancer in front of your
Logstash cluster.

Placing Logstash *after* Kafka can streamline your security consumer
planning by focusing only on messages going into the SIEM. It also allows
message enrichment post-Kafka, so the security team only needs to focus
on its requirements when enriching, or "adding bytes," to messages. This
design lets Kafka handle load balancing but requires the cluster to be
reachable by all hosts that need to send or receive data. Consumers also
have access to raw, original messages, which may be preferable for some
compliance-based policies. You might prefer this placement when a SIEM
is just one of the many Kafka consumers and the organization has already
widely implemented Kafka pipelines.

Enrichment in the middle lets Logstash, Filebeat, or other tools shuttle data between topics. In this middle placement, Logstash consumes topics, applies various transformations and enrichments, and then writes to any number of post-transformation topics. This may be beneficial for security analytics, preprocessing, or enrichments that require coalescing large amounts of inflight data to one actionable data stream. It also allows consumers to subscribe to raw messages, transformed messages, or both, depending on compliance regulations. This placement requires creating more topics; however, Kafka's data retention policies can shorten unprocessed topics to keep only days' or hours' worth of messages, depending on your risk appetite.

You may use all or none of these placement ideas. Weigh the pros and cons of each setup carefully; it's easier to ask your system administrators to make a change once rather than flip-flop on designs.

SAVING CONFIGURATIONS WITH GIT

In your local Git repository, make a directory for your Kafka files, then copy your *server.properties* and *client.properties* configurations into it, along with any command notes you may have created, and remove any sensitive credentials. Track the files with `git add . && git status`. Commit the new files using `git commit -am "added Kafka files"`. Finally, use `git push` to send the files to your remote repository.

Summary

Apache Kafka is a powerful tool for moving data across the enterprise. It creates one central location to which your organization can send streaming data and allows multiple consumers to access the data simultaneously. Tools you've used previously, such as Rsyslog and Logstash, integrate seamlessly as producers, consumers, or both at the same time.

In this chapter, you created your own Kafka cluster. You used TLS connections to send and receive data from the cluster management tools included with Kafka. You also used Rsyslog, Filebeat, and Logstash to send Kafka real events and receive events in return. Finally, you stored your Kafka configurations using Git.

Next, we'll cover Ansible, an automation tool for deploying software, updates, or system changes across multiple servers at once.

11

AUTOMATING TOOL CONFIGURATIONS

By automating the installation, updating, and maintenance of your tools, you can save time, prevent human error, and ensure that a system's configuration meets your requirements. This chapter covers Ansible, a tool that can script software deployments, run updates, transfer files, and more. It automates many IT operations that would otherwise require hands-on-keyboard interaction or the creation of unique configuration files. In the following sections, you'll install Ansible and explore its syntax. In the next chapter, you'll use it to automate many of the actions you performed throughout this book.

Working with Ansible

Ansible is a Python-based tool that automates system administration tasks. It uses modules that each perform a specific action, like creating a directory, downloading compressed file packages, managing users, and more. Using Secure Shell, it can connect to and administer hundreds of servers at a time.

Many of Ansible's modules are *idempotent*, meaning they achieve the same outcome no matter the number of times they're executed. Modules that support idempotency achieve a state once executed, and any additional executions of the module check for this desired state, then skip any actions that would alter it.

One example of an idempotent task is copying a local file to remote hosts; if the file is already present on the host and matches the local version, Ansible won't copy it across the network multiple times. Similarly, if a given package is installed on a system, Ansible won't reinstall it. Idempotency allows Ansible to enforce standard configuration without causing chaos on the network by accidentally running an installation command multiple times.

With few exceptions, you could automate every process covered so far in this book with Ansible. If you need to deploy Filebeat or Elastic Agent on dozens, or even hundreds, of hosts reachable over SSH, Ansible can do so. Ansible can simplify pulling multiple Git repositories, deleting departed employees' SSH keys from dozens of servers, or installing packages on a lab virtual machine.

Ansible can also generate dynamic text files using *Jinja templating*, which uses placeholder strings in a template file that you can fill with variable values that you specify. A Jinja template might look like this: "Hello my name is {{ first_name }}." A script with a first_name variable assigned the value James could use the template to create the string "Hello my name is James."

Jinja templating is useful for creating multiple versions of a tool's configuration. For example, in Chapter 10, you manually created several copies of Kafka's *server.properties* file, altering the host-specific lines to apply to each virtual machine on which Kafka was running. Ansible can use a single standard Jinja template to generate unique copies of the file for each Kafka server. We'll cover Jinja templates later in this chapter.

Inventories

Ansible *inventories* are files that store IP addresses, hostnames, ports, and other variables that identify all of the hosts Ansible should connect to when executing a task or playbook. Ansible supports two inventory formats: YAML and flat, INI-style text files. You'll create inventories using both layouts shortly, and you'll use YAML inventories in this chapter.

Commands, Playbooks, and Roles

Ansible modules perform one or more specific tasks, such as copying files, managing services, or updating access lists. You may execute one task at a time using ad hoc commands or perform a collection of tasks in sequence using a *playbook*. Playbooks execute one or more tasks at a time during a run, or *play*. You may also use playbooks to run multiple other playbooks at once.

To further abstract these components, you could use *roles*, or reusable, grouped bundles of variables, tasks, playbooks, and other items. We won't use roles in this chapter, but you could use the content you'll create in this chapter to make your own roles. You can find useful examples in the "Roles" section of the Ansible documentation.

Gathering System Facts

When Ansible connects to a remote host, it doesn't automatically execute module code. First, it collects facts about a system, such as the operating system build, network information, mounted volume names, AppArmor and SELinux status, and more. This allows you to build conditions into your playbooks, such as running Uncomplicated Firewall commands if the operating system is Ubuntu or Firewalld if the system is RHEL. Importantly, facts allow Ansible's modules to determine if their success is even feasible on a system; if there's no disk space and you're about to transfer several gigabytes of data, Ansible should warn you. You can choose to disable fact gathering if you don't need it.

Templates

Ansible can use any number of variables stored in a dedicated file, encrypted vault, inventory, task, or playbook, as well as variables issued on the command line. *Templates* are individual files to which Ansible dynamically adds variables during runtime for each host or variable condition. For example, you might use a single template for Kafka's main configuration files to generate all the individual brokers' settings.

Temporary Files

Ansible pushes temporary Python files to each host for every task it executes, including ad hoc commands and playbook tasks. The issuing workstation sends these files to the remote hosts over SSH, and the remote hosts execute them. These temporary files are typically placed in the user's *~/.ansible/tmp* directory or in */tmp* and then a randomly generated subdirectory.

The temporary filenames generally begin with *AnsiballZ* and end with the Ansible module currently executing, such as *AnsiballZ_user.py* or *AnsiballZ_command.py*. They contain a large base64-encoded ZIP file within each deployed script, which the temporary script extracts, revealing all the code necessary to execute on the remote system. The temporary files self-delete once complete.

SSH Requirements

Ansible requires no TLS setup, as it relies on SSH, with some support for WinRM and other remote access protocols. Ensure that any host you wish to connect to, including the workstation running Ansible, is accessible using the SSH keys you created in Chapter 2. (You could use a username and password instead, but you'd have to specify them every time you make a remote connection.)

To follow along with this chapter, make sure your SSH agent is running and has your private key loaded; otherwise, Ansible will prompt you for your private key for each system you access. Also ensure that you have access to superuser accounts on your various servers. Ideally, you would use the same username or service account on all systems, although both Ansible and SSH allow you to specify different users for each system.

Some Ansible resources suggest giving this user password-less sudo access, or even not requiring sudo at all, to modify system files; follow your organization's policies on superuser access privileges. To err on the side of caution, you should avoid granting password-less superuser access; the commands in this chapter will prompt you for your remote sudo passwords.

Installation

Begin by running the following command to create the directories you'll use for files and any notes from this chapter:

```
$ mkdir -p ~/ansible/{files,logs,output,tasks,templates,vars}
```

At the end of this chapter, you'll push any files you created to your remote Git repository for safekeeping. Alternatively, create these directories and any chapter-related files in your local Git repository and just work from there. This way, you can commit your notes and files as you work through the chapter.

Ansible is available via `apt` and `dnf` and as a package from the PyPi Python package repository. Two main versions of Ansible are available: plain Ansible and Ansible Core. Ansible includes built-in standard packages, such as those for copying files and adding users, but also highly rated community modules that do things like modify firewall rules or generate X.509 certificates. Ansible Core includes only the built-in modules.

On Ubuntu and Debian, use `apt` to install the full Ansible package:

```
$ sudo apt install ansible
```

On Red Hat Enterprise Linux, CentOS, and Rocky Linux, substitute `dnf` for `apt` and install `ansible-core`, but note you won't have access to community features. If you want to install Ansible using Python (this may be a better idea on RHEL), which also allows you to import its code in other scripts, use Python 3's `pip` module:

```
$ python3 -m pip install --user ansible
```

This `pip` command should install Ansible for the current user only. If you want to make it available to all users on the system, omit the `--user` argument and run the command with `sudo`. Next, let's cover the main parts of Ansible.

Creating Inventories

Let's create an Ansible inventory for an example Kafka cluster. The following snippet defines a group of hosts called `kafka`, numbered `01` to `03`. In your *~/ansible* directory or local repository, add the following lines to a new file named *inventory.conf*:

```
[kafka]
kafka01 ansible_host=192.168.8.30 broker_id=211
kafka02 ansible_host=192.168.8.31 broker_id=212
kafka03 ansible_host=192.168.8.32 broker_id=213
```

Note this example references three Kafka nodes; if you made fewer than that in Chapter 10 or want to use other servers or IP addresses altogether, alter the entries accordingly. Inventories place the group name inside square brackets and then list the hosts. The `ansible_host` variable indicates the IP addresses Ansible should connect to, similar to the `Hostname` statement in an SSH configuration file. Ansible uses the specified hostnames to target assets for particular plays.

The previous inventory snippet is in the INI format, but Ansible comes with a tool to convert INI inventories to YAML. Run the following command to generate a YAML inventory from the text files you just created:

```
$ ansible-inventory -i inventory.conf --list --yaml | tee inventory.yml
```

You should see the following YAML output both on your terminal and inside the new *inventory.yml* file that the tee command created:

```
all:
  children:
    kafka:
      hosts:
        kafka01:
          ansible_host: 192.168.8.30
          broker_id: 211
        kafka02:
          ansible_host: 192.168.8.31
          broker_id: 212
        kafka03:
          ansible_host: 192.168.8.32
          broker_id: 213
```

YAML formatting relies on whitespace and indentation to communicate relationships; this example uses two spaces at each new indentation level, as will the following examples. We'll use YAML-formatted inventories throughout the rest of the chapter.

In the inventory we just created, let's add variables we'll use shortly to demonstrate loops. Between `ansible_host` and `broker_id`, add `basename` and `hostname` values for each host, as shown here for `kafka01`:

```
--snip--
      kafka01:
        ansible_host: 192.168.8.30
        basename: kafka01
        hostname: kafka01.local
        broker_id: 211
--snip--
```

These new variables are somewhat contrived and used primarily for the sake of example. However, they address potential issues with treating the inventory name as the actual machine hostname. Inventory names may not accurately reflect a machine's hostname, as they exist solely for your reference in the inventory files, and underlying network connections made by Ansible use IP addresses. For example, if you copy hostnames from Active Directory to create your inventory, those names should be accurate; by contrast, if you name your inventory hosts something ambiguous like *host1* or *server2*, you might not want to add those names to critical configuration files.

In the previous snippet, because each member of the hosts tier has a short name, such as `kafka01`, it's tempting to just use that term combined with a domain name variable, such as `.local`, when writing to templated configurations. If you instead created your inventory using true fully qualified domain names for the Ansible hosts, you could just use the `inventory_hostname` special variable (which holds something like `kafka01.local`) to write the FQDN wherever it's needed, such as adding it to a configuration file like */etc/hosts*.

If your inventory hosts are randomly named, silly, or ephemeral (for example, based on AWS instance IDs), you'll need to find other ways to reference the hostnames you need. You can gather these from the hosts, manually create them using variables, or query a Lightweight Directory Access Protocol (LDAP) tool for them. There is a wealth of information in the official Ansible documentation and elsewhere on the internet about creating dynamic inventories, but this topic is beyond the scope of this chapter.

Configuration Files

Ansible's configuration files expand its default behaviors, such as its SSH login options and error handling. The tool checks four locations for settings in a specific order: the environment variable `ANSIBLE_CONFIG`, a file named *ansible.cfg* in the current directory, a hidden file *~/.ansible.cfg* (note the dot before *ansible*) in your home directory, and a */etc/ansible/ansible.cfg* file added during installation, which should be empty by default.

Let's practice modifying Ansible's configuration. Say you're using an SSH configuration that defines the keys to use with various remote hosts but wish to instead use a password to log in. You can use a local configuration to modify Ansible's SSH settings. Create *ansible.cfg* in your local working Ansible directory and add the following lines to it:

```
[ssh_connection]
ssh_args = -F none -o PreferredAuthentications=password
```

The `-F none` option tells Ansible not to load a configuration, and the `PreferredAuthentications` option tells it to log in using a password, if the remote system allows it. If you don't want to make an entire SSH configuration file, the Ansible command line option `--ssh-common-args` lets you specify SSH options for ad hoc commands, which we'll cover shortly:

```
$ ansible --ssh-common-args "-F none -o PreferredAuthentications=password"...
```

SSH options defined in this way override the ones in *~/.ssh/config* as if you used them in a manual SSH connection. You can find in-depth descriptions of these SSH options at *https://linux.die.net/man/5/ssh_config*. To keep these features in your notes but disable them while running Ansible, comment the lines with a hash mark or rename the file to *ansible .cfg.disabled*.

Running Ad Hoc Commands

Ad hoc commands are single command lines that use one module at a time to perform one specific task. This might include copying a file to several hosts, updating system packages, or restarting services on a specific group of servers. Ad hoc commands are useful for making unexpected or minor changes to multiple servers at a time, performing routine maintenance, and running individual shell commands. In this section, we consider examples of common ad hoc commands.

Enabling Check Mode

Check mode lets you run simulations of any changes a command or playbook will make. This setting lets you test for unexpected behaviors or check whether errors occur when running a new or complicated command. Invoke check mode on the command line with `--check` or `-C`, or in a task with `check_mode: true`. There's also a `--diff` option, which lists all changes made in a before-and-after style output. Whether you're running ad hoc commands or large playbooks, check mode should be a regular part of your workflow to ensure you don't break anything on your network.

Distributing Files

The copy module copies a file from your Ansible workstation to the hosts listed in the inventory. We'll revisit the copy module throughout this chapter. In your *~/ansible* directory, create an empty text file named *CopyMe.txt*, then run the following command to transfer it to your remote hosts, changing the dest directory value as necessary:

```
$ touch CopyMe.txt
$ ansible all -i inventory.yml -m copy -a "src=CopyMe.txt dest=/home/j/"
```

The keyword all, called a *pattern* in Ansible's terminology, indicates that every host in the inventory should receive the file, but you could also specify an inventory group, such as kafka, or an individual host, like kafka01. The -m option specifies the module, copy, and -a includes module arguments in quotations. Success is indicated by "changed": true appearing in the command's output. You should see the following message meaning the transfer worked:

```
"changed": true,
"checksum": "da39a3ee5e6b4b0d3255bfef95601890afd80709",
"dest": "/home/j/CopyMe.txt",
--snip--
```

Ansible won't transfer the file again if you repeat the command unless the file's hash has changed, indicating that the file's content is different, such as if you added new text. Running the previous command again should show "changed": false:

```
"changed": false,
"checksum": "da39a3ee5e6b4b0d3255bfef95601890afd80709",
"dest": "/home/j/CopyMe.txt",
--snip--
```

The copy module also supports changing file ownership and access permissions, forcibly copying existing files, backing up remote files before being overwritten, and many more options. Here is an example that uses these options:

```
$ ansible all -i inventory.yml -m copy -a "src=records.txt dest=/home/jerry/
owner=jerry group=scta-bni mode=0640 force=true backup=true"
```

In this snippet, the new owner of the *records.txt* file is *jerry*, the group is *scta-bni*, and the access mode is 0640, meaning *jerry* can read and write to the file and *scta-bni* can only read the file. The force option copies the file to the remote host even if it's already present there, and backup stores a temporary copy of the original file, with the addition of a date and timestamp in the backup's filename. Next, let's discuss running commands on remote hosts.

Executing Commands

At first glance, Ansible's command and shell modules appear to do the same thing: run commands on remote systems. The modules have a minor difference, however; shell loads a new shell session, which lets commands pipe values to each other, whereas command uses Python's subprocess module to spawn processes directly and doesn't support piping.

The following command uses the command module to list the contents of the remote user's home directory, the default directory Ansible connects to when accessing a remote host. Note the presence of the *CopyMe.txt* file, which you just distributed using the copy module:

```
$ ansible all -i inventory.yml -m command -a "ls -lh"
--snip--
kafka01 | CHANGED | rc=0 >>
total 36K
-rw-r--r-- 1 j j    0 Feb 28 22:50 CopyMe.txt
drwxr-xr-x 2 j j 4.0K Jan  4  2040 Desktop
drwxr-xr-x 2 j j 4.0K Jan  4  2040 Documents
--snip--
```

In the previous command, the output CHANGED refers to the fact the command succeeded. (Had we done something other than list filenames, we likely would have altered the listed resources.)

In the following command, attempting to pipe the listing into a grep command fails because the underlying Python subprocess module's code doesn't support using pipes in this manner, instead interpreting the pipe character as a filename:

```
$ ansible all -i inventory.yml -m command -a "ls -lh | grep txt"
kafka01 | FAILED | rc=2 >>
Documents:
total 0ls: cannot access '|': No such file or directory
ls: cannot access 'grep': No such file or directory
```

The shell module properly interprets the pipe because it first loads a shell session and then passes the ls output through grep:

```
$ ansible all -i inventory.yml -m shell -a "ls -lh | grep txt"
kafka01 | CHANGED | rc=0 >>
-rw-rw-r-- 1 j j 4.0K Jan  2 2040 CopyMe.txt
```

If you have a custom use case that existing modules don't support, the command and shell modules may allow you to perform those activities on multiple hosts at once. The commands they run aren't idempotent, however, so it's best to use Ansible's dedicated modules when possible.

Updating Packages

When a new security advisory or alert appears in the news, a patching frenzy occurs. System administrators and service owners must dive into the patch status of every asset for which they're responsible and update out-of-date software immediately.

Ansible has modules dedicated to package managers such as Apt and RPM, but it also includes the package module, which runs either Apt or RPM behind the scenes as needed. Package names often differ between package managers, so we'll use the apt module in the subsequent examples.

The following command updates the local apt cache listing of available packages and doesn't upgrade or install anything:

```
$ ansible all --become --ask-become-pass -i inventory.yml -m apt
-a "update_cache=true"
```

The --become argument makes Ansible a superuser, using sudo by default to elevate privileges. The argument --ask-become pass means Ansible should prompt for the remote account's sudo password.

The next command updates the cache and installs Nmap; there is an implied argument, state=present, meaning Ansible should install the tool if it's not already present:

```
$ ansible all --become --ask-become-pass -i inventory.yml -m apt
-a "update_cache=true name=nmap"
```

The explicit argument state=absent uninstalls Nmap:

```
$ ansible all --become --ask-become-pass -i inventory.yml -m apt
-a "name=nmap state=absent"
```

The apt module's name argument supports wildcards. When used while changing state to latest, these can direct Ansible to install all available upgrades:

```
$ ansible all --become --ask-become-pass -i inventory.yml -m apt
-a "update_cache=true name='*' state=latest"
```

You'll find the state keywords present, absent, and latest used throughout Ansible's module library. They're generally synonymous with *install* or *add*, *uninstall* or *remove*, and *update* or *upgrade*, respectively, when managing packages and files.

Managing Services

Ansible's systemd_service module supports common service actions like starting and restarting, stopping, reloading, enabling, and disabling systemd services. The following command restarts the Rsyslog service, which you must do every time you update its configurations:

```
$ ansible all --become --ask-become-pass -i inventory.yml -m systemd_service
-a "name=rsyslog state=restarted"
```

This module is useful for handling service restarts across groups of servers. You can install updates and restart services on any number of servers in a controlled manner by grouping hosts in your inventory.

Rebooting Servers

Ansible has a built-in module for rebooting hosts and a community-created module for shutting them down. As when running service restarts, grouping your hosts in your inventory can make it easier to reliably manage rolling server restarts with ad hoc commands or playbooks.

The following command reboots the kafka group in your inventory. By default, Ansible will check a server's availability for 10 minutes to make sure the reboot worked:

```
$ ansible kafka --become --ask-become-pass -i inventory.yml -m reboot
```

Similarly, the following command powers off the group:

```
$ ansible kafka --become --ask-become-pass -i inventory.yml -m
community.general.shutdown -a "delay=60"
```

If you choose to run the shutdown module without arguments, the server will immediately begin to safely power down.

Playbooks for Task Execution

Now that you've explored some of Ansible's modules with ad hoc commands, let's make a playbook to execute multiple tasks in order. We'll create the user *kafka* on all hosts in the inventory. In a text editor, add the following line to *vars/vars.yml*, a file containing variables, to specify the new username:

```
user: kafka
```

Next, let's create a *vault*, or encrypted file containing secrets, such as passwords or API keys. The ansible-vault command opens the default system text editor, likely vi. You'll be prompted for a password before entering the text editor:

```
$ ansible-vault create vars/vault.yml
```

If you'd like to change the text editor used, you can specify it using the export command:

```
$ export EDITOR=/usr/bin/nano
```

You can add the export command to *~/.profile* (note the period after the slash) so it's loaded every time you start a new shell session.

Once you've created the vault, in a separate terminal, create a SHA-512 hash for the password *abcd1234*. Ansible will use this hash to safely provide the user's password to the remote systems, without compromising its actual value. Ansible requires the `passlib` Python module for creating hashes, so let's install it and then use the module to generate the password's hash:

```
$ python3 -m pip install passlib
$ python3 -c "from passlib.hash import sha512_crypt; import getpass;
print(sha512_crypt.using(rounds=5000).hash(getpass.getpass()))"
Password:
$6$8Jn2A6bMtynSS...
```

In your vault file, open in your other terminal, add the hash to the password variable in quotation marks. Note that I've truncated the value here for brevity:

```
user_password: "$6$8Jn2A6bMtynSS..."
```

If you need to add further entries to this vault, substitute `edit` for `create` in the previous command. Shortly, we'll cover a dynamic way to enter the user's password as the playbook runs and hash the password before connecting to the remote systems.

Create the *playbook_newuser.yml* playbook file and add the following lines:

```
❶ - hosts: all
    become: yes
❷ gather_facts: yes
❸ vars_files:
    - vars/vars.yml
    - vars/vault.yml

❹ tasks:
    ❺ - name: Create User and Set Password
        ansible.builtin.user:
        ❻ name: "{{ user }}"
        ❼ password: "{{ user_password }}"
          home: "/home/{{ user }}"
          shell: /bin/bash
```

The playbook opens by declaring the inventory hosts it uses (in this case, all of them) ❶, then uses `become: yes` to invoke sudo. Playbooks gather facts from hosts by default, but we specify the option here to demonstrate you can disable the setting if you desire by changing yes to no ❷, which speeds up playbook execution.

Next, we specify the relative locations of the variable and vault files ❸ containing the new user's name and password, respectively. The tasks block contains the actions the playbook should perform ❹. Each task begins with a name and then names the module, in this case user, followed by its settings ❺. The second name parameter uses Jinja templating to load the user variable ❻, and the password parameter uses the password's SHA-512 hash ❼ when providing the password to the remote system.

NOTE *You can reference modules by their shorthand notation, such as by using copy instead of ansible.builtin.copy, in both ad hoc commands and playbooks. Ansible documentation recommends using the module's full name, however, to avoid naming conflicts with community modules.*

Run the playbook using the following command:

```
$ ansible-playbook --ask-become-pass --ask-vault-pass -i inventory.yml playbook_newuser.yml
```

Ansible should prompt you for the become (sudo) password and the vault password, *abcd1234*. It should then gather facts and create the *kafka* user. The scrolling output should list each affected host as changed, with a final status of ok=2 indicating that both fact gathering and user creation tasks succeeded. With that command, you've just created a new user on multiple hosts at once. If needed, the user module can also update the user's password, lock the account, or delete it altogether.

If you wish to specify the password when the playbook runs instead of adding its hash to the vault, change the beginning of the playbook to the following lines:

```
- hosts: all
  become: yes
  gather_facts: no
❶ vars_files:
    - vars/vars.yml
❷ vars_prompt:
    - name: "user_password"
      prompt: "Enter a password for the new user"
❸     private: yes
      encrypt: sha512_crypt
      confirm: yes
      salt_size: 7
```

Notice that the vault is no longer present ❶ and that there's a new heading, vars_prompt ❷. The name parameter sets the variable's name to user_password, and you define a prompt that appears before entering the new password. Setting private to yes ❸ means the typed password will be invisible; setting it to no displays the password on screen. We want a SHA-512 hash, salted to increase hash complexity, and a prompt to confirm the password before continuing.

Reusable Tasks

Task files are YAML files that contain one or more Ansible tasks. They're intended to be playbook agnostic and reusable; playbooks can import task files and run them as if they were part of the playbook file itself. These files let you write, store, and update a useful task once, instead of re-creating the same task for any new playbooks.

Create the directory *~/ansible/tasks* or make a folder in your repository to store the task files you'll make throughout the remainder of this chapter. Task files contain a task just as they would appear in a playbook, except the first line of the task has no indentation. Subsequent lines should be indented as necessary using two spaces. In the previous section, the user module's opening hyphen (-) started four spaces from the left, nested underneath tasks.

Create a new file, *tasks/newuser.yml*, and add the following lines:

```
- name: Create User and Set Password
  ansible.builtin.user:
    name: "{{ user }}"
    password: "{{ user_password }}"
    home: "/home/{{ user }}"
    shell: /bin/bash
```

Playbooks use the import_tasks module to import tasks from external files. The following code shows the previous *playbook_newuser.yml*, updated to read the task file:

```
- hosts: all
  become: yes
  gather_facts: yes
  vars_files:
    - vars/vars.yml
    - vars/vault.yml

  tasks:
    - name: Create User and Set Password
      ansible.builtin.include_tasks:
        file: tasks/newuser.yml
```

We can use the same command as before to run this playbook, but we'll take the opportunity to demonstrate the use of short options instead of long ones:

```
$ ansible-playbook -J -K -i inventory.yml playbook_newuser.yml
```

The -J option is short for --ask-vault-password, and -K is short for --ask-become-pass, which asks for your sudo password. If you don't want to include become: yes in your playbook, you can use -b or --become on the command line. As with most command line programs, you may also group the options together, like this: -Jkbi.

Delegating Tasks

Ansible typically executes tasks on remote hosts specified in the inventory. You may also delegate execution to a specific host if desired and make the action run only once. The following task file snippet would run the task only on your local workstation and only one time:

```
- name: Perform Some Task
  delegate_to: localhost
  run_once: true
--snip--
```

Tasks like querying APIs, running commands affecting a server cluster, or writing results to a file are good candidates for delegating tasks and running them one time. For example, consider creating Kafka topics, which you did in Chapter 10; you needed to create topics only once, and trying to do so multiple times would have returned errors. In that case, you could pick just one of your Kafka nodes and then delegate the topic-creation commands.

Performing Tasks Locally

Ansible includes the shorthand syntax local_action for delegating a task to *localhost*. The following task uses the copy module as a one-liner inside the local_action task to save facts for each host to a local file. Note that the ansible_host variable references the IP address of the host listed in the inventory, not its hostname:

```
- name: Save Facts
  local_action: copy content="{{ ansible_facts }}" dest="logs/facts_{{ ansible_host }}.json"
```

You can rewrite the same task to specify the module parameter, as well as the parameters for that module to use:

```
- name: Save Distribution
  local_action:
    module: copy
    content: "{{ ansible_facts['distribution'] }}"
    dest: "logs/distribution_{{ ansible_host }}.json"
```

If you need to save variables, facts, or module output, you could store it locally using this method. You should see the following output if you run this local task in a playbook:

```
-rw-rw-r-- 1 j j  6 Jan 14 12:15 distribution_192.168.8.130.json
-rw-rw-r-- 1 j j  6 Jan 14 12:15 distribution_192.168.8.132.json
-rw-rw-r-- 1 j j 24K Jan 14 12:14 facts_192.168.1.30.json
-rw-rw-r-- 1 j j 23K Jan 14 12:14 facts_192.168.1.31.json
--snip--
```

Next, let's write blocks of text to files.

Writing Dynamic Data to Files

Throughout this book, we've manually added new entries to the */etc/hosts* file on multiple servers and appended lines to various configuration files. Let's now use Ansible loops and the `blockinfile` module to do the same thing with less risk of human error. In this section, we'll use Jinja templating variables to write dynamic data to files.

Modifying hosts Files

We've previously used the */etc/hosts* file to record hostname resolution information for IP addresses. Generally, it's best to use a DNS server instead of relying on keeping each server's */etc/hosts* files in sync. If you don't have a DNS server, however, you can use Ansible to enforce configurations based on inventory files and variables. First, add the domain *.local* to *vars/vars.yml* so the task can reference it:

```
domain: .local
```

Create the task file, *tasks/etchosts-all.yml*, and add the following lines to it:

```
- name: Add All Hosts to /etc/hosts
  blockinfile:
    path: /etc/hosts
    block: |
❶ {% for item in groups['all'] %}
    {{ hostvars[item].ansible_host }}    {{ hostvars[item].hostname }}
❷ {% endfor %}
    {% for item in groups['all'] %}
    {{ hostvars[item].ansible_host }}    {{ hostvars[item].basename }}
    {% endfor %}
```

Recall that your inventory has `basename` and `hostname` variables representing short names and FQDNs, respectively. Because we want to add both values to the hosts file, we'll need two loops.

We first begin a Jinja for loop over every host's dictionary of variables in the inventory group `all` ❶. We then write a Jinja template to specify the IP address and hostname to add to the file. Jinja's syntax begins and ends blocks with percent signs (%) nested between curly brackets ({}). The Jinja statement {% endfor %} terminates both for loops ❷.

The `hostvars` dictionary object contains all variables and facts associated with the current host, and `ansible_host` is the IP address listed in the inventory for the current inventory entry. The second loop also adds every host's IP address and its `basename` variable to */etc/hosts*.

Note that there are simpler ways to achieve the same result than referencing the `hostname` and `basename` variables for each host. The special Ansible variable `inventory_hostname` holds the name you gave to each host in the inventory, such as `kafka01` in the inventory configured previously. A similar variable, `inventory_hostname_short`, captures everything before the first period in an FQDN. In other words, if you named each inventory host using its FQDN, such as `kafka01.local`, `inventory_hostname_short` would return `kafka01`. Alternatively, you could use gathered facts to reference the machine's hostname, write them all to a file, then circle back with another task or playbook to insert the values in */etc/hosts* and a local log.

Inventories may contain dozens or hundreds of hosts, and you may not want to add all of them to every */etc/hosts* file. If you want to add hosts in the current play only, such as Kafka brokers but not Rsyslog servers, use `ansible_play_batch` instead of `groups['all']` in the for loop. You could also use different patterns to target different groups of servers, such as by specifying `kafka` instead of `all` in an ad hoc command. As an alternative to this process, use a DNS server.

Automatically Generating Encryption Keys

In Chapter 6, you generated random, 32-character encryption keys for Kibana to safeguard its internal objects and session data. Instead of using `command` or `shell` modules to execute the key generation command, let's use `blockinfile` to generate output text and the Jinja `lookup` function to create random strings. Create a new task file, *tasks/kibana-encryption-keys.yml*, and add the following to it:

```
- name: Generate and Append Kibana Encryption Keys to kibana.yml
  run_once: true
  blockinfile:
    state: present
    path: /etc/kibana/kibana.yml
    block: |
      xpack.encryptedSavedObjects.encryptionKey: "{{ lookup('password' ,'/dev/null chars=
hexdigits length=32') }}" ❶
      xpack.reporting.encryptionKey: "{{ lookup('password' ,'/dev/null chars=hexdigits
length=32') }}"
      xpack.security.encryptionKey: "{{ lookup('password' ,'/dev/null chars=hexdigits
length=32') }}"
```

Please note that each key generation function should appear on a single line; we've broken them here due to space constraints.

Jinja includes many built-in functions, including a password generator. To make use of it, each of the encryption keys runs the `lookup` function inside of a Jinja variable ❶ with the first parameter set to `password`. Specifying */dev/null* means the function won't log the password anywhere, as that path doesn't keep any data sent to it. The passwords are all mixed-case `hexdigits`, and the whole string is limited to 32 characters, the same length as the keys generated by Kibana's key generator. This task runs once, as you need to generate encryption keys only once for Kibana.

If you run this task in a playbook, the following snippet should appear at the end of */etc/kibana/kibana.yml*:

```
# BEGIN ANSIBLE MANAGED BLOCK
xpack.encryptedSavedObjects.encryptionKey: "bB0139b17Bb899E6F57da93dC855aa16"
xpack.reporting.encryptionKey: "5fF652D1eecF247e6ddeD42dadCAdA8A"
xpack.security.encryptionKey: "9bfAfCaFCe1B19CB93cf3cDE7E9DEbAC"
# END ANSIBLE MANAGED BLOCK
```

Notice the lines of text containing BEGIN and END surrounding the new keys, called *markers*. Ansible uses markers to identify where to place the text created by the blockinfile module. It checks for the presence of these markers and overwrites the contents between them with the most recent blockinfile module executed, or adds the text to end of a file if no markers are present. You can change or disable the marker text or use markers to add custom comments to your files.

Appending Text

When the blockinfile module identifies markers in a file, it overwrites everything between the markers, even when executing tasks in the same playbook. This means that if you use blockinfile to write text to a log, you'll get the output of the most recent execution only, not an aggregated result.

You can remove markers by setting them to empty quotes, which tricks Ansible into appending text:

```
- name: Add All Hosts to /etc/hosts
  blockinfile:
❶ marker: ""
    path: /etc/hosts
    block: |
      {% for item in groups['all'] %}
--snip--
```

If you were to run this task multiple times, the empty marker ❶ parameter would let blockinfile append the hosts to */etc/hosts* multiple times. In Chapter 12, we'll explore this concept further to write output logs.

SAVING CONFIGURATIONS WITH GIT

If you're not already working out of a Git repository, copy your Ansible directory to your local repository. Modify or create a new *.gitignore* file as well to prevent pushing your vault to the remote repository, if desired. Track new changes with **git add .**, then commit your changes with **git commit -am "added Ansible files"**. Finally, use **git push** to send the changes to your remote repository. As you work from your local repository and add new tasks you find useful, remember to push them to the remote repository.

Summary

Ansible is useful for automating tool deployments; managing configurations; transferring, downloading, and creating files; and performing system administrator tasks. In this chapter, you used Ansible to install updates, add a new user, write variables and dynamic strings to a file, and more. Ansible allows you to deploy your entire data logging infrastructure in minutes, as opposed to manually in hours, days, or weeks.

Next, you'll use Ansible to update firewall rules, download files from the internet, create TLS keys and signed certificates, and explore new modules. We'll cover automating activities from earlier in this book and introduce several new Ansible features.

12

ANSIBLE TASKS AND PLAYBOOKS

Ansible playbooks enable you to automate the multistep installation instructions you've performed while following along with this book. In this chapter, you'll update firewall rules, distribute and extract compressed files, download files from the internet, create dynamic files based on templates, and more. You'll also implement the TLS infrastructure you created in Chapter 2 by using Ansible tasks and write custom logs based on module output.

Allowing Firewall Traffic

Ansible has several firewall modules, including community-created ones for Firewalld and Uncomplicated Firewall. You could use these to easily deploy firewall changes across your network, ensuring that all devices provide the same level of access regardless of the operating systems they're running.

Before taking any other firewall actions, it's important to avoid locking yourself out of Secure Shell by allowing traffic on TCP port 22. Without SSH access, neither you nor Ansible will be able to reach remote hosts. In a datacenter or business environment, you may even need to visit the server in person to allow access again.

The following tasks allow TCP traffic on port 22 for RHEL, which uses Firewalld, and Ubuntu, which uses UFW. Save this task as *tasks/firewall -allow-ssh.yml*:

```
- name: Open Port 22/TCP
  ansible.posix.firewalld: ❶
    state: enabled
    port: 22/tcp
    permanent: true
    immediate: true
  when: ❷
    ansible_facts['distribution'] == "RedHat" or ansible_facts['distribution'] ==
    "Rocky" or ansible_facts['distribution'] == "CentOS"

- name: Open Port 22/TCP
  community.general.ufw: ❸
    rule: allow
    port: 22
    proto: tcp
  when: ❹
    ansible_facts['distribution'] == "Ubuntu"

- name: Enabled FirewallD
  ansible.builtin.systemd: ❺
    state: restarted
    daemon_reload: true
    name: firewalld
  when:
    ansible_facts['distribution'] == "RedHat" or ansible_facts['distribution'] ==
    "Rocky" or ansible_facts['distribution'] == "CentOS"

- name: Enable UFW
  #command: ufw enable
  community.general.ufw: ❻
    state: enabled
  when:
    ansible_facts['distribution'] == "Ubuntu"
```

The ansible.posix.firewalld module ❶ accepts the same parameters as the command line version of Firewalld. Note this module requires the python3-firewall package to work, which may be missing on older versions of RHEL. The when statement ❷ ensures that the firewalld module runs only on RHEL hosts. You can chain together or statements here if you also plan to also use CentOS or Rocky Linux, which use Firewalld as well. The community .general.ufw module ❸ similarly allows TCP port 22 traffic on hosts running Ubuntu ❹.

After adding the firewall rules, restart the Firewalld service using the systemd module ❺ on Red Hat and the ufw module ❻ on Ubuntu, as the UFW module contains a reloaded state option.

Automatic File Transfers

In Chapter 10, you downloaded a Kafka tarball package, then copied it to each of your remote systems. Using Ansible, you can automatically transfer files to hosts. We'll cover two methods of doing so: directly copying the files and forcing hosts to download the files themselves. We'll also use Ansible to retrieve files from a Git repository.

Distributing the Kafka Package

Let's use Ansible to automate the distribution of the Kafka tarball package and then extract the tarball remotely. To make this task as file agnostic as possible, we'll use variable substitution. Add the following to the same *vars/vars.yml* variable file you worked with in Chapter 10, where you set the user variable to kafka. Be sure to substitute version numbers for the placeholders italicized in the snippet:

```
user_group: kafka
filename: kafka_A.B-X.Y.Z.tgz
destination_directory: /opt/kafka
```

These variables define what user group will own the Kafka tarball, the name of the tarball file, and the directory in which to extract it. Next, create a file called *tasks/tarball.yml* and add the following two tasks:

```
- name: Copy Tarball to Remote
  copy:
❶ src: "files/{{ filename }}"
    dest: /tmp/
    owner: "{{ user }}"
❷ group: "{{ user_group }}"
    mode: 0700

- name: Extract Tarball
❸ unarchive:
❹ remote_src: true
    src: "/tmp/{{ filename }}"
❺ dest: "{{ destination_directory }}"
    owner: "{{ user }}"
    group: "{{ user_group }}"
    mode: 0700
❻ extra_opts:
    - --strip
    - 1
```

The first task copies the local file described in the variables file to the remote hosts' */tmp* directory ❶, setting ownership and access mode

permissions for the *kafka* user and group ❷. The task references the ansible
.builtin.copy module using the short name copy. Ansible recognizes these
shorter names so long as they don't conflict with community modules that
use the same short name.

To extract the tarball, we use the unarchive module ❸. We set remote_src to
true ❹ to tell the module to look for the file on the remote hosts, rather than
locally. The unarchive module uses GNU Tar to decompress and then extract
the tarball's contents into the output directory ❺. It also uses extended Tar
options to place the files directly into */opt/kafka* instead of in subdirectories
contained within the archive ❻.

Because we created these tasks using variables, we could download a
different file, change the permissions to set on it, or update the destination
directory by simply changing the variables or referencing entirely different
variable files; we don't need to alter or re-create the tasks themselves.

Downloading Files from the Internet

If you want each inventory host to download its own files instead of receiving them from a central workstation via copy, use the get_url module. The
following task makes each inventory host download the Kafka tarball to its
/tmp directory. Once again, be sure to substitute appropriate version numbers for the included placeholders:

```
- name: Fetch Web File
  get_url:
    url: https://downloads.apache.org/kafka/A.B.C/kafka_E.F-X.Y.Z.tgz
    dest: /tmp/
```

Making hosts download their own files is beneficial on networks that
have fast internet connections but slow site-to-site network tunnels. It's also
useful for fetching files shared internally on web servers.

Cloning Git Repositories

Ansible's git module pulls or clones repositories onto each remote host. To
practice using it, save the following as *tasks/git-clone.yml*:

```
- name: Git Clone
  ansible.builtin.git:
    repo: "https://github.com/swisskyrepo/PayloadsAllTheThings.git"
    dest: tools/PayloadsAllTheThings/
    force: true
```

Ansible connects to the remote user's home directory by default. This
git task will create a new directory, *~/tools/PayloadsAllTheThings/*, referenced
using a relative path that omits the *~/* portion. The module then clones the
repository into this new path and forcibly replaces any alterations or deleted
items.

Combined with the copy and get_url modules, the git module allows
you to rapidly provision or update analyst and operator workstations. The

git module is especially useful if you centrally manage configurations, as it makes pulling new, unscheduled configuration updates on dozens or even hundreds of hosts trivial. Similarly, if a tool becomes misconfigured, you can roll back the change by running this module.

Creating Kafka Configuration Templates

Chapter 11 discussed Jinja templates: files that use variable placeholders instead of concrete values, allowing Ansible to generate unique configurations for each host. For example, you generated multiple *client-ssl.properties* files for each node of your Kafka cluster in Chapter 10. The following code snippets use Ansible to automate the creation of these configuration files.

Add the following properties to *vars/vars.yml*. These are the same settings you manually defined previously:

```
ports:
  ssl: 9094
directories:
  kafka:
    certs: /opt/kafka/certs/
```

To reference nested YAML variable values, Ansible uses dotted notation. For example, the template will reference the variables you defined using ports.ssl and directories.kafka.certs, respectively.

In your *vars/vault.yml* vault file, add the following passwords, which you'll use to access the password-protected TLS private key:

```
$ ansible-vault edit vars/vault.yml
Vault password: abcd1234
--snip--
ssl_key_password: abcd1234
keystore_password: abcd1234
truststore_password: abcd1234
```

Within your *~/ansible* directory, make a new subdirectory named *templates*. Informally, the Jinja community uses the file extension *j2* for templates. Create a file called *templates/client-ssl.properties.j2* and add the following lines to it:

```
bootstrap.servers={% for node in groups['kafka'] %}{% if loop.last %}{{
hostvars[node].basename }}{{ domain }}:{{ ports.ssl }} ❶
  {% else %}{{ hostvars[node].basename }}{{ domain }}:{{ ports.ssl }},{% endif %}{% endfor %}
security.protocol=SSL
ssl.keystore.location="{{ directories.kafka.certs }}{{ ❷
hostvars[inventory_hostname].basename }}{{ domain }}.keystore.jks"
ssl.keystore.password="{{ keystore_password }}"
ssl.key.password="{{ ssl_key_password }}"
ssl.truststore.location="{{ directories.kafka.certs }}truststore.jks"
ssl.truststore.password="{{ truststore_password }}"
```

We use a `for` loop to create a comma-joined list of brokers ❶. It loops over all of the broker basename variables and dynamically adds the Kafka brokers to them. Note that we define the `if` statement on a single line (broken here due to space constraints) but insert a line break before the `else` statement, which is necessary due to Jinja templating quirks. Without this line break, the `security.protocol` line would join the `bootstrap.servers` line as the loop executes, appended to the last hostname, and prevent Kafka from starting.

The nested directory variable ❷ precedes the dynamic hostname variable to create keystore names. Note that this line shouldn't contain a line break either.

For the sake of this example, let's delegate the creation of these files to your local machine. Create a file called *tasks/kafka-configs.yml* and add the following lines to it:

```
- name: Generate and Copy client-ssl.properties to Remote
  delegate_to: localhost ❶
  template:
    src: templates/client-ssl.properties.j2
    dest: "output/client-ssl.properties_{{ hostvars[inventory_hostname].basename ❷
}}{{ domain }}"

- name: Remote Double Quotes in server.properties
  delegate_to: localhost
  replace: ❸
    path: "output/client-ssl.properties_{{ hostvars[inventory_hostname].basename ❹
}}{{ domain }}"
    regexp: '\"'
    replace: ""
```

This task runs on *localhost* ❶ and creates one *client-ssl.properties* file per inventory host, appending the hostname to the filename ❷. This naming convention will make the files easier to identify in your local *output* directory.

We also use the `replace` module ❸ to eliminate any double quotes introduced by the `template` module. Replacing double quotes is optional, but it's a best practice to clean up any unnecessary characters you wouldn't include if you were entering the configuration manually. We use the same variables as in the `template` module to reference the dynamic hostname path ❹.

The following file, *playbook_template.yml*, executes the Kafka task; note that it doesn't elevate its privileges via `become` and doesn't gather any facts because the example Kafka task runs locally:

```
- hosts: all
  become: no
  gather_facts: no
  vars_files:
    - vars/vars.yml
    - vars/vault.yml
```

```
tasks:
  - name: Generate File From Template
    ansible.builtin.include_tasks:
      file: tasks/kafka-configs.yml
```

Execute the playbook using the following command:

```
$ ansible-playbook -Ji inventory.yml playbook_template.yml
```

Once the task completes, list the *output* directory's contents. You should see configuration files created for each host:

```
$ ls -lh output/
total 16K
-rw-rw-r-- 1 j j 309 Dec  6 15:58 client-ssl.properties__kafka01.local
-rw-rw-r-- 1 j j 309 Dec  6 15:58 client-ssl.properties__kafka02.local
-rw-rw-r-- 1 j j 309 Dec  6 15:58 client-ssl.properties__kafka03.local
```

The contents of *client-ssl.properties__kafka01.local* should look like the following:

```
bootstrap.servers=kafka01.local:9094,kafka02.local:9094,kafka03.local:9094
security.protocol=SSL
ssl.keystore.location=/opt/kafka/certs/kafka01.local.keystore.jks
ssl.keystore.password=abcd1234
ssl.key.password=abcd1234
ssl.truststore.location=/opt/kafka/certs/truststore.jks
ssl.truststore.password=abcd1234
```

Because you delegated this task to *localhost*, the template module wrote the files to your local *output* directory. Without delegation, this module would generate the file and copy it to the remote host, saving you from having to also use the copy module to transfer the file and from needing to store a bunch of output files. If you're using this task without local delegation, be sure to remove the dynamic hostname in the output filename.

Installing GPG Keys

In Chapter 6, you manually installed GNU Privacy Guard keys so you could download Elastic applications using package managers. Let's create a reusable task that handles this installation for you.

Each GPG key has a unique ID, and Ansible's two GPG modules refer to this ID using different terms. The apt_key module uses the id parameter, whereas rpm_key calls it a fingerprint. In this section, we'll demonstrate the use of both modules. Add the following lines to *vars/vars.yml*:

```
gpg:
  fingerprint: 46095ACC8548582C1A2699A9D27D666CD88E42B4
  url: https://artifacts.elastic.co/GPG-KEY-elasticsearch
```

You can look up these values yourself in the Elastic documentation. Next, add the following Ansible instructions to *tasks/gpg-add.yml*:

```
- name: Print Package Manager
❶ debug:
    msg: "{{ ansible_facts['pkg_mgr'] }}"

# Apt
- name: Import Apt Signing Key from URL, If Fingerprint Not Present
❷ ansible.builtin.apt_key:
  ❸ id: 46095ACC8548582C1A2699A9D27D666CD88E42B4
    url: https://artifacts.elastic.co/GPG-KEY-elasticsearch
    state: present
  when:
    ansible_facts['pkg_mgr'] == "apt"

# RPM
- name: Import RPM Signing Key from URL, If Fingerprint Not Present
  ansible.builtin.rpm_key:
  ❹ fingerprint: 46095ACC8548582C1A2699A9D27D666CD88E42B4
    key: https://artifacts.elastic.co/GPG-KEY-elasticsearch
    state: present
  when:
    ansible_facts['pkg_mgr'] == "rpm" or ansible_facts['pkg_mgr'] == "dnf"
```

First, the debug task ❶ prints each host's package manager fact. We'll cover debug messages later in this chapter. Next, the apt_key module ❷ installs a key from a URL if the ID isn't present ❸. The rpm_key module then installs the same key ❹. Each task uses a when statement to control execution.

Responding to Prompts

Ansible's expect module detects prompts and provides answers to their questions. For example, it can respond to prompts asking you to change your password. In Chapter 6, you reset passwords for the *elastic* and *kibana_system* service accounts. The expect module can automate this manual process.

In *vars/vars.yml*, add the following line, which specifies an individual Elasticsearch server on which Ansible will run the command. You also installed this node in Chapter 6:

```
elastic_testnode: elasticsearch01.local
```

In *vars/vault.yml*, add the new password for the user *elastic*:

```
$ ansible-vault edit vars/vault.yml
elastic_user_password: abcd1234
```

Now create the *tasks/elasticsearch-user-passwords.yml* task file and add the following lines to it:

```
- name: Reset Password for User elastic
  delegate_to: "{{ elastic_testnode }}"
  run_once: true
  expect:
    command: /usr/share/elasticsearch/bin/elasticsearch-reset-password -u elastic ❶
    -i --url "https://{{ elastic_testnode }}:9200" -f
    responses: ❷
      (?i)Please confirm: y ❸
      (?i)Enter password: "{{ elastic_user_password }}"
      (?i)Re-enter password: "{{ elastic_user_password }}"
  when:
    ansible_facts['distribution'] == "Ubuntu"
```

The password reset command parameter ❶ is a single line, but we've wrapped it here due to space constraints. The responses parameter ❷ uses case-insensitive matching via (?i) to add values to the lines as Ansible reads them, entering y for the first prompt ❸ and variables for the rest. In other words, each prompt is missing the data you provide. By completing each prompt, Ansible can successfully interact with the *elasticsearch-reset-password* program.

Accessing APIs and Web Services

Ansible can connect to remote API services and process the response data. In this section, you'll use multiple tasks to connect to API endpoints so you can automate working with network services, whether inside or beyond your organization.

In Chapter 8, you made a small Python web server for testing API responses that runs on *https://localhost:5000*. The main file for that project is named *app.py*; navigate to its directory, then edit it to include the following functions, which we'll use to test the code in this section:

```
@app.route('/new_api_request')
def requestapipage():
    message = {"new_key":"b33fb33f"}
    return json.dumps(message)

@app.route('/validate', methods=['POST'])
def validateapipage():
    d = request.get_json(force=True)
    api_key = d["api_key"]
    return json.dumps({"status":"valid"})

@app.route('/api/fleet/outputs', methods=['POST'])
def fleetapipage():
    d = request.get_json(force=True)
    return json.dumps(d)
```

These functions create three API endpoints: one that returns a simulated API key, another that validates it, and a third that simulates sending an HTTP POST request to Kibana. Together, these functions mimic the process of requesting API keys from Elasticsearch and Kibana to configure a fleet server and then using the key to configure Elastic Agent. The `fleetapipage` function returns the JSON you send it, so you can visually check what the remote server receives. After you've added the functions, restart your web server by running the following command in the directory where it's stored:

```
$ ./app.py
```

Let's use a single playbook, *playbook_api_interaction.yml*, to demonstrate how these items interact with one another:

```
- hosts: localhost
  become: no
  gather_facts: no

  tasks:

    - name: Get Simulated API Key
    ❶ uri:
      ❷ validate_certs: false
        method: GET
        url: https://localhost:5000/new_api_request
        http_agent: "curl/7.81.0"
      ❸ return_content: true
    ❹ register: api_result_unparsed

    - name: Parse API Key from JSON, Set Fact
      set_fact:
      ❺ api_key: "{{ (api_result_unparsed.content|from_json).new_key }}"
        cacheable: yes

    - name: Show API Key
      debug:
        msg: "{{ ansible_facts['api_key'] }}"

    - name: Save Facts - API Key Only
      local_action: copy content="{{ ansible_facts['api_key'] }}"
                    dest="logs/api_{{ ansible_host }}"

    - name: Validate API Key
      uri:
      ❻ method: POST
        url: https://localhost:5000/validate
        validate_certs: false
      ❼ headers:
          Content-Type: application/json
        return_content: true
      ❽ body_format: json
```

```
❾ body: {"api_key":"{{ansible_facts['api_key']}}"}
   register: validate_response

 - name: Show Validation Status
   debug:
     var: (validate_response.content|from_json).status
```

We delegate this playbook to *localhost*, since we need only one API key, we'll run the tasks only once, and we won't collect any facts. The uri module ❶ makes an HTTP GET to the Flask web server, ignoring TLS validation issues ❷, as the web server uses its own self-signed certificate. We also set our own user agent string, since many web services ignore Python user agent strings. We must specify that we want the server to return content to us ❸. That content will be our new API key, and we save the results in a variable named api_key_unparsed ❹.

As the web server returns the API key in JSON, we perform a Jinja operation in parentheses to access the content attribute from the uri variable's registration. The set_fact module ❺ creates a variable we can access later in the playbook, named api_key. We parse the content string into JSON. Then, outside the parentheses, we extract the new_key attribute, which contains the API key value. The parentheses operation makes a dictionary object available, allowing us to call .new_key to access the key's value, b33fb33f.

After displaying the API and logging it to a file, another instance of the uri module sends a POST request ❻ to the web server. We also include the outgoing content type header ❼, require that Ansible save the HTTP response data, and specify outgoing data is in JSON format ❽. We include the API key, stored in a JSON object in the body parameter ❾ of the POST request. We save the response back using the variable validate_response. Finally, we use a debug task to display the API's validation status.

Run this playbook with the following command:

```
$ ansible-playbook playbook_api_interaction.yml
```

You should see requests like these in your Flask terminal:

```
127.0.0.1 - - [19/Feb/2040 22:35:56] "GET /new_api_request HTTP/1.1" 200 -
127.0.0.1 - - [19/Feb/2040 22:35:58] "POST /validate HTTP/1.1" 200 -
```

Ansible should show the following output:

```
--snip--
TASK [Show New Simulated API Key Parsed From JSON] ************************
ok: [localhost] => {
    "msg": "b33fb33f"
}

TASK [Save Facts - API Key] **********************************************
changed: [localhost]

TASK [Use API] ***********************************************************
ok: [localhost]
```

```
TASK [Show Validation Status] *********************************************
ok: [localhost] => {
    "(validate_response.content|from_json).status": "valid"
}
--snip--
```

Finally, view the logfile containing the "new" API key:

```
$ cat logs/api_localhost
b33fb33f
```

The uri module also supports HTTP basic authentication, which allows you to provide a username and password to access web resources. In Chapter 6, you manually configured an Elastic Agent fleet server and set up service accounts for both Elasticsearch and Kibana. One step in that process involved manually setting TLS filepaths, hostnames, and default logging and monitoring outputs. The following JSON contains those same configurations, which we can send to our simulated Kibana API over HTTP POST to instead make these changes remotely. Add the following to *files/ fleet_output_elasticsearch.json*:

```
{
  "type": "elasticsearch",
  "id": "fleet-elasticsearch",
  "name": "elasticsearch",
  "hosts": ["https://elasticsearch.local:9200"],
  "is_default": true,
  "is_default_monitoring": true,
  "ssl": {
    "certificate": "/opt/Elastic/Agent/certs/wildcard.local.flex.cert.pem",
    "key": "/opt/Elastic/Agent/certs/wildcard.local.flex.key.pem",
    "certificate_authorities": ["/opt/Elastic/Agent/certs/ca-chain.cert.pem"]
  }
}
```

The following playbook, *playbook_basicauth.yml*, uses basic authentication to access a Kibana API that configures fleet settings. Note that the test endpoint doesn't require authentication; to access an endpoint that does require it, you'd need to change the url parameter to a real domain, such as kibana .local (shown commented out) and change validate_certs from false to true:

```
- hosts: localhost
  become: no
  gather_facts: no

  tasks:

    - name: Update Fleet Default Outputs and TLS Filepaths (POST)
      delegate_to: localhost
```

```
  run_once: true
  uri:
    method: POST
    #url: https://kibana.local:5601/api/fleet/outputs
    url: https://127.0.0.1:5000/api/fleet/outputs
❶ force_basic_auth: true
    user: elastic
    password: abcd1234
❷ validate_certs: false
    #ca_path: tls/certs/ca-chain.cert.pem
❸ headers:
      kbn-xsrf: reporting
      Content-Type: application/json
    return_content: true
    body_format: json
❹ body: "{{lookup('file','files/fleet_output_elasticsearch.json') |
      to_json}}"
  register: api_output

- name: Show Results
  debug:
❺ var: api_output.content|from_json
```

We use a POST request to the new */api/fleet/outputs* endpoint on the
test server to force basic authentication ❶ and set the *elastic* username and
password. Remember, you may either use a vault or enter this password
in a prompt. We're using validate_certs: false here ❷, as the test server
has its own self-signed certificate, but this parameter defaults to true if
omitted. Remove this parameter when testing on systems that use basic
authentication.

After defining the CA chain file (commented out for our test API), we
add the HTTP headers that Kibana expects when using the API ❸. The body
parameter contains the Jinja function lookup with the file argument ❹, meaning it will read the contents of the JSON file we just created. The lookup
converts the file's contents to a JSON string for transmission using the
to_json Jinja function. Finally, we save the response body as the variable
api_output ❺, then use debug to show it on the terminal.

Execute the playbook:

```
$ ansible-playbook playbook_basicauth.yml
```

Ansible should display the following output, indicating it succeeded, as
we see our JSON file's contents mirrored back to us in the response:

```
TASK [Update Fleet Default Outputs and TLS Filepaths (POST)] ****************
ok: [localhost]

TASK [Show Results]
***************************************************************************
ok: [localhost] => {
    "api_output.content|from_json": {
```

```
    "hosts": [
        "https://elasticsearch.local:9200"
    ],
    "id": "fleet-elasticsearch",
--snip--
localhost : ok=2 ...
```

The Flask web server terminal should show the following log:

```
127.0.0.1 - - [15/Feb/2040 12:37:03] "POST /api/fleet/outputs HTTP/1.1" 200 -
```

The full playbook is available on GitHub with the rest of the code from this book.

TLS Automation

Ansible has community modules for OpenSSL and X.509, and we can use these to generate CAs, certificate signing requests, keys, and signed certificates. The OpenSSL module doesn't require configuration files; instead, each step in the setup process, from creating a root CA to creating and signing a certificate, uses an idempotent module function.

Ensure that you're in *~/ansible* before following along with this section. The tasks will reference relative filepaths and output data to the relative subdirectory *tls*, which you'll create shortly.

Setting Up the Directory

Create a file called *tasks/tls-setup.yml* and add the following lines, which create the same directory structure used in Chapter 2:

```
- name: Create TLS Required Local Directories
  delegate_to: localhost
  run_once: true
  file:
    state: directory
❶ path: "{{ item }}"
❷ loop:
    - tls/caroot
    - tls/caintermediate
    - tls/certs
    - tls/keys
    - tls/csr
    - tls/configs
```

The file module's path parameter ❶ uses a local variable named item, which acts as a placeholder for the loop parameter ❷. The loop runs each line in the list, automatically creating each directory. If the directories already exist, the module makes no changes.

Creating the Root CA

The root CA task file should perform three tasks: generate a key, create a certificate signing request, and then self-sign the certificate signing request. (Recall that all root certificates are self-signed.) Create *tasks/tls-caroot.yml* and then add the key-creation task:

```
- name: Generate Root CA 4096-bit Private Key
  delegate_to: localhost
  run_once: true
  community.crypto.openssl_privatekey:
    path: tls/caroot/ca.key
    passphrase: "{{ ssl_key_password }}"
    type: RSA
    size: 4096
    cipher: auto
```

This task uses the openssl_privatekey module to generate a 4,096-bit key, as in Chapter 2. Next, create the certificate signing request using the openssl_csr module in the same file, which involves adding subject information such as locality and organization names:

```
- name: Generate Root CA CSR
  delegate_to: localhost
  run_once: true
  community.crypto.openssl_csr:
    path: tls/caroot/ca.csr
    privatekey_path: tls/caroot/ca.key
    privatekey_passphrase: "{{ ssl_key_password }}"
    digest: sha512
    country_name: US
    state_or_province_name: MO
    locality_name: St. Louis
    organization_name: Business, Inc.
    organizational_unit_name: Information Technology
    common_name: Root CA
    email_address: none@localhost
  ❶ basicConstraints:
      - "CA:TRUE"
    key_usage_critical: true
    key_usage:
      - keyCertSign
      - cRLSign
```

These settings should look familiar by now. Most are optional, save for basicConstraints ❶ and both key-usage parameters, which CAs require. Next, sign the certificate signing request using the x509_certificate module:

```
- name: Create Self-Signed Root CA from CSR
  delegate_to: localhost
  run_once: true
  community.crypto.x509_certificate:
    path: tls/caroot/ca.cert.pem
```

```
csr_path: tls/caroot/ca.csr
privatekey_path: tls/caroot/ca.key
privatekey_passphrase: "{{ ssl_key_password }}"
❶ provider: selfsigned
```

The selfsigned provider value ❶ means the task won't use an issuer or a signing CA. Rather, OpenSSL creates the new, signed certificate using the certificate signing request. By default, the certificate remains valid for 10 years.

Creating the Intermediate CA

The steps to create the intermediate CA are identical to those for creating the root CA, save for the certificate signing request signature. Create *tasks/ca-intermediate.yml* and add three tasks to it, starting with key generation:

```
- name: Generate a 4096-bit OpenSSL Private Key
  delegate_to: localhost
  run_once: true
  community.crypto.openssl_privatekey:
    path: tls/caintermediate/ca-int.key
    passphrase: "{{ ssl_key_password }}"
    type: RSA
    size: 4096
    cipher: auto
```

This task creates a 4,096-bit private key, protected with the passphrase *abcd1234* taken from the vault, and defines where the module saves the key file. Next, create the certificate signing request task, which you'll recall from Chapter 2 contains attributes to apply to the signed certificate:

```
- name: Generate Intermediate CA CSR
  delegate_to: localhost
  run_once: true
  community.crypto.openssl_csr:
    path: tls/caintermediate/ca-int.csr
    privatekey_path: tls/caintermediate/ca-int.key
    privatekey_passphrase: "{{ ssl_key_password }}"
    digest: sha512
    country_name: US
    state_or_province_name: MO
    locality_name: St. Louis
    organization_name: Business, Inc.
    organizational_unit_name: Information Technology
    common_name: Intermediate CA
    email_address: none@localhost
    basicConstraints:
      - "CA:TRUE"
❶    - "pathlen:0"
    key_usage_critical: true
    key_usage:
      - keyCertSign
      - cRLSign
```

These properties should look familiar. They include the location, digest, and various key extensions ultimately passed from the certificate signing request to the signed certificate once it's signed by the CA. Note the pathlen:0 constraint ❶, which means that no subordinate certificate authorities exist below this one. Finally, use the root certificate to sign the intermediate certificate:

```
- name: Generate Intermediate CA Signed Certificate
  delegate_to: localhost
  run_once: true
  community.crypto.x509_certificate:
    path: tls/caintermediate/ca-int.cert.pem
❶ csr_path: tls/caintermediate/ca-int.csr
❷ ownca_path: tls/caroot/ca.cert.pem
    ownca_privatekey_path: tls/caroot/ca.key
    ownca_privatekey_passphrase: "{{ ssl_key_password }}"
❸ ownca_not_after: "+3650d"
    ownca_digest: sha512
    provider: ownca
```

The ownca options mean you're using your own CA for these actions, instead of other module options specific to commercial certificate providers. Specify the intermediate CA's certificate signing request ❶, the root CA's certificate ❷, and the private key and then set the final certificate to be valid for 3,650 days ❸, or 10 years.

Generating the CA Chain

Let's use the reliable blockinfile module to combine the two CA certificates into the CA chain. Add the following tasks to *tasks/tls-cachain.yml*:

```
- name: Create CA Chain File - Add Root CA
  delegate_to: localhost
  run_once: true
  blockinfile:
    path: tls/certs/ca-chain.cert.pem
❶ create: yes
    state: present
    marker: ""
    block: "{{ lookup('file', 'tls/caroot/ca.cert.pem') }}"

- name: Create CA Chain File - Add Intermediate CA
  delegate_to: localhost
  run_once: true
  blockinfile:
    path: tls/certs/ca-chain.cert.pem
    create: yes
    state: present
    marker: ""
    block: "{{ lookup('file', 'tls/caintermediate/ca-int.cert.pem') }}"
```

Previously, we used file and its state touch to create a new file. Here, we're using the create parameter ❶ to make the file, though you may instead use a separate task to create the file if you so desire.

Creating a Flex Certificate

Now let's make the task for flex certificates. Create *tasks/tls-cert-flex.yml* and add the following key, certificate signing requests, and signature tasks:

```
- name: Generate Flex 4096-bit Private Key
  delegate_to: localhost
  community.crypto.openssl_privatekey:
  ❶ path: "tls/keys/{{ hostvars[inventory_hostname].hostname }}.flex.key.pem"
    passphrase: "{{ ssl_key_password }}"
    type: RSA
    size: 4096
    cipher: auto
```

As these tasks create files unique to each inventory host, include a dynamic hostname in the path ❶ parameter for all three tasks. Next, add the certificate signing request task:

```
- name: Generate Flex CSR
  delegate_to: localhost
  community.crypto.openssl_csr:
    path: "tls/csr/{{ hostvars[inventory_hostname].hostname }}.flex.csr"
    privatekey_path: "tls/keys/{{ hostvars[inventory_hostname].hostname
      }}.flex.key.pem"
    privatekey_passphrase: "{{ ssl_key_password }}"
    digest: sha512
    country_name: US
    state_or_province_name: MO
    locality_name: St. Louis
    organization_name: Business, Inc.
    organizational_unit_name: Information Technology
    common_name: "{{ hostvars[inventory_hostname].hostname }}"
    email_address: none@localhost
    subject_alt_name: "DNS:{{ hostvars[inventory_hostname].basename }},DNS:{{
      hostvars[inventory_hostname].hostname }}"
    basicConstraints:
  ❶ - "CA:FALSE"
    key_usage:
      - digitalSignature
      - keyEncipherment
      - nonRepudiation
  ❷ extended_key_usage:
      - clientAuth
      - serverAuth
```

Here, we state that this file is specifically not a CA ❶, and we add the clientAuth and serverAuth extensions ❷. Note that we're creating a dynamic common name only for the sake of example, as common name verification is deprecated.

Use the intermediate CA to sign the flex certificate signing request:

```
- name: Generate Flex Signed Certificate
  delegate_to: localhost
  openssl_certificate:
    path: "tls/certs/{{ hostvars[inventory_hostname].hostname }}.flex.cert.pem"
    csr_path: "tls/csr/{{ hostvars[inventory_hostname].hostname }}.flex.csr"
    ownca_path: tls/caintermediate/ca-int.cert.pem
    ownca_privatekey_path: tls/caintermediate/ca-int.key
    ownca_privatekey_passphrase: "{{ ssl_key_password }}"
    ownca_not_after: "+3650d"
    ownca_digest: sha512
    provider: ownca
```

These signed certificates should also remain valid for 10 years.

Adding Container Files

To include all TLS files we've created throughout this book, let's make PKCS#12 and Java KeyStore container files. First, let's add some variables inside the inventory file, underneath the group name kafka, which affect the remaining tasks in this section:

```
all:
  children:
    kafka:
      vars:
        requires_pkcs12: yes
        requires_jks: yes
      hosts:
        kafka01:
          ansible_host: 192.168.8.30
          broker_id: 211
--snip--
```

These variables state that everything in the kafka group requires PKCS#12 and Java KeyStore files. Next, create *tasks/tls-pkcs12.yml* and add the following, which uses the openssl_pkcs12 module:

```
- name: Generate PKCS12 Container File
  delegate_to: localhost
❶ when: hostvars[inventory_hostname].requires_pkcs12
  community.crypto.openssl_pkcs12:
  ❷ action: export
    path: "tls/certs/{{ hostvars[inventory_hostname].hostname }}.flex.pkcs12"
    friendly_name: "{{ hostvars[inventory_hostname].hostname }}"
    privatekey_path: "tls/keys/{{ hostvars[inventory_hostname].hostname
      }}.flex.key.pem"
    privatekey_passphrase: "{{ ssl_key_password }}"
    certificate_path: "tls/certs/{{ hostvars[inventory_hostname].hostname
```

```
    }}.flex.cert.pem"
  other_certificates_parse_all: true
  other_certificates:
    - tls/certs/ca-chain.cert.pem
  state: present
```

When a host has the variable requires_pkcs12 set to true ❶, this task runs. The container includes each host's private key, its signed certificate, and its own copy of the CA chain file. The action ❷ parameter indicates that this task should explicitly create a new PKCS#12 container file, rather than attempt to parse an existing one. The other parameters list the files to import and provide friendly identifier names for these files.

Let's also create Java KeyStore files. Create *tasks/tls-jks.yml*, which runs if any host requires such a file:

```
- name: Generate Java KeyStore (JKS) Container File
  delegate_to: localhost
  when: hostvars[inventory_hostname].requires_jks
  community.general.java_keystore:
    name: "{{ hostvars[inventory_hostname].hostname }}"
    dest: "tls/certs/{{ hostvars[inventory_hostname].hostname }}.flex.jks"
    certificate_path: "tls/certs/{{ hostvars[inventory_hostname].hostname
      }}.flex.cert.pem"
    private_key_path: "tls/keys/{{ hostvars[inventory_hostname].hostname
      }}.flex.key.pem"
    private_key_passphrase: "{{ ssl_key_password }}"
    password: "{{ ssl_key_password }}"
```

Finally, let's build the TLS playbook and run these tasks.

Creating the TLS Playbook

Create *playbook_tls.yml* and import the tasks you just created:

```
- hosts: all
  become: no
  gather_facts: no
  vars_files:
    - vars/vars.yml
    - vars/vault.yml

  tasks:

    - name: Create TLS Required Local Directories
      include_tasks:
        file: tasks/tls-setup.yml

    - name: Create TLS Root Certificate Authority
      include_tasks:
        file: tasks/tls-caroot.yml
```

```
  - name: Create TLS Intermediate Certificate Authority
    include_tasks:
      file: tasks/tls-caintermediate.yml

  - name: Generate CA Chain
    include_tasks:
      file: tasks/tls-cachain.yml

  - name: Generate Flex Private Key
    include_tasks:
      file: tasks/tls-cert-flex.yml

  - name: Create PKCS12/PFX Container Files
    include_tasks:
      file: tasks/tls-pkcs12.yml

  - name: Create JKS Container Files
    include_tasks:
      file: tasks/tls-jks.yml
```

Now run the playbook:

```
$ ansible-playbook --ask-vault-pass -i inventory.yml playbook_tls.yml
```

If you'd like to watch Ansible create the files in real time, use the following watch command:

```
$ watch -n 1 -d ls -lh tls/*
```

Once the playbook finishes, you should see the following Ansible output:

```
--snip--
PLAY RECAP *********************************************************************
filebeat : ok=11 changed=5 unreachable=0 failed=0 skipped=0 rescued=0 ignored=0
logstash : ok=20 changed=14 unreachable=0 failed=0 skipped=0 rescued=0 ignored=0
rsyslog  : ok=11 changed=5 unreachable=0 failed=0 skipped=0 rescued=0 ignored=0
--snip--
```

Listing the *tls* directory's contents should show something like the following:

```
$ ls -lhR tls/
tls/:
total 24K
drwxrwxr-x 2 j j 4.0K Feb 15 15:55 caintermediate
drwxrwxr-x 2 j j 4.0K Feb 15 15:55 caroot
drwxrwxr-x 2 j j 4.0K Feb 15 15:55 certs
drwxrwxr-x 2 j j 4.0K Feb 15 15:55 configs
drwxrwxr-x 2 j j 4.0K Feb 15 15:55 csr
drwxrwxr-x 2 j j 4.0K Feb 15 15:55 keys

tls/caintermediate:
total 12K
```

```
-rw-rw-r-- 1 j j 2.2K Feb 15 15:55 ca-int.cert.pem
-rw-rw-r-- 1 j j 1.9K Feb 15 15:55 ca-int.csr
-rw------- 1 j j 3.3K Feb 15 15:55 ca-int.key
--snip--
```

Just like that, you've automated your entire TLS infrastructure! As an exercise, create a separate playbook containing only the task *tls-cert-flex.yml*, and create a copy of the inventory called *inventory-oneshot.yml* that contains only new hosts that need certificates. Run the flex-only playbook and the *oneshot* inventory to generate new signed certificates as you need them, saving you from having to run the CA tasks every time. As an additional exercise, try creating a wildcard flex certificate for your domain.

Troubleshooting with debug

You may need to troubleshoot variables, facts, and unexpected module output. You can increase Ansible's output verbosity levels using one to four -v options (up to -vvvv). You can also use the debug module to print variable values on the terminal, as you did earlier in this chapter.

I mentioned that when Ansible gathers facts from each host it connects to, it stores those values in a Python dictionary named ansible_facts. The debug module can make use of these facts to display informative messages. You can access individual fact values using the dictionary format *key*['*value*'], such as ansible_facts['*hostname*'], which would provide the machine's stored hostname, and ansible_facts['*distribution*'], which you used in Chapter 11 to gather distribution names.

Previously in this chapter, we set gather_facts to no; change this setting in your playbooks to **gather_facts: yes** to collect this information from remote hosts.

The debug module's var parameter has implied Jinja brackets, so you should use it to specify only a single variable to display during a playbook's execution. For example, the following task prints the operating system distribution for each host in play:

```
- name: Print Facts - distribution
  debug:
    var: ansible_facts['distribution'] }}
```

When run as part of a playbook, this task would display the following output:

```
TASK [Print Facts - distribution] ************************
ok: [kafka01] => {
    "ansible_facts['distribution'] }}": "RedHat}}"
}
ok: [kafka02] => {
    "ansible_facts['distribution'] }}": "Rocky}}"
}
--snip--
```

The `msg` parameter accepts a string and requires Jinja brackets around variables, so you can use it to display multiple variables at once in the terminal output. For example, the following task uses `msg` to print both `hostname` and `distribution` variables at the same time, then registers a new variable you'll write to a file shortly:

```
- name: Print Facts - hostname and distribution
  debug:
    msg: "{{ ansible_facts['hostname'] }} - {{ ansible_facts['distribution'] }}"
  register: hostname_and_distribution
```

Running this task should show the following output:

```
TASK [Print Facts - hostname and distribution] *******
ok: [kafka01] => {
    "msg": "kafka01 - RedHat"
}
ok: [kafka02] => {
    "msg": "kafka02 - Rocky"
}
--snip--
```

Let's use two `local_action` tasks to create a logfile containing this hostname and distribution information. Use your trusty `blockinfile` module with an empty `marker` parameter to append each host's information to a single file, *logs/hostname_and_distribution.log*:

```
- name: Create logs/hostname_and_distribution.log
  local_action: file path="logs/hostname_and_distribution.log" state="touch"

- name: Save Host and Distribution Information
  local_action:
    module: blockinfile
    marker: ""
    path: logs/hostname_and_distribution.log
    block: |
      {{ hostname_and_distribution.msg }}
```

Within the `block` parameter, the pipe character (|) indicates the presence of multiple lines for Ansible to write into the output file. The variable in brackets includes the `msg` attribute; this attribute refers to the variable you previously registered using `debug`, which contains the hostname and distribution string. Also note that `marker` is set to empty quotes; subsequent executions of this playbook will append data to the logfile instead of overwriting a specific entry each time. A new file, *logs/hostname_and_distribution.log*, should contain entries like the following, with your hostnames and OS types as appropriate:

```
kafka01 - Rocky
kafka02 - RedHat
kafka03 - Ubuntu
```

Capturing module output is especially useful when running new tasks for the first time or saving certain actions required by auditing and compliance policies. It's also useful for saving API results and dynamic text like cluster IDs, or even passwords, if your organization's policy allows logging such secrets.

SAVING CONFIGURATIONS WITH GIT

Ensure Git is tracking your files by using **git add ..** Next, run **git status** to check for any outstanding items, such as adding your *vars/vault.yml* file to *.gitignore* if you wish to prevent your lab secrets from uploading to the remote repository. Run **git commit -am "uploading Ansible tasks and playbooks"** and then push the files to the remote repository using **git push**.

Summary

Ansible supports data engineers by automating many of their tool deployment and configuration tasks. Whether you're working in a home lab or business environment, Ansible can save you dozens or hundreds of hours of configuration time simply by allowing you to create tasks and playbooks that perform scripted actions on your servers. In this chapter, you updated firewall rules, downloaded files, worked with APIs, created TLS infrastructure, copied files, created configurations from templates, and more. In the next chapter, you'll explore the caching tools Redis and Memcached and then use them along with Filebeat and Logstash to create a cyber threat intelligence framework inside your data pipelines.

13

CACHING THREAT INTELLIGENCE DATA

Caching tools allow you to store key-value data pairs in RAM. Your data pipelines can then access that data directly from memory, which is orders of magnitude faster than reading data from a hard drive and enables you to compare values in your data pipelines against the cache in near-real time. Caches generally hold frequently accessed data, such as the top news stories on a popular website, DNS resolution addresses, active user login sessions, or video game session statistics.

In this chapter, you'll use cache tools to store threat indicators such as malicious web domains and IP addresses, use filters to check for matches, and apply tags to events where matches occur. You'll work with two caching tools, Memcached and Redis, and revisit Filebeat and Logstash to receive, process, and disseminate indicators to each server that processes streaming data.

Speeding Up Lookups with Caching

When it comes to checking in-flight events for threat intelligence values, you might initially think to use Logstash's translate filters, introduced in Chapter 9. These translate filters read the contents of a structured text file, such as YAML or JSON, into RAM and then compare values from streaming data to the memory contents.

But translate filters can take anywhere from seconds to almost a minute to load if they contain hundreds of thousands of entries, as they must read text files from disk. Also, the only way to update an entry held in memory is to first update the file on disk, which requires creating some process to distribute the new file to every Logstash instance in a cluster. Lastly, large translate tables necessitate changing certain memory-related Logstash settings, which may affect other areas of performance.

A dedicated cache, such as Redis or Memcached, allows Logstash (or another tool) to offload the responsibilities of managing data in memory. The cache receives and stores key-value pairs, manages deduplication, and ages out old data. Most importantly, it's designed to optimize speed. Caching tools also manage their own backups, clustering, replication, and security through dedicated configuration files. This separation of duties lets tools like Logstash handle the input, transformation, and output of data, while caches act as in-memory lookup databases.

Installing Redis and Memcached

Let's install the tools needed for the Redis and Memcached projects in this chapter. We'll start by ensuring that hostnames properly resolve so that TLS connections succeed.

Dividing the Project Servers into Nodes

We'll divide the project servers into two groups: one single cyber threat intelligence node and the data nodes. The cyber threat intelligence node, named *threatintel.local*, is responsible for receiving, retrieving, and disseminating threat indicators. The data nodes represent servers on which Logstash processes streaming data, and we'll number them sequentially, beginning with *logstash01.local*.

These projects use one cyber threat intelligence node and two data nodes. Let's configure *threatintel.local*, *logstash01.local*, and *logstash02.local*. Add entries to your own DNS server, or add the following lines to */etc/hosts* on your main workstation, cyber threat intelligence node, and data nodes:

```
$ sudo nano /etc/hosts

192.168.8.130    threatintel
192.168.8.130    threatintel.local
192.168.8.131    logstash01
```

```
192.168.8.131    logstash01.local
192.168.8.134    logstash02
192.168.8.134    logstash02.local
```

Be sure to change the IP addresses as necessary for your environment, then save and exit the */etc/hosts* file.

On your cyber threat intelligence host, install Filebeat, Logstash, and Redis:

```
$ sudo apt install filebeat logstash redis-server -y
```

On your data nodes, install the same tools, as well as Memcached:

```
$ sudo apt install filebeat logstash redis-server memcached -y
```

Finally, on all servers, install the *redis* gem using the Ruby version that comes packaged with Logstash:

```
$ sudo /usr/share/logstash/bin/ruby -S gem install redis
```

Both caching tools may start automatically and run in the background as a service. If you want to stop them or prevent either tool from starting automatically, use the following commands; otherwise, you can leave them running for the examples in this chapter, as we'll restart them anyway after changing configurations:

```
$ sudo systemctl stop redis-server memcached
$ sudo systemctl disable redis-server memcached
```

On RHEL systems, use dnf instead of apt and redis instead of redis-server. Next, let's configure TLS for these tools.

Enabling TLS

Until this point, you've mostly used one tool at a time or run multiple instances of the same tool on different servers. In this chapter, however, you'll run multiple tools on each of the servers, and these tools will use TLS, when able, even to communicate with other tools on the same host.

Rather than using TLS or SSH tunnels, each Logstash node connects locally to Redis over a Unix socket. The *threatintel* server replicates its cache keys to *logstash01* and *logstash02* over a TLS connection across the network, but each Logstash server still connects only to its local, co-installed Redis instance. You won't use a TLS connection for Memcached, as you'll connect to it locally using a Logstash filter.

For the sake of simplicity, we'll use the wildcard certificate created in Chapter 6 that each application can access. Ensure the wildcard certificate contains the hostnames *threatintel*, *logstash01*, and *logstash02* and entries for each tool, including the *.local* domain, as you may encounter security tools in the future that reject wildcard certificates. Although multiple applications will access the TLS files, they're intended to act as one cohesive unit, so let's add them to a group to share access to the key and certificate files.

The following commands create a new group called *bookproject* that can access the TLS files and then adds to the group your username, the *logstash* user, and both *redis* and *memcached* users (which should have been created automatically when you installed Redis and Memcached). The last command executes a new login shell so your group memberships take effect immediately. Run these commands on your cyber threat intelligence and data nodes:

```
$ sudo addgroup bookproject
$ for i in {j,logstash,redis,memcached}; do sudo usermod -aG bookproject $i; done
$ exec su -l j
```

Note that a lowercase L comes after su. Next, make a new directory */etc/ssl/bookproject*, give your new group permissions to it, change the ownership, and then change directories into it:

```
$ sudo mkdir -p /etc/ssl/bookproject
$ sudo chmod 0775 /etc/ssl/bookproject
$ sudo chown root:bookproject /etc/ssl/bookproject
$ cd /etc/ssl/bookproject
```

On the host that has your TLS files, start a Python web server one directory level above where the TLS files are located:

```
$ python3 -m http.server 8080
```

On each of your data nodes and your cyber threat intelligence node, download the TLS wildcard files into */etc/ssl/bookproject*:

```
$ wget 192.168.8.133:8080/tls/certs/ca-chain.cert.pem
$ wget 192.168.8.133:8080/tls/certs/wildcard.local.flex.cert.pem
$ wget 192.168.8.133:8080/tls/certs/wildcard.local.flex.pkcs12
$ wget 192.168.8.133:8080/tls/keys/wildcard.local.flex.key.pem
$ wget 192.168.8.133:8080/tls/keys/wildcard.local.flex.key.nopass.pem
```

Finally, change permissions and ownership of the files:

```
$ sudo chmod 0640 *
$ sudo chown root:bookproject *
```

Try viewing the CA chain to ensure you can still access it:

```
$ cat ca-chain.cert.pem
```

If you can't, your group membership might not have updated properly, so log out and then log back in, or use the exec su -l <username> command you ran previously to launch a new login shell, followed by `id` or `groups` to view your group memberships.

Optionally, you can add your CA chain to your system's list of trusted authorities. This lets applications you may use in the future trust your custom CA. On Ubuntu, the following commands update your system-wide trusted CAs. The `update-ca-certificates` command requires first changing from `pem` to `crt` extensions:

```
$ sudo cp ca-chain.cert.pem /usr/local/share/ca-certificates/ca-chain.crt
$ sudo update-ca-certificates
```

On Red Hat and similar flavors of Linux, use the following commands:

```
$ sudo cp ca-chain.cert.pem /etc/pki/ca-trust/source/anchors/
$ sudo update-ca-trust
```

With the TLS files in place, let's start configuring Redis.

Configuring Redis

Let's configure Redis before we dive into its various commands. Generate a 50-character password you'll use later to authenticate to Redis:

```
$ openssl rand 50 | openssl base64 -A
ZtyziOSFGAcbGy807...
```

This command generates random characters, then base64-encodes them into a single line with the `-A` switch. Next, back up the original Redis configuration file, aptly named *redis.conf*, and make changes to it using your editor of choice:

```
$ sudo cp /etc/redis/redis.conf /etc/redis/redis.conf.original
$ sudo nano /etc/redis/redis.conf
```

By default, Redis listens on *localhost*, but if the following bind statement is commented out for some reason, Redis listens on all available interfaces. Ensure the following line is uncommented, meaning it doesn't have a leading hash mark:

```
bind 127.0.0.1 ::1
```

If you choose to disable IPv6, you may omit the `::1`. Next, let's tell Redis it will be managed by *systemd* so that you can use commands such as `systemctl restart redis` to restart the service:

```
supervised systemd
```

Further down the file, add the random string you just generated. We'll use this password shortly on the command line. Uncomment the line requirepass foobared, and change foobared to your 50-character string:

```
requirepass ZtyziOSFGAcbGy807...
```

Finally, let's enable a Unix socket in addition to localhost. The Unix socket will allow programs on the same host to interact with Redis without the overhead of using the TCP network stack. Uncomment the unixsocket and unixsocketperm lines, and change the permissions to 0666 so that any program on the same host may reach Redis; be sure to reassess these permissions if you use Redis in production:

```
unixsocket /var/run/redis/redis-server.sock
unixsocketperm 0666
```

Save your configuration file, and restart Redis. Let's also use the ss command, or netstat on older systems, to view active TCP listeners:

```
$ sudo systemctl restart redis-server
$ sudo ss -lnp | grep redis
u_str LISTEN 0 511 /var/run/redis/redis-server.sock 34173 * 0
users:(("redis-server",pid=947,fd=7))
tcp   LISTEN 0 511 127.0.0.1:6379 0.0.0.0:*
users:(("redis-server",pid=947,fd=6))
```

This output shows the Unix and *localhost* sockets. Note that in the command checking for listening sockets, the 0.0.0.0:* following the localhost address doesn't mean Redis is listening on all interfaces, but rather that any host-local address can connect.

Configuring Memcached

Memcached is a much simpler caching system than Redis, as it doesn't support features such as clustering or replication.

On Ubuntu- and Debian-based systems, the main configuration file is */etc/memcached.conf*. The default configuration includes many helpful comments describing each of the various options. By default, Memcached listens on all available interfaces. On your data nodes, add -l 127.0.0.1 to the configuration to listen only on localhost instead of allowing external connections, -U 0 to disable UDP, and -m 128 to increase the default memory maximum from 64MB to 128MB, though you'll want that value much higher in production:

```
$ sudo nano /etc/memcached.conf
--snip--
-l 127.0.0.1
-U 0
--snip--
-m 128
--snip--
```

On RHEL, CentOS, and similar systems, the main configuration, /etc/sysconfig/memcached, is dramatically different. Whereas the Ubuntu configuration was a top-down list of arguments to tweak, the RHEL configuration places these arguments in the *key=value* pairs in /etc/sysconfig/memcached:

```
$ sudo vi /etc/sysconfig/memcached
PORT="11211"
USER="memcached"
MAXCONN="1024"
CACHESIZE="64"
OPTIONS="-l 127.0.0.1,::1"
```

The previous lines should be the defaults in /etc/sysconfig/memcached, but you may change them as desired. After making any changes to the configuration, restart the memcached service for changes to take effect:

```
$ sudo systemctl restart memcached
```

Next, let's explore using Redis and Memcached using command line tools, before continuing with connecting via Logstash.

Working with Redis

To connect to the Redis command line interface, use **redis-cli**. By default, the command connects to *localhost* over TCP, but let's use the faster Unix socket to better emulate local services connecting to Redis:

```
$ redis-cli -s /var/run/redis/redis-server.sock
redis /var/run/redis/redis-server.sock>
```

Authenticate as the default user using the long string you previously created; a successful login should show OK:

```
> auth default ZtyziOSFGAcbGy807...
OK
```

Once authenticated, run a test command to ensure you can interact with Redis:

```
> ping
PONG
```

Redis stores key-value pairs, among other data. Use the set command to add a new key; in this example, we create the key abcd with a value of 1234. Then, use get to retrieve the key:

```
> set abcd 1234
> get abcd
"1234"
```

You can set a time-to-live (TTL), or expiration value, using the EX *<number>* option after providing the key you want to set. The following command gives abcd a lifespan of five seconds, after which Redis drops it from the cache:

```
> set abcd 1234 EX 5
> get abcd
"1234"
```

Immediately running get abcd returns its value, but if you wait six seconds, Redis won't return anything:

```
> get abcd
(nil)
```

You can also view system utilization using the info command, which lets you specify a resource type, such as system memory (RAM):

```
> info memory
# Memory
used_memory:2859704
used_memory_human:2.73M
used_memory_rss:13369344
used_memory_rss_human:12.75M
used_memory_peak:2921880
used_memory_peak_human:2.79M
used_memory_peak_perc:97.87%
--snip--
```

This chapter won't include user access control lists (ACLs), which can further restrict how applications access Redis, but the following commands demonstrate how to add them in the form of users:

```
> acl setuser setonly on allkeys +set >abcd1234
> acl setuser getonly on allkeys +get >abcd1234
```

The first command creates a new user, *setonly*, which can add any key but only has access to the set command and has an account password of *abcd1234*. The second command is similar, except the *getonly* user can use only the get command.

You'll need to exit Redis using CTRL-C, then run *redis-cli* again to see this new account in action. Authenticate as *setonly*, set a new key, and then attempt to use get; Redis should return an error:

```
> auth setonly abcd1234
OK
> set wxyz 5678
OK
> get wxyz
(error) NOPERM this user has no permissions to run the 'get' command
or its subcommand
```

Redis also includes a benchmark utility that can measure performance using given criteria:

```
$ redis-benchmark \
-s /var/run/redis/redis-server.sock \
-t get \
-n 1000000 \
-d 100 \
-c 1 \
-a ZtyziOSFGAcbGy807nY6Ap21Qd42SJa7Uthsfly9S1LbvflkevvDvTGRBC69qatZGQo=
====== GET ======
  1000000 requests completed in 62.23 seconds
  1 parallel clients
  100 bytes payload
  keep alive: 1
  host configuration "save": 900 1 300 10 60 10000
  host configuration "appendonly": no
  multi-thread: no

95.51% <= 0.1 milliseconds
--snip--
100.00% <= 4 milliseconds
16069.94 requests per second
```

This command connects to the Unix socket (-s), then uses the get operation (-t) one million times (-n). It specifies that each response has 100 bytes (-d), a single connection (-c), and the *requirepass* password (-a) you created earlier in this chapter. On a very old laptop running Ubuntu, a single Unix socket connection achieved about 16,069.94 get requests per second, completing in just over a minute. The same command using set achieved approximately 14,852.22 requests per second. These numbers would likely be different with real data and system strain, however.

Working with Memcached

Now let's practice working with Memcached. You must use *telnet* to interact with the Memcached program, so operations like using the up arrow to access previous commands aren't supported. Connect to Memcached on port 11211:

```
$ telnet localhost 11211
Trying 127.0.0.1...
Connected to localhost.
Escape character is '^]'.
```

The set command requires a 32-bit flag that Memcached will store along with the data, a TTL in seconds, and the bytes for the data to be stored. In the following command, let's set the flag to 0, as we don't need to store any application-specific bytes with each value. Set a new 4-byte value, abcd, with a 30-second TTL:

```
# set VALUE FLAGS(INT) TTL(SECONDS,INT) BYTES(INT)
> set abcd 0 30 4
> 1234
> STORED
```

Next, use **get** to retrieve the value you just stored:

```
> get abcd
> VALUE abcd 0 4
> 1234
> END
```

To exit, use CTRL-], then use CTRL-D to exit telnet. Next, let's begin the first of two caching architectures covered in this chapter.

Populating and Replicating Redis for Threat Lookups

In this section, you'll use Filebeat and Logstash to populate a *leader* Redis instance, which will act as the source of key-value pairs containing threat indicators. *Follower* Redis instances will copy, or *replicate*, the leader database onto each Logstash node. This design, diagrammed in Figure 13-1, lets Logstash check incoming data against an up-to-date cache of malicious indicators, populate alerts, and inform your security operations center. By putting the responsibility of indicator replication solely on Redis, you can ensure that caches remain synchronized after an unexpected outage or reboot.

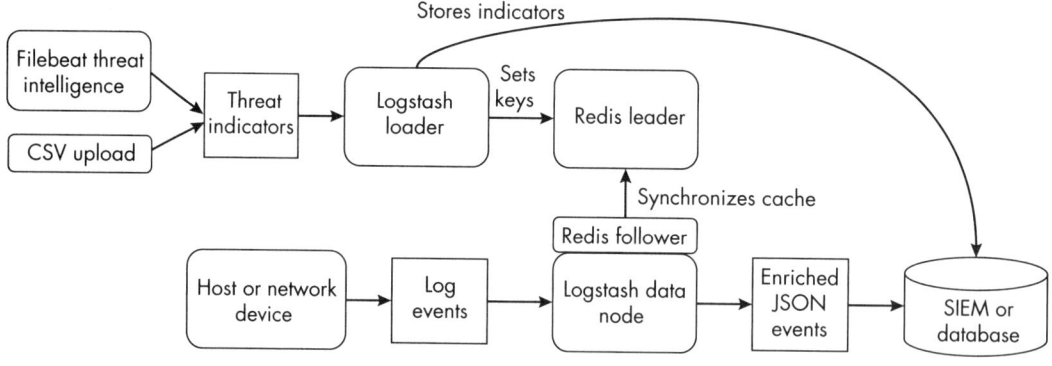

Figure 13-1: Using the Redis leader-follower model to check data for threat intelligence indicators

One downside to the leader-follower approach is if the leader database gets flushed or emptied somehow, all followers will dump their keys too. Note, however, that this would most likely occur as the result of an administrator action, and the Logstash instance that sets keys in Redis is also responsible for sending them to Elasticsearch or another database, meaning the data should be backed up.

Logstash doesn't have a built-in filter for Redis, but because Logstash has a Ruby filter, you'll create your own Redis filter in this project. You'll use Ruby logic to write key-value pairs into Redis and to check streaming data against the cache.

You'll also add a Logstash input that will enable analysts to send their own indicators to Redis in a CSV file. You could use this input to repopulate the cache if emptied or, more importantly, add indicators uncovered by your cyber investigations directly into your data pipelines for enrichment.

Creating the Leader Cache

We'll start with the cyber threat intelligence node. This node will run Filebeat, which will periodically pull indicators from a list you'll configure. Filebeat will send these indicators to a Logstash host running on the same server. The Logstash instance will parse the indicator values to create key-value pairs, store them in the Redis leader, and send the indicators to Elasticsearch for safekeeping.

Let's create the Redis instance that will serve as the leader copy of the key-value pairs used in your pipelines. Make the following configuration changes to */etc/redis/redis.conf*:

```
--snip--
bind 0.0.0.0
port 0
unixsocket /var/run/redis/redis-server.sock
unixsocketperm 0666
tls-port 6379
tls-cert-file /etc/ssl/bookproject/wildcard.local.flex.cert.pem
tls-key-file /etc/ssl/bookproject/wildcard.local.flex.key.nopass.pem
tls-ca-cert-file /etc/ssl/bookproject/ca-chain.cert.pem
supervised systemd
requirepass ZtyziOSFGAcbGy807...
tls-replication yes
--snip--
```

Note that these options don't necessarily appear consecutively, but I've placed them in the order you'll likely find them as you scroll through the file.

This configuration tells Redis to listen on 0.0.0.0, meaning all interfaces. Note that if you comment out the bind entry, Redis would also listen on all interfaces, but for the sake of being explicit and keeping the configuration readable, we'll tell Redis exactly how we want it to operate. In a production environment, the cyber threat intelligence and data nodes shouldn't be reachable from the open internet. Even though Redis listens on all interfaces, only hosts on the same network segment should be able to reach it.

The port 0 statement disables all plaintext TCP traffic, and we enable the Unix socket and its permissions, as we did earlier in the chapter. The tls-port 6379 line reestablishes a TCP listener, but one expecting only TLS traffic.

The TLS certificate, nopass key, and CA chain come next. Redis won't automatically read all trusted certificates on the host unless you specify a directory of CAs or an individual file, such as your chain file. Next are the supervised and requirepass options discussed earlier. The tls-replication statement specifically tells Redis to use encryption between the leader and its read-only followers.

Redis likely started running immediately after you installed it. Allow port 6379/TCP through your firewall and then restart *redis-server* to make your changes take effect. Check its status and then enable Redis to start automatically on boot:

```
$ sudo ufw allow 6379/tcp
$ sudo systemctl restart redis-server
$ systemctl status redis-server
$ sudo systemctl enable redis-server
```

With the Redis configuration complete, let's set up Logstash.

Receiving Threat Indicators with Logstash

We'll create an instance of Logstash to receive indicators, either from Filebeat or from custom analyst uploads. It will then format the indicators, add them to the Redis leader cache, and then optionally store them in Elasticsearch. Logstash will act as a *setter* in this role, adding key-value pairs to the Redis leader cache. Later, Logstash *getters* will read these values to compare against streaming data.

If you're still running Elasticsearch from Chapter 6 and want to connect this Logstash to it, test the connection using the CA chain file:

```
$ echo -n | openssl s_client -CAfile /etc/ssl/bookproject/ca-chain.cert.pem
-connect elasticsearch01.local:9200
--snip--
SSL handshake has read 5646 bytes and written 403 bytes
Verification: OK
--snip--
DONE
```

Check the contents of */etc/logstash/pipelines.yml* to ensure Logstash detects new configurations in */etc/logstash/conf.d* when started:

```
$ cat pipelines.yml
--snip--
- pipeline.id: main
  path.config: "/etc/logstash/conf.d/*.conf"
```

We don't need to make any adjustments to *logstash.yml*. If you wish to change individual pipeline worker thread counts in production, do so in that file.

Defining Inputs

This configuration will accept indicators from Filebeat and Elastic Agent and custom indicators uploaded by analysts. We'll work through the configuration in sections, so create */etc/logstash/conf.d/redis-set-indicators.conf* and add the following inputs:

```
input {
  elastic_agent {
    port => 5044
    type => "external_ioc" ❶
    ssl_enabled => true
    ssl_client_authentication => "required"
    ssl_certificate => "/etc/ssl/bookproject/wildcard.local.flex.cert.pem"
    ssl_key => "/etc/ssl/bookproject/wildcard.local.flex.key.pem"
    ssl_key_passphrase => "abcd1234"
    ssl_certificate_authorities => [ "/etc/ssl/bookproject/ca-chain.cert.pem" ]
  }
  http {
    port => 8080
    type => "custom_ioc" ❷
    ssl_enabled => true
    ssl_client_authentication => "required"
    ssl_certificate => "/etc/ssl/bookproject/wildcard.local.flex.cert.pem"
    ssl_key => "/etc/ssl/bookproject/wildcard.local.flex.key.pem"
    ssl_key_passphrase => "abcd1234"
    ssl_certificate_authorities => [ "/etc/ssl/bookproject/ca-chain.cert.pem" ]
  }
}
```

These inputs accept Elastic Agent and Beats data on port 5044 and HTTP requests on port 8080. The types external_ioc ❶ and custom_ioc ❷ allow you to separately query Elasticsearch for indicators acquired by Filebeat and Elastic Agent and for the custom ones uploaded by your cyber analysts using CSV files. We'll cover handling CSV files shortly.

Processing Indicators

Next, we'll add a filter to preprocess data from Filebeat. The threatintel module in Filebeat stores actual indicators in the message field, which is JSON-encoded into a single string. Add the following filter after the input block:

```
filter {
❶ if [agent][type] == "filebeat" and [service][type] == "threatintel" {
  ❷ json {
      source => "[message]"
      target => "[labels]"
      skip_on_invalid_json => true
    }
  ❸ if [event][dataset] {
      mutate {
        add_field => { "[labels][cti_message]" => "%{[event][dataset]}" }
      }
```

```
        } else {
          mutate {
            add_field => { "[labels][cti_message]" => "threatintel" }
          }
        }
   ❹ if [labels][signature] {
          mutate {
            update => { "[labels][cti_message]" =>
            "%{[labels][cti_message]}-%{[labels][signature]}" }
          }
        }
   ❺ if [processed][file_type] and [processed][file_type] != "unknown" {
          mutate {
            update => { "[labels][cti_message]" =>
            "%{[labels][cti_message]}-%{[labels][file_type]}" }
          }
        }
      }
    }
}
```

First, we check whether the data came from Filebeat and its service type is `threatintel` ❶, meaning it originated from the Filebeat module we'll enable shortly. The filter parses the JSON-encoded `message` contents into individual labels fields ❷.

Next, we begin to build the string stored in Redis. We use any given indicator as the value your data nodes will add to streaming events if a match occurs. To construct this value, we use the `labels` fields we just created, then append certain values if their fields exist.

The first `mutate` filter adds a new field ❸, `labels.cti_message`, and sets it to the value of `event.dataset`. It uses `threatintel` as a fallback to guarantee that at least some value will be set when Logstash adds the indicator to the cache. An update operation adds `labels.signature` if the field is present ❹. This field contains the name of a malware family. If the `file.type` field exists and isn't unknown, the filter appends that field to `labels.cti_message` via `mutation` update ❺.

We construct `labels.cti_message` as a string because we're ultimately holding this value in a cache based entirely inside RAM. Instead of creating a string, you could encode the entire event and parse it downstream if a match occurs, but that would consume vast amounts of valuable memory. As there's a high likelihood of never encountering most of the values you'll store in this cache (which is a good thing), the value-construction technique used here errs on the side of using less RAM.

Handling Custom Uploads

Next, add a filter to handle custom indicator uploads, which analysts can provide via CSV files:

```
filter {
  if [type] == "custom_ioc" {
  ❶ split {}
  ❷ csv {}
```

```
❸ if [column1] == "indicator" and [column2] == "cti_message" { drop {} }
❹ ruby {
     id => "ruby_remove_nil"
     code => '
       hash = event.to_hash
       hash.each do |k,v|
         if v == nil
           event.remove(k)
         end
       end
     '
   }
❺ mutate {
     rename => {
       "column1" => "[labels][indicator]"
       "column2" => "[labels][cti_message]"
     }
   }
❻ if ![labels][indicator] {
     mutate {
       add_field => { "[labels][indicator]" => "missing" }
     }
   }
   if ![labels][cti_message] {
     mutate {
       add_field => { "[labels][cti_message]" => "threatintel" }
     }
   }
  }
 }
}
```

This filter runs its plug-ins if the type is custom_ioc, which the http input
should add when a file is sent to Logstash. As the HTTP input receives the
whole file at once, split converts each row into its own event ❶. The csv
filter ❷ recognizes the row's columns should parse into their own JSON
fields.

The if statement ❸ checks for the column names and drops them if
present. Note that because split occurs before csv, the latter's skip_header
option, which does the same thing, has no effect here. Next, a Ruby filter
removes nil, or nonexistent, values from each event ❹. (CSV files may
contain empty sets of quotes or consecutive commas indicating blank
columns.)

A mutate filter ❺ renames the two columns in the uploaded file to labels
.indicator and labels.cti_message, respectively. You could expect your analyst
to provide notes, case numbers, or potentially even initials with any custom
upload. If either of those fields don't exist ❻, we set default values to something always sent to the cache.

We'll cover how to format a sample CSV file containing indicators in
"Handling Analyst-Submitted Indicator Data" on page 303. We'll also cover
using cURL to send the CSV to Logstash.

Populating Redis with Key-Value Pairs

The next filter contains the Ruby code we'll use to populate the leader
Redis instance with key-value pairs:

```
# init runs once when Logstash starts.
filter {
  ruby {
    id => "ruby_redis"
    init => '
  ❶ require "uri"
    require "redis"
  ❷ redis_requirepass = "<YOUR-REDIS-REQUIREPASS>"
    # Unix socket
  ❸ $r = Redis.new(path: "/var/run/redis/redis-server.sock", db: 0,
      password: redis_requirepass)
    # Network socket
  ❹ #$r = Redis.new(host: "localhost", port: 6379, db: 0,
    # Password: redis_requirepass)
    # Keys expire after 30 days.
    # 60 seconds * 60 minutes * 24 hours * 30 days = 2,592,000 seconds
  ❺ @ttl = 2592000
    '

    code => '
  ❻ val = event.get("[labels][cti_message]")
    # Stores full url and domain (host)
    if event.get("[labels][url]")
  ❼ $r.set(event.get("[labels][url]").downcase, val, ex: @ttl)
  ❽ uri = URI(event.get("[labels][url]"))
  ❾ $r.set(uri.host.downcase, val, ex: ttl)
    end
    # Stores custom indicators
  ❿ if event.get("[labels][indicator]")
      $r.set(event.get("[labels][indicator]").downcase, val, ex: @ttl)
    end
    # Stores IP address
    if event.get("[labels][ip]")
      $r.set(event.get("[labels][ip]").downcase, val, ex: @ttl)
    end
    # Stores SHA256 hash
    if event.get("[labels][sha256_hash]")
      $r.set(event.get("[labels][sha256_hash]").downcase, val, ex: @ttl)
    end
    # Stores MD5 hash
    if event.get("[labels][md5_hash]")
      $r.set(event.get("[labels][md5_hash]").downcase, val, ex: @ttl)
    end
    # Stores import hash
    if event.get("[labels][imphash]")
      $r.set(event.get("[labels][imphash]").downcase, val, ex: @ttl)
    end
    # Stores ssdeep
    if event.get("[labels][ssdeep]")
      $r.set(event.get("[labels][ssdeep]").downcase, val, ex: @ttl)
```

```
      end
  '
  }
}
```

Recall the `init` statement executes when Logstash loads; we don't want to load modules and make Redis connections for every event, so we place those commands here. Ruby comes bundled with the `uri` module, which this configuration uses to extract domains from full URLs ❶. We also load the redis module we just installed and define the `redis_requirepass` variable ❷, which contains the `requirepass` value you set in */etc/redis/redis.conf.*

The variable r connects to the Redis Unix socket using Redis database 0 (the default) and authenticating with the Redis password ❸. A comment demonstrates using a TCP connection to reach Redis ❹. If you add your own Redis ACL users, insert the `username` and `password` arguments to these connection objects. We're using the Unix socket, since it's faster than TCP but also doesn't require TLS. Closing out the `init` section, we set the TTL to 30 days, measured in seconds ❺.

In the `code` block, which processes each event passing through the filter, we retrieve the value of `labels.cti_message`, the field constructed in the previous filter ❻. Next begins a series of `if` statements to check for the various types of indicators you'll encounter, such as domains and IP addresses. If you don't first check whether a field exists, you'll produce `_rubyexception` tags in your downstream database, as Ruby doesn't know how to handle adding a nonexistent field to the cache.

If Filebeat's `threatintel` module sends a URL ❼, it's converted to lowercase via the `.downcase` method and added to the cache with the value of `labels.cti_message` with the 30-day TTL. The uri module parses the web address ❽, then the HTTP `host` object, or domain, is lowercased (again, `downcase`) and added to the cache ❾. This ensures that either a full URL or just the domain is available for your data feeds. We make another `if`-exists check and add an IP field. Next, we add the logic to submit your custom `labels.indicator` values ❿ and several hash fields.

As you add threat intelligence feeds to your data pipelines, ensure you know what indicators are available and add them to your cache if you deem them valuable. Keep in mind that attackers can trivially change hashes by adding or removing even a single byte in a file, and IP addresses are only marginally harder to alter with proxying, DNS rotation, or server hijacking, so these indicators might not always reliably detect future attacker activity. Use your best judgment for return on investment in your environment.

Also note that you may encounter data flagged as malicious despite being hosted on an otherwise legitimate domain. Use discretion when considering these cases; while it's technically possible that a subdomain of google.com might inadvertently host malware, you probably don't want google.com to trigger intelligence alerts in your SIEM. Consider adding custom logic to pretag or drop unwanted items entering your intelligence feed, use scripted checks for domains you don't want in your cache, or manually delete bad entries when you notice a spike in unwanted cache matches.

Creating Custom API Keys

If you intend to store your indicators in Elasticsearch, you need to create an API key so Logstash can write data into your cluster. In Kibana, click the hamburger menu at the top-left corner and then click **Dev Tools**. In the left panel, add the following text to create a POST request, then press CTRL-ENTER to submit it to Elasticsearch:

```
POST /_security/api_key
{
  "name": "logstash_cti",
  "role_descriptors": {
    "logstash_writer": {
      "cluster": ["monitor"],
      "index": [
        {
          "names": ["*"],
          "privileges": ["auto_configure", "create", "create_doc",
                        "read", "view_index_metadata"]
        }
      ]
    }
  }
}
```

This API will let Logstash write data from Beats, Elastic Agent, and other inputs to various Elasticsearch indexes and data streams, then read events from Elasticsearch if needed. This is a more permissive version of the API created in Chapter 6 to facilitate testing in your environment. It can allow you to automatically trigger *retro hunts* (searches of old data for new indicators) when new indicators pass through the pipeline. The API should return a response that includes your ID and key:

```
{
  "id": <some_value>,
  "api_key": <some_value>,
--snip--
```

Keep track of the id and api_key values, as you'll need them for the output section.

Outputting Data to Elasticsearch

By default, Logstash sends data stream traffic to a stream called logs -generic-default in Elasticsearch. This data stream unfortunately doesn't automatically exist. To add it, create the following API request in Kibana's Dev Tools, after the previous API request, then press CTRL-ENTER to send it to Elasticsearch:

```
PUT /_data_stream/logs-generic-default
```

You should see the following response in the right window:

```
{
  "acknowledged": true
}
```

Finally, add an `elasticsearch` output at the end of your Logstash configuration and a commented-out `stdout` output in case you'd like to perform manual testing. Format the response from your previous API request like this: *id:api_key*. Then, set your formatted *id:api_key* value using the (confusingly named) `api_key` option in the output:

```
output {
  #stdout { codec => rubydebug { metadata => true }}
  elasticsearch {
    hosts => "https://elasticsearch01.local:9200"
    api_key => "NH4uN5ABEoX7gabm9s2k:jEn2EBEUSeaMBPwjVA4vsA"
    data_stream => true
    ssl_enabled => true
    ssl_certificate_authorities => "/etc/ssl/bookproject/ca-chain.cert.pem"
  }
}
```

This output ensures that your indicators will be stored in a database, so you don't need to jam the whole JSON event into the cache, just the constructed indicator value, `labels.cti_message`. Save and exit the file, then test the configuration:

```
$ sudo /usr/share/logstash/bin/logstash -f
/etc/logstash/conf.d/redis-set-indicators.conf --config.test_and_exit
[INFO ] 2040-05-15 21:34:57.227 [LogStash::Runner] runner – Using
config.test_and_exit mode. Config Validation Result: OK. Exiting Logstash
```

With the file working, start the Logstash service, check its logfile for any errors starting up, and enable it so it starts automatically:

```
$ sudo systemctl start logstash
$ sudo tail -f /var/log/logstash/logstash-plain.log$ sudo systemctl enable logstash
```

Next, let's configure Filebeat.

Reading Threat Intelligence

The Filebeat instance running on the cyber threat intelligence server will periodically request threat intelligence indicators from a list of intelligence providers you'll configure shortly. Begin by backing up the original */etc/filebeat/filebeat.yml* file, then create a new one with the following contents:

```
output.logstash:
  enabled: true
  hosts: [ "threatintel.local:5044" ]
```

```
ssl.enabled: true
ssl.verification_mode: full
ssl.certificate: /etc/ssl/bookproject/wildcard.local.flex.cert.pem
ssl.key: /etc/ssl/bookproject/wildcard.local.flex.key.pem
ssl.key_passphrase: abcd1234
ssl.certificate_authorities:
  - /etc/ssl/bookproject/ca-chain.cert.pem

filebeat.config.modules:
  path: ${path.config}/modules.d/*.yml
  reload.enabled: true
  reload.period: 15s
```

These settings instruct Filebeat to send threat intelligence data to the Logstash instance at *threatintel.local*. They also define TLS options and the default path of Filebeat's modules. For the sake of testing, values in modules you decide to update will take effect in one second. Next, disable Filebeat's system module and enable the threatintel module, as we'll use this host only for threat intelligence processing:

```
$ sudo filebeat modules disable system
$ sudo filebeat modules enable threatintel
```

Let's tell Filebeat to request indicators from publicly available indicator services. Set enabled to **true** for the abuseurl, abusemalware, and malwarebazaar provider settings in *threatintel.yml*; if you have personal API keys for the other services listed in the file, feel free to enable those as well:

```
$ sudo nano /etc/filebeat/modules.d/threatintel.yml
--snip--
  abuseurl:
    enabled: true
--snip--
  abusemalware:
    enabled: true
--snip--
  malwarebazaar:
    enabled: true
--snip--
```

Filebeat is just about complete. Test the configuration:

```
$ sudo filebeat test config
Config OK
$ sudo filebeat test output
logstash: threatintel.local:5044...
  connection...
    parse host... OK
    dns lookup... OK
    addresses: 192.168.8.130
    dial up... OK
  TLS...
```

```
   security: server's certificate chain verification is enabled
   handshake... OK
   TLS version: TLSv1.3
   dial up... OK
  talk to server... OK
```

If you receive any connection errors, try restarting Logstash and check-ing firewall access and DNS entries. Finally, start and enable the Filebeat service:

```
$ sudo systemctl start filebeat && systemctl status filebeat
  filebeat.service - Filebeat sends log files to Logstash or directly to
  Elasticsearch.
    Loaded: loaded (/lib/systemd/system/filebeat.service; disabled;
    vendor preset: enabled)
    Active: active (running) since Tue 2040-05-25 20:45:28 UTC
--snip--
$ sudo systemctl enable filebeat
```

With Filebeat sending indicators to Logstash and Logstash writing keys into Redis, we can begin configuring the data nodes.

Creating Redis Followers

Let's move from the leader node to the follower data nodes. The data nodes run as Redis followers, which are read-only copies of the threat intelligence data in the leader instance. We'll use Logstash as a *getter* in this section to retrieve values from Redis to compare against streaming pipeline data.

On the data nodes, make the following configuration changes to */etc/redis/redis.conf* to run Redis as a follower. The followers should receive updated key-value pairs within milliseconds any time new data enters the leader cache. Note once again that I've organized these lines in the order you'll likely encounter them, but they won't appear consecutively in the file:

```
bind 127.0.0.1
port 0
unixsocket /var/run/redis/redis-server.sock
unixsocketperm 0666
tls-port 6379
tls-cert-file /etc/ssl/bookproject/wildcard.local.flex.cert.pem
tls-key-file /etc/ssl/bookproject/wildcard.local.flex.key.nopass.pem
tls-ca-cert-file /etc/ssl/bookproject/ca-chain.cert.pem
tls-replication yes
supervised systemd
replicaof 192.168.8.130 6379
masterauth ZtyziOSFGAcbGy8O7nY6Ap21Qd42SJa7Uthsfly9S1LbvflkevvDvTGRBC69qatZGQo=
requirepass ZtyziOSFGAcbGy8O7nY6Ap21Qd42SJa7Uthsfly9S1LbvflkevvDvTGRBC69qatZGQo=
```

These options should look similar to those in the master Redis configu-ration, with a few tweaks. The followers listen only on *localhost*, using TLS and its Unix socket. The replicaof statement uses the leader's IP address and port, meaning this Redis instance replicates all keys from the leader, and masterauth is the leader node's requirepass value you created previously.

Restart Redis, then enable it to start on boot:

```
$ sudo systemctl restart redis-server && systemctl status redis-server
$ sudo systemctl enable redis-server
```

On both the cyber threat intelligence and data nodes, run the following command on the Redis command line interface to view replication status:

```
$ redis-cli -s /var/run/redis/redis-server.sock
> auth default ZtyziOSFGAcbGy807...
> info replication
```

Next, let's configure the data node Logstash, which checks in-flight values against Redis for matches.

Configuring a Logstash Getter

The following configuration contains filters you could include in any of the existing Logstash pipelines that process flowing data. These filters will enrich events with cyber threat intelligence context and generate alerts.

On your data nodes, create the file */etc/logstash/conf.d/redis-get-indicators .conf*. Use the same elastic_agent input and elasticsearch output statements as the Logstash instance running on the Redis leader (the threat intelligence node) in "Defining Inputs" on page 283.

The first part of the filter looks similar to the setter configuration you created on the cyber threat intelligence node, but it includes a few changes to the connection objects; be sure to update the requirepass value to the one you created previously in this chapter:

```
# init runs once when Logstash starts.
filter {
  ruby {
    id => "ruby_redis_get"
    init => '
      require "redis"
      redis_socket = "/var/run/redis/redis-server.sock"
      redis_requirepass = "ZtyziOSFGAcbGy807n..."
      # Make a dedicated connection for each field to check.
❶     $r_domain = Redis.new(path: redis_socket, db: 0, password:
        redis_requirepass)
      $r_sourceip = Redis.new(path: redis_socket, db: 0, password:
        redis_requirepass)
      $r_destinationip = Redis.new(path: redis_socket, db: 0, password:
        redis_requirepass)
    '
    code => '
      # Use dedicated Redis connections for each field.
      #
```

```
      # Track cti hits using tags.
❷ arr = ["cti_match"]
      #
      # Domain; uses destination.domain
❸ if event.get("[destination][domain]")
        hit = $r_domain.get(event.get("[destination][domain]").downcase)
        if hit
❹         event.set("[labels][cti_message]", hit)
❺         arr.append("cti_destination.domain")
        end
      end
      #
      # Source IP address
      if event.get("[source][ip]")
        hit = $r_sourceip.get(event.get("[source][ip]").downcase)
        if hit
          event.set("[labels][cti_message]", hit)
          arr.append("cti_source.ip")
        end
      end
      #
      # Destination IP address
      if event.get("[destination][ip]")
        hit = $r_destinationip.get(event.get("[destination][ip]").downcase)
        if hit
          event.set("[labels][cti_message]", hit)
          arr.append("cti_destination.ip")
        end
      end
      #
      # Check if arr has more than 1 item in it.
      if arr.length > 1
        # Add arr to tags; create tags first if it does not exist.
❻       if not event.get("[tags]")
          event.set("[tags]", [])
        end
❼       arr.each do |item|
          event.set("[tags]", event.get("[tags]") << item)
        end
      end
      '
  }
}
```

In the init section, we establish multiple connection objects for each of
the fields ❶ we need to check. For the sake of brevity, we'll retrieve only the
domain and IP address fields, but you could add other fields, such as hash
formats.

In the code section, we configure an array ❷ for tags applied at the end
of the code block. This array enables automation beyond the scope of this
book, such as leveraging the cti_source.ip tag to identify a source.ip field
you wish to analyze further.

We use if statements ❸ to first check if a field exists in the current event being processed. If there's a cache match, we add the value from the cache ❹ as `labels.cti_message`, which is the value we constructed earlier, on the leader node. We also append a tag to the array ❺ using the format `cti_<field>` for automation downstream; a hypothetical tool could look for tags prefixed with `cti_` and then perform actions based on the field containing the match.

Note that this example uses only a domain and two IP address fields; add cache checks for any hash fields you may be interested in, filenames, and other data your analysts find useful. The filter closes out by checking if the array containing matches has more than a single item inside (recall it's initialized with a default value of `cti_match`); if so, it checks if the tags field exists ❻ and, if not, creates it. Then, we append each item from the array to the tags field ❼.

Deduplicating and Enriching Data

Next, let's add some utility Ruby filters to the Logstash configuration that deduplicate tags and add the hostname of the Logstash server processing an event. The duplication of tags might occur if multiple indicators match an event; deduplicating them saves storage bytes. You may wish to include these Ruby filters inside of the larger one you just created, but for the sake of readability, we'll keep them separate:

```
# Deduplicate tags.
filter {
  ruby {
    id => "ruby_tag_dedup"
    code => '
      if event.get("[tags]")
    ❶ event.set("[tags]", event.get("[tags]").uniq)
      end
    '
  }
}

# Add the hostname of the logstash server if not present using a loose
# approximation of an ecs field.
filter {
  ruby {
    id => "ruby_add_agentforwarder"
    init => '
      require "socket"
    ❷ @@hostname = Socket.gethostname
    '
    code => '
    ❸ event.set("[agent][forwarder]", @@hostname)
    '
  }
}
```

The first Ruby block deduplicates the tags field in case your tagging process uses the same field multiple times ❶. The next filter is the same as the one in Chapter 9; it adds the hostname ❷ of the current Logstash instance as the field agent.forwarder ❸ in the final event JSON sent to your SIEM.

Just like the Logstash instance feeding the leader Redis, save and then test the configuration:

```
$ sudo /usr/share/logstash/bin/logstash -f
/etc/logstash/conf.d/redis-get-indicators.conf --config.test_and_exit
[INFO ] 2040-05-15 23:25:44.131 [LogStash::Runner] runner - Using
config.test_and_exit mode. Config Validation Result: OK. Exiting Logstash
```

With the file working, start the Logstash service and enable it so it starts automatically:

```
$ sudo systemctl start logstash && systemctl status logstash
$ sudo systemctl enable logstash
```

Logstash may take a few moments to start again. You can follow Logstash's bootup process by tailing its logfile to look for errors:

```
$ tail -f /var/log/logstash/logstash-plain.log
```

Once your data nodes are up and running, you'll have threat indicator enrichment baked directly into your data pipeline, hopefully shortening the time gap between an incident occurring and detection.

Check Elasticsearch to ensure data is flowing correctly and that the Redis getter configuration isn't slowing anything down. You can also load a test value into your leader Redis instance, such as *localhost* or a busy internal IP address, so you can verify that cache matching is working. As an exercise, try simulating cache matches by adding otherwise legitimate domains to your Redis leader via Logstash CSV upload. Navigate to a few websites in your browser, then check for matches in Kibana.

Taking down your leader Redis for maintenance shouldn't affect the accessibility of the threat intelligence data, as Redis saves its current state to disk (though you can change this behavior to set your own backup policies). If your leader Redis loses all its values, you can pull indicators from Elasticsearch and add them to a CSV file to repopulate your cache; I'll leave this task to you as an exercise. Next, let's explore creating a threat intelligence cache with Memcached.

Distributing Threat Intelligence with Memcached

In this section, you'll use Memcached to once again send Filebeat data to Logstash on a cyber threat intelligence node. This time, however, Logstash will distribute the indicators to each data node instead of loading a leader database. The data nodes will be responsible for loading their own caches, as Memcached doesn't use replication. We'll discuss strategies for preventing cache *drift*, or differences between each data node's cache values, at the end of this section.

Configuring the Cyber Threat Intelligence Node

We'll begin on the cyber threat intelligence node, which will fetch and receive malicious indicators, then disseminate them to the data nodes. Like in the previous architecture, the node will function as the environment's hub, but this time, communication will flow in only one direction, from the cyber threat intelligence node outward. This design reduces the node's responsibilities, as the node doesn't need to maintain the Redis leader instance; instead, it pushes database maintenance down to the consumer data nodes.

Configure Filebeat in the same way you did in the previous section. Keep the same Logstash output, enable the threatintel module, and use the same *threatintel.yml* configuration. Recall that Filebeat doesn't support sending data to multiple destination servers at the same time; this is why you still need Logstash to distribute indicators to the follower nodes.

Alternatively, you can use the file output in *filebeat.yml* to write indicators to disk. Then, Logstash can read the files and distribute them as necessary. This would let you automatically compress and rotate logs, so you can archive the files somewhere, in lieu of storing them in Redis. Here, we'll rely on the SIEM for long-term storage.

Create a new file at */etc/logstash/conf.d/intel-distribute.conf*. Use the same elastic_agent and http inputs and elasticsearch output as in the previous section. Also use the same CSV-processing filter block from "Handling Custom Uploads" on page 284 to support loading custom indicators. In the output block, add the following code to send events to your data nodes' Logstash instances:

```
output {
  if [labels][cti_message] {
--snip--
    logstash {
      id => "output_to_logstash01"
      hosts => [ "logstash01.local:9800" ]
      ssl_enabled => "true"
      ssl_verification_mode => "full"
      ssl_keystore_path => "/etc/ssl/bookproject/wildcard.local.flex.pkcs12"
      ssl_keystore_password => "abcd1234"
      ssl_certificate_authorities => [ "/etc/ssl/bookproject/ca-chain.cert.pem" ]
    }
--snip--
  }
}
```

Adding more than one address in the `hosts` option would load-balance, or evenly distribute, your indicators across all listed servers. Since we want all hosts to have the same data, we add one `logstash` output per host.

We need either a PKCS#12 or a Java KeyStore container file to communicate downstream when using an encrypted private key with the Logstash output. Strangely, this output doesn't have an `ssl_key_password` option like plug-ins covered in previous chapters. Without that option, you can't specify the key's passphrase in the configuration or in Logstash's keystore. If you wish to use a PKCS#12 file, transfer it to your cyber threat intelligence node, place it in */etc/ssl/bookproject*, and set the same access permissions as the other files there. Otherwise, just use the nopass private key along with the `ssl_key`, `ssl_certificate`, and `ssl_certificate_authorities` options to follow along.

Notice that this `output` block has an `if` statement that checks for `labels .cti_message`; Logstash outputs this event only if the field is present. This is optional both here and in the Redis project and restricts this configuration to being solely for this project. This demonstrates using logical statements to restrict the outward flow of data to prevent errant tags or type fields from being applied to the wrong logs.

When you're using Ansible, you might find it handy to use a `template` or `blockinfile` to complete the Logstash output section based on an inventory file. You could store the output as an Ansible template using Jinja syntax, and an Ansible playbook could fill in the inventory details, Next, let's cover setting and getting Memcached values on the data nodes.

Configuring the Data Node

Let's begin by configuring the data nodes that work with Memcached to process streaming data. The data nodes will receive indicators from the cyber threat intelligence node, then write them into their own Memcached instances. Unlike the Redis project covered previously, these nodes don't reach out to the cyber threat intelligence node to synchronize databases. Instead, Logstash has a built-in filter to form a connection with Memcached and then set and retrieve key-value pairs. Each data node's Logstash instance will connect to its own local Memcached instance to access its indicators. Different Logstash pipelines can then compare streaming data to the locally cached values.

On your data nodes, install Memcached as you did in "Installing Redis and Memcached" on page 272 and then make it start automatically at bootup using **sudo systemctl enable memcached**. Memcached should automatically start when the installation is complete. As we covered previously, Memcached uses TCP port 11211, which Logstash connects to by default. You may double-check or change this value in */etc/memcached.conf* on Ubuntu and Debian or */etc/sysconfig/memcached* on Red Hat.

The Logstash output and input use TCP port 9800 by default, so ensure your firewall rules allow this port. Add the following lines to */etc/logstash/conf.d/memcached-set-indicators.conf*:

```
input {
  logstash {
    id => "input_logstash"
    port => 9800
    ssl_enabled => true
    ssl_client_authentication => "required"
    ssl_certificate => "/etc/ssl/bookproject/wildcard.local.flex.cert.pem"
    ssl_key => "/etc/ssl/bookproject/wildcard.local.flex.key.pem"
    ssl_key_passphrase => "abcd1234"
    ssl_certificate_authorities => [ "/etc/ssl/bookproject/ca-chain.cert.pem" ]
  }
}
```

Next, add the following filter, which begins to add your indicators to Memcached:

```
filter {
  if ([agent][type] == "filebeat" and [service][type] == "threatintel" and
  [labels][cti_message]) or [type] == "custom_ioc" or [type] == "external_ioc" {
    # Store sha256
    if [labels][sha256_hash] { ❶
      mutate {
        lowercase => [ "[labels][sha256_hash]" ] ❷
      }
      memcached { ❸
        hosts => [ "localhost:11211" ]
        ttl => 2592000
        set => {
          "[labels][cti_message]" => "%{[labels][sha256_hash]}" ❹
        }
      }
    }
    # Store MD5
    if [labels][md5_hash] {
      mutate {
        lowercase => [ "[labels][md5_hash]" ]
      }
      memcached {
        hosts => [ "localhost:11211" ]
        ttl => 2592000
        set => {
          "[labels][cti_message]" => "%{[labels][md5_hash]}"
        }
      }
    }
    # Store imphash
    if [labels][imphash] {
      mutate {
        lowercase => [ "[labels][imphash]" ]
```

```
    }
    memcached {
      hosts => [ "localhost:11211" ]
      ttl => 2592000
      set => {
        "[labels][cti_message]" => "%{[labels][imphash]}"
      }
    }
  }
}
# Store ssdeep
if [labels][ssdeep] {
  mutate {
    lowercase => [ "[labels][ssdeep]" ]
  }
  memcached {
    hosts => [ "localhost:11211" ]
    ttl => 2592000
    set => {
      "[labels][cti_message]" => "%{[labels][ssdeep]}"
    }
  }
}
# Store urls (full)
if [labels][url] {
  mutate {
    lowercase => [ "[labels][url]" ]
  }
  memcached {
    hosts => [ "localhost:11211" ]
    ttl => 2592000
    set => {
      "[labels][cti_message]" => "%{[labels][url]}"
    }
  }
}
# Store domain parsed from a URL
if [labels][url_domain] {
  mutate {
    lowercase => [ "[labels][url_domain]" ]
  }
  memcached {
    hosts => [ "localhost:11211" ]
    ttl => 2592000
    set => {
      "[labels][cti_message]" => "%{[labels][url_domain]}"
    }
  }
}
# Store IP
if [labels][ip] {
  mutate {
    lowercase => [ "[labels][ip]" ]
  }
  memcached {
```

```
      hosts => [ "localhost:11211" ]
      ttl => 2592000
      set => {
        "[labels][cti_message]" => "%{[labels][ip]}"
      }
    }
  }
}
# Store custom indicators
if [labels][indicator] {
  mutate {
    lowercase => [ "[labels][indicator]" ]
  }
  memcached {
    hosts => [ "localhost:11211" ]
    ttl => 2592000
    set => {
      "[labels][cti_message]" => "%{[labels][indicator]}"
    }
  }
}
```

After checking whether the indicator field received from Filebeat's threatintel module (via Logstash) exists in the current event ❶, we lowercase the value ❷ to standardize what goes into the cache, as we need to reliably check for it in other configurations. Inside the memcached filter ❸, we declare hosts to be localhost port 11211, the default Memcached port. The set statement ❹, which adds keys to the cache, adds the value of the field on the left of the arrow (labels.cti_message) to the key on the right of the arrow, which should be a received indicator. We use a variable to reference the actual value of the labels.sha256_hash field as a string. This means that the hash value in labels.sha256_hash becomes the key and labels.cti_message becomes the value. The remaining statements add key-value pairs for hashes, URLs, IP addresses, and custom indicators.

Use a null output to wrap up this configuration:

```
output {
  null {}
}
```

We don't use an output because all indicators should already be in Elasticsearch, as the *intel-distribute.conf* Logstash configuration should have sent them there. Sending them again in the Logstash configuration would cause duplicate entries. For manual testing, however, you might want to use a stdout output instead of the null one to display the indicators in the terminal.

Next, make a new configuration named */etc/logstash/conf.d/memcached -get-indicators.conf* to check the streaming data for threat intelligence values. Use the same elastic_agent input and elasticsearch output as the previous configurations and an optional stdout output for manual testing. As mentioned previously, the getter configuration is meant to be representative of what you might use in an actual pipeline that processes live data. Like the Redis getter, the following filter may be placed into any other configuration you wish to begin checking for cached matches:

```
filter {
❶ if [file][hash][sha256] {
    memcached {
      get => {
      ❷ "%{[file][hash][sha256]}" => "[labels][cti_message]"
      }
    ❸ add_tag => [ "cti_match", "cti_file.hash.sha256" ]
    }
  }
  if [file][hash][md5] {
    memcached {
      get => {
        "%{[file][hash][md5]}" => "[labels][cti_message]"
      }
      add_tag => [ "cti_match", "cti_file.hash.md5" ]
    }
  }
  if [file][hash][imphash] {
    memcached {
      get => {
        "%{[file][hash][imphash]}" => "[labels][cti_message]"
      }
      add_tag => [ "cti_match", "cti_file.hash.imphash" ]
    }
  }
  if [url][original] {
    memcached {
      get => {
        "%{[url][original]}" => "[labels][cti_message]"
      }
      add_tag => [ "cti_match", "cti_url.original" ]
    }
  }
  if [url][full] {
    memcached {
      get => {
        "%{[url][full]}" => "[labels][cti_message]"
      }
      add_tag => [ "cti_match", "cti_url.full" ]
    }
  }
  if [url][domain] {
    memcached {
      get => {
        "%{[url][domain]}" => "[labels][cti_message]"
      }
      add_tag => [ "cti_match", "cti_url.domain" ]
```

```
      }
    }
    if [destination][domain] {
      memcached {
        get => {
          "%{[destination][domain]}" => "[labels][cti_message]"
        }
        add_tag => [ "cti_match", "cti_destination.domain" ]
      }
    }
    if [tls][client][server_name] {
      memcached {
        get => {
          "%{[tls][client][server_name]}" => "[labels][cti_message]"
        }
        add_tag => [ "cti_match", "cti_tls.client.server_name" ]
      }
    }
    if [source][ip] {
      memcached {
        get => {
          "%{[source][ip]}" => "[labels][cti_message]"
        }
        add_tag => [ "cti_match", "cti_source.ip" ]
      }
    }
    if [destination][ip] {
      memcached {
        get => {
          "%{[destination][ip]}" => "[labels][cti_message]"
        }
        add_tag => [ "cti_match", "cti_destination.ip" ]
      }
    }
  }
}
```

As with the setter script, we first check whether a field we want to compare, such as source.ip or destination.ip, exists ❶. Inside the memcached filter, in the get statement ❷, we get the value of the field to check and then label any identified matches as the labels.cti_message field. The filter also adds several tags ❸ if it finds a match: the cti_match tag and cti_<*field*> tags that contain the matching field name, such as cti_source.ip.

For the sake of example, the previous filters include other fields that contain domains you may find in your data, such as tls.client.server_name, which often contains the name of a remote server a client is trying to reach during a TLS connection. Also included are several hash varieties, IP address fields, and URL and domain fields. These fields may not appear in every log source, but they'll certainly appear in some of them. Be sure to become familiar with the data in your pipelines and add other fields as necessary.

Preventing Drift

Because the data nodes don't check themselves against a leader database, drift may occur if one node is down for maintenance when an indicator push occurs. In this case, you might want to create a custom script to back-fill any missed items. You could query your SIEM for the time at which the server was down, then push any indicators found, new or not, into the caches via custom upload to Logstash. This might be a good opportunity for an Ansible task to alleviate missed detection concerns by baking in such backfills to your maintenance playbooks.

Handling Analyst-Submitted Indicator Data

Both projects in this chapter used a Logstash HTTP input to add new indicators to the cache. The following CSV file provides an example of the data an analyst might upload using this input. It includes expected values, missing values, and an unexpected third column in the last row:

```
"indicator","cti_message"
"333.333.333.333","bad ip"
"4444.exe","meterpreter"
"5.local","bad website"
"6.local",
,"only a description"
1,2,3
```

The Redis setter and Memcached distribution configurations would remove the first row, which includes column names. The configurations would add default values to the missing fields in the third-to-last and second-to-last rows. Lastly, the configurations would truncate the last row, containing three values, from the third column onward.

The following curl command uploads a file named *iocs.csv* to a plaintext HTTP listener; a successful upload should show a completion percentage of 100 and the word ok:

```
$ curl localhost:8080 -T iocs.csv
% Total
100
--snip--
ok
```

Logstash should show output like the following:

```
--snip--
"message" => "\"4444.exe\",\"meterpreter\"",
"labels" => {
    "indicator" => "4444.exe",
  "cti_message" => "meterpreter"
},
--snip--
```

To connect to a Logstash listener expecting TLS with client authentication, you'll need to add `https://` to the URL and the options `--cacert`, `--cert`, and `--key`; if you don't need to verify hostnames for testing, you may use the option `-k` as well:

```
$ curl https://threatintel.local:8080 -T iocs.csv \
--cacert /etc/ssl/bookproject/ca-chain.cert.pem \
--cert /etc/ssl/bookproject/wildcard.local.flex.cert.pem \
--key /etc/ssl/bookproject/wildcard.local.flex.key.nopass.pem
```

You can easily add more columns to the custom indicator upload filters covered previously. These options may include analyst initials or names, case numbers, custom TTLs, priority and confidence levels, or CVE numbers. As we've covered previously, strive to automate clunkiness and don't overengineer your requirements to the point that they become burdensome for your team.

Going Beyond

You could expand the pipelines created in this chapter in several ways. For example, Kafka could be an ideal tool for receiving indicators from Filebeat and other sources. Your consumers, including Logstash pipelines, could then be lone members of their own consumer groups, each of which receives every new indicator and updates their caches. This approach would allow your consumers to reliably keep their caches updated, even during server restarts or outages, although you should still have a process in place to recover from drift. You may even use tools such as Apache Flink, which is beyond the scope of this book, to watch data streaming through Kafka, perform lookups, and write enriched data back into Kafka to topics that Logstash consumes.

The Logstash configurations in this chapter store indicators in Elasticsearch, so you could choose to read indicators from the SIEM and push them into your caches instead of using setters. Using your preferred scripting language, you could query Elasticsearch on a schedule, then write any indicator results into the cache. This technique loosely centralizes populating the cache and ensures that any servers undergoing maintenance receive backfilled updates. Also, using Ansible to populate Redis and Memcached may allow you to bypass the need for the distributor and setter configurations entirely.

You could use the `cti_<field>` tags to automate actions, such as triggering retro hunts for new indicators in old data or retrieving suspicious files for analysis mere milliseconds after they're detected. You could also trigger a SIEM alert, queue a network block for approval, push an aggressive Elastic Agent policy that captures network metadata, or open an incident case and populate its relevant fields with data from events. You may even quarantine a host if you trust certain indicators in your cache enough to block users.

> **SAVING CONFIGURATIONS WITH GIT**
>
> If you aren't already working from a Git repository, add your working files to one, redact any credentials, and track the files with `git add .`, then check them with `git status`. Commit changes using `git commit -am <message>`, then use `git push` to send your notes and files to your remote repository.

Summary

Caching adds direct value to your cyber data pipelines by enabling real-time lookups for malicious values in your streaming data. Redis provides replication and synchronization of data between nodes, and Memcached lookups are built into Logstash.

In this chapter, you used Redis and Memcached to store and look up data. You created a threat intelligence caching pipeline with Filebeat, Logstash, a Redis leader database, and Redis followers that check streaming data. You also used Filebeat, Logstash, and Memcached to create a distribution system for disseminating indicators of compromise directly to each data node. You learned about potential automation ideas, benefits and drawbacks of various implementations, and ways that Ansible could save you time.

INDEX

firewall
    clutter, 55
    ports, 27
Firewalld, 27, 103, 208, 248
    allowing SSH, 28
fleet servers
    Ansible simulation, 256
    Elastic Agent, 99
    installation, 112–113
    integrations, 111
    new service tokens, 111
    output settings, 111
    role, 99
Flink, 304

G

Git, 172
    adding, 34, 37, 38
    branches, 34, 41
        deleting, 44
    checkout, 41
    cloning, 34
    commands
        config, 35
        fetch, 47
        init, 36
        log, 39
    commits, 34, 37, 39
    initializing locally, 36
    merges, 34, 44
    pulls, 34
        rebasing, 47
        rejected, 46
    pushes, 34, 39
        deleting, 44
        rejected, 46
        set-upstream origin, 37
    remote, 43
        remote add origin, 36
    repository, 34
    resetting, 47
    stashing, 48
        stash pop, 48
    status, 38
        status --short, 38, 40
GitHub, xxv, 35
.gitignore file, 40
GitLab, 35

GNU Privacy Guard (GPG), 104
Golang, 54
groups, 275

H

hosts file
    on Linux, 103
    on Windows, 86, 103
    remembering to update, 119
Hypertext Transfer Protocol (HTTP), xxv
    basic authentication, 258
    input in Logstash, 154
    output in Logstash, 156
hypervisor, xxiv

I

id command, 275
indentation, 9
integrations, 99, 116
    assets, 116, 123
    Elastic Agent, 116
    fleet server, 111
    guidelines, 117
    Iptables, 117
    monitor processes, 116
    Network Packet Capture, 116
intel-distribute.conf file, 296
Invoke-WebRequest command, 78
iocs.csv file, 303
Iptables, 117

J

Java, 54
Java Development Kit, 209
Java KeyStores (JKS), 210
JavaScript, 67
JavaScript Object Notation (JSON), 9
    dotted field names, 61
    newline-delimited, 58
Java Virtual Machine (JVM), 106
Jinja, 228
    from_json function, 259
    lookup function, 243, 259
    Python, 228
    syntax, 242
    to_json function, 259
jq tool, 11, 109
jvm.options file, 152

PuTTY, 11
Python
  Flask, 157
  Jinja, 228
  passlib module, 238
  subprocess module, 235
  virtualenv package, 157
  web server, 87, 104, 211, 274

R

RainerScript, 133
README.md file, 37
Red Hat Enterprise Linux (RHEL), 10
  Memcached configuration files, 277
Redis, 162, 272
  channel mode, 162
  commands
    acl, 278
    get, 278
    info, 278
    set, 277
  configuration files, 275
  cyber threat intelligence node, 281
  Filebeat output, 74
  followers, 280, 291
  installation, 273
  leaders, 280
  list mode, 162
  Logstash input, 163
  Logstash output, 164
  maintenance, 295
  redis.conf file, 275, 291
  redis-get-indicators.conf file, 292
  replication, 280
  Ruby filters, 287
  Ruby gem, 273
redis-benchmark command, 279
redis-cli command, 277, 292
regular expressions, 142, 176, 190
retro hunts, 288, 304
RFC 3164 format, 62, 128, 175
RFC 5424 format, 62, 128, 137, 191
RHEL (Red Hat Enterprise Linux), 10
  Memcached configuration
    files, 277
Rsyslog, 6, 129, 219
  actions, 137, 141
  advanced format, 133

basic format, 132
case-insensitive
  match, 145
  regex, 142
  string, 141
compressing whitespace,
  140
configuration
  client, 144
  main, 132
  OpenSSL, 130
  server, 144
  testing, 133
constant keyword, 139
creating new variables, 142
dynamic filenames, 140
/etc/rsyslog.d/ directory, 132
files
  /etc/rsyslog.conf, 132
  rsyslog-imkafka.conf, 220
  rsyslog-omkafka.conf, 219
  send-to-filebeat.conf, 63
global TLS settings, 134
input modules, 134
  imfile, 136
  imkafka, 135, 220
  imptcp, 134–135, 145
installation, 129
Kafka, 219
OpenSSL configuration file,
  130
output modules, 136
  jsonify, 140
  omfile, 136
  omfwd, 137, 144
  omkafka, 219
properties, 138
  global, 133
  rawmsg, 140
property keyword, 139
property replacer, 138, 142
publishing to Kafka, 219
regular expressions, 142
replacing text, 141
rulesets, 141
sp-if-no-1st-sp modifier, 142
stream drivers, 135
subscribing to Kafka, 220

RESOURCES

Visit *https://nostarch.com/data-engineering-cybersecurity* for errata and more information.

More no-nonsense books from **NO STARCH PRESS**

DEVOPS FOR THE DESPERATE
A Hands-On Survival Guide
BY BRADLEY SMITH
176 PP., $29.99
ISBN 978-1-7185-0248-2

WINDOWS SECURITY INTERNALS
A Deep Dive into Windows Authentication, Authorization, and Auditing
BY JAMES FORSHAW
608 PP., $59.99
ISBN 978-1-7185-0198-0

AUTOMATE THE BORING STUFF WITH PYTHON, 3RD EDITION
Practical Programming for Total Beginners
BY AL SWEIGART
672 PP., $59.99
ISBN 978-1-7185-0340-3

EFFECTIVE SHELL
A Practical User's Guide to Working Smarter on the Command Line
BY DAVE KERR
472 PP., $49.99
ISBN 978-1-7185-0414-1

PRACTICAL LINUX FORENSICS
A Guide for Digital Investigators
BY BRUCE NIKKEL
400 PP., $59.99
ISBN 978-1-7185-0196-6

FROM DAY ZERO TO ZERO DAY
A Hands-On Guide to Vulnerability Research
BY EUGENE LIM
344 PP., $59.99
ISBN 978-1-7185-0394-6

PHONE:
800.420.7240 OR
415.863.9900

EMAIL:
SALES@NOSTARCH.COM

WEB:
WWW.NOSTARCH.COM